THE ENGLISH COACH'S INSTRUCTIONAL *Playbook*

CLASSROOM STRATEGIES INFORMED BY NEUROSCIENCE, ATHLETICS, AND PSYCHOLOGY

IAN BERRY & MICHAEL DEGEN

Telemachos Publishing

Copyright ©2024 by Ian Berry and Michael Degen

No portions of this book may be reproduced or transmitted in any form or by any means, electronic or mechanical, including photocopying, recording, or by an information storage and retrieval system without permission from the publisher.

First Edition

First Printing 2024

Telemachos Publishing
Garland, TX 75046-0387
www.telemachospublishing.com

Library of Congress Catalog Card Number: 2022944418

ISBN: 9780985384968

For English teachers

willing to ditch their roles as "sage on the stage."

CONTENTS

Foreword   7
Charlie DeLong

CHAPTER 1
Neuroscience, Psychology, and Coaching Meet: the Initial Idea   12

   Brain Research   16
   The Psychology of Expert Performance   21
   Athletic Coaching   31
   Neuroscience, Psychology, and Coaching: Application   45

CHAPTER 2
What We Need to Know About the Brain   46

CHAPTER 3
Defining the Core Plays   62

   L1, L2, L3 Plays   64
   Executing Additional Writing Plays   82
      L2-L1-L2 Play   82
      To the Right Play   82
      Modified L1 Play   83
      The Thesis (TH) Play   92
      Topic Sentence (TS) Play   94
      Organization Play   96
      Topic String Play   100
      Word and Logic Glue Play   103

CHAPTER 4
Daily Practice: The Fundamentals   106

   Practicing the Plays   107
   Movement Variations for Any Unit   108
   The Writing Journal   112
   The Brain Break   114
   Musical Chairs   116

How to Engage "Difficult" Texts	124
The Evidence-Association Chart (EAC)	132
Paragraph Chart	140
Teaching Aristotle's Topics of Invention	144
Practicing Four Syntactical Patterns	162
Get Creative with Organizing Evidence	166
Sentence Imitation	170
Sentence Combination	175
Grammar Dice	181
Human Sentences	188
Labeling	194
Memory Work	197
Isolating Plays in Sentence Creation	201
Peer-Editing / Critic's Walk	204
Writing Conference Memo	210

CHAPTER 5
Putting the Plays Together: Scrimmage & Reflection Activities — 216

The Scrimmage	217
Types of Questions to Consider When Reading	219
The Discussion Quiz	223
The Literary News Conference	233
The Tournament of Scholars	242
The Quotation Game	250
The Revision Chart	258

APPENDIX

Keeping the Plays Close—Bookmarks for Students	267
The Scoring Guide & Mastery Handout	270
Playbook Quiz	284
Feedback Memo	287
What Did the Teacher Say?	288
Glossary	290

References	**292**
Acknowledgments	**300**
Index	**303**

FOREWORD
DRAWING THEM BACK FOR MORE

In the late 1950s, Sepp Herberger, one of the greatest soccer coaches of all time (1954 FIFA World Cup winning coach), had this to say when asked to describe the perfect soccer practice: "Leave the players on the field exhausted and laughing."

Environment

As a coach, I want my students to want to come to practice so I need to create an environment that is enjoyable, fulfilling, and demanding. Practice should be understood and readily applied to the game; the outcome should lead the players to think about the how, what, when, and why of the practice. It is by this process that we can give them ideas and encourage them to develop their own. Then they will produce something new or at least original; therefore, it will be effective for some time.

One of the most important components of a learning environment is that of positive coaching. In the book *Positive Coaching* by Jim Thompson, the author contends that all coaches need to be relentlessly positive, looking for teachable moments where the coach will point out those times when things are done correctly. This positive environment increases the receptivity of the learners. Thompson gives the example of a group of dolphins that, when faced with a negative hostile training environment at SeaWorld, would withdraw to the furthest, deepest part of their tank and refuse to practice. But when the training environment was changed to one of positive reinforcement, those very same dolphins far exceeded all training expectations, going as far as creating their own innovative tricks and routines, much to the surprise and delight of their trainers.

So what should an effective practice environment be composed of? In the world of sports, we have two training principles that help shape and design training environments that can and will bring about the desired results.

You Get What You Train For

The first principle is the SAID principle of training: Specific Adaptation to Imposed Demands (you get what you train for).

The coach must decide what specific adaptations are wanted/needed, then design the "imposed demands" that will bring about the desired adaptations. These practices should incorporate one, some, or all four of the pillars of the game—the technical, the tactical, the physical, and the psychological.

These practices must be game-like in their design. The problems that are presented, the patterns of movement observed, the solutions that are created, will be practiced repeatedly to the point of a near automatic response.

Yet we must allow for spontaneity and creativity; for instance, playing a game where before anyone may score everyone must be over the halfway line (goalie not included). Players will still need to pass, dribble, attack, and defend, but it will require a lot of running by all players, the ability to possess the ball in the opponent's half, and all teammates getting across the half line. This practice will emphasize fitness (physical) and ball possession (technical, tactical). As with all practices, as players adapt and improve, then practices must become more challenging. In the above practice, for example, one can make the game more challenging by making the field smaller or by adding more players, thus reducing the time and space. This new condition would require all players to make quicker decisions (tactical) and improve their technique, pass, trap, and dribble (technical). The challenge is to keep success just out of reach, yet visible enough to inspire the effort needed to attain it.

Deliberate Practice

The second training principle is that of deliberate practice, a universal technique intended to improve performance, inspire players to reach objectives just beyond their competence, and provide feedback from a respected expert. It involves high levels of repetition.

While engaging in deliberate practice, we are always looking for errors or areas of weakness. Once we identify one, we establish a plan for improving it. If one approach does not work, we keep trying new ones until something does. Using deliberate practice, we can overcome many limitations that we might view as fixed. We can go farther than we thought possible when we began. Kicking a soccer ball a lot is not deliberate practice, which is why a lot of soccer players do not get better. However, we can set up a practice where, from twenty-five yards out, a player must chip the ball fifty times over the goal into a 10-foot diameter circle, with the goal of doing so 80% of the time. We continually observe results and make appropriate adjustments. Doing this repeatedly is deliberate practice. The more we engage in deliberate practice, the greater our capabilities become.

To develop creative players is part of deliberate practice that works well, the "embrace and extend approach." This method starts with mimicry: having your athletes observe more proficient players, then challenging them to copy and master the techniques they see from their higher-level role models. When players acquire a reasonable repertoire of ability, you can challenge them to combine or otherwise modify these skills and ideas to produce new skills and ideas that they can make their own. Remember that it is not creative simply to do what someone else has told you to do.

Coaches must allow their players to produce their own ideas at the risk of failing. This trial-and-error self-discovery is best achieved in what is called "free play." A game-like situation (highly competitive) yet without the fear of losing. The only pressure comes from within. The player is allowed—encouraged—to be curious, try new things, take risks, see what works and does not work. In all practices this free play must be done a lot so a player will become confident with what does and does not work for him in game-like situations.

When you sense that the players have run out of ideas, then you can use guided self-discovery techniques to lead them in the right direction. Ask them why something did not work, what else could have been done, and get them to think about the game. But you must let them solve the problem if you want them to develop creative, critical thinking and playing skills.

Introducing competition automatically increases task complexity because players must now factor in the actions of others as they make decisions about their own actions. Adding chaos to the environment increases contextual interference, which increases the learning potential for the activity. Competition will stimulate the athlete's enjoyment and the creativity of the learning process.

This philosophy not only ensures that the players are prepared for the rigorous demands of a 90-minute game, but that they also enjoy the demands of the practice in a way that draws them back for more.

Why would a coach want to write a foreword for a book about writing? For two reasons: (1) Dr. Degen and Mr. Berry are good friends of mine, and (2) because during my 35 years as department chair for the Physical Education Department, I have enjoyed many discussions concerning the learning process with these two colleagues.

———

We have discussed concepts like repetition, collaboration, guided self-discovery and "only perfect practice makes perfect," concepts that are near and dear to all coaches.

It is evident to us that the academic learning process has much in common with the athletic learning process. After many conversations where we shared ideas and experiences concerning the learning process in many different endeavors, it slowly dawned on us that teachers and coaches should work together to refine, grow, and help each other in order to better serve our students.

Charles DeLong
2022

01

NEUROSCIENCE, PSYCHOLOGY, & COACHING MEET

—THE INITIAL IDEA—

In this book, neuroscience, the psychology of expert performance, and coaching in athletics converge to inform a new instructional paradigm for the secondary English classroom.

These fields, which the secondary language arts world has not extensively considered, have valuable insights to offer teachers. Listening to them allows us to design instruction that both energizes our classrooms and enhances student learning, providing all students a pathway to higher achievement.

What do neuroscientists, psychologists, and athletic coaches have to tell English teachers about their instruction?

They invite us to consider a classroom shaped by *movement*, in both a literal and figurative sense.

First, considerable expanding research on the brain convincingly demonstrates that literal, physical movement should play a part in our instruction, designing class activities where students must physically get out of their seats, change seats, gallery walk past whiteboards, position themselves physically in various marked locations of the room. These choices don't merely keep students awake: movement also assists the brain in learning complex tasks, strengthening memory, building more resilient neurons, and enhancing the brain's overall health.

Second, the psychology of expert performance and the methodologies of coaching in athletics shape our thinking about movement in a more figurative sense.

Psychologists have examined the most successful athletes, artists, and scientists, and have uncovered that expertise in *any* field is achieved through a specific mode of training. They have broken down the thought processes and training protocols of these top performers, identifying the movements involved in acquiring expertise: these individuals intentionally acquire specific skills, internalize them through repetition, and ultimately achieve an ability to strategically execute them with a level of excellence that surpasses most of their competition.

Coaches have methodically developed training programs that bring out the best in their athletes, by visualizing the winning performance and considering all of the adaptations (technical, tactical, psychological, physical) that their players must make to be able to achieve it. They have then designed practice to focus solely on these aspects of performance, which form the playbook that their athletes must internalize, then execute successfully, in order to win.

Psychologists and coaches of athletes help us to envision how expert performance in English may be trained:

- First, by breaking down performance in reading and writing into specific, smaller "movements," visualizing the thought processes involved in these complex intellectual behaviors;

- Second, by designing a playbook of these movements for our students;

- Third, by creating lesson plans that actively engage students in practicing and internalizing the playbook, while we adopt the role of the coach.

Note that, when we speak figuratively of reading and writing "movements" or "plays," we are no longer referring to physical actions (standing up, going to the board, switching desks, passing a marker to a partner), but intellectual ones, movements of the mind. Throughout this book, we will be using the words "movement" and "play" interchangeably. Both words are synonymous with the word *skill*.

Just as football players know by heart several plays that direct their physical movement about the field, high-performing English students have mastered a different set of movements or plays. The playbook in English class includes but is not limited to

- Creating parallel structure within a sentence

- Identifying important diction, detail, or imagery within a literary passage

- Making interpretive associations for a piece of textual evidence

- Organizing evidence within a paragraph.

We find this physical, athletic analogy to be helpful for us and our students.

For one thing, the word "skill" is abstract; it does not create a picture in our students' minds. "Movement" and "play" are far more visual words. They evoke images of action. They have parts. They can be broken down into smaller steps.

Using these words communicates to students that reading and writing are not magical or genetically bestowed gifts, but activities that involve a process, abilities that can be acquired through training. It also tells students that they are entering a space that will engage them in practice. Finally, it orients our thinking about instruction, focusing us on engaging students in learning *how* to read, write, and think, rather than lecturing to them about *what* to notice, what to write, or what to think.

But to teach them, *coach* them in this way, we need a playbook.

A playbook that breaks apart the thought processes of the ideal reader or writer is something that the English classroom has lacked, yet it has never been more needed.

Those who lack proficiency in writing cannot see the thought process of the ideal student who drafts a distinctive thesis statement. Many students do not know how the top performers even make sense of a Shakespearean soliloquy, let alone explain its meaning with insightful commentary. To students like these, the movements of reading and writing are obscure.

Our students are changing: many of them have a lower reading level, weaker vocabulary, and shorter attention span than their predecessors of even a decade ago. More and more, they experience the English language primarily through a digital world that does not give them a working knowledge of grammar, syntax, and style, but rather tends to distort or dull their understanding of these, and even do the work for them.

More than ever, our students need teachers who can elucidate the process of reading and writing, and show them the plays that lead to success.

- How does the ideal reader enter a difficult literary text and understand the associative ideas that the author conveys?

- How does the ideal writer develop an essay that states a precise interpretive claim about the literary text?

If we do not visualize and articulate these movements for our students, not only will they be confused about them, but we will also have no strategies to give them effective feedback. The teacher without a playbook has only imprecise comments to offer:

- "This paper needs more development."
- "You need to go deeper."
- "This paragraph makes no sense."
- "Read between the lines."
- "This is just summary."

Few, if any, young writers can understand how to respond to these statements.

What young writers can respond to, however, are specific "plays" that cue them toward concrete actions to improve the clarity of a sentence, the coherence of a paragraph, the precision of an interpretive idea.

The following sections of this chapter expand upon these two categories of physical and figurative movement while the subsequent chapters provide concrete lesson plans based on these principles.

Brain Research

Certain concepts from neuroscience research help explain the basis for the application of physical movement to the design of classroom activities. Teaching strategies that incorporate movement into our lessons engage with the science linking the cognitive and motor components of the brain.[1]

The Cerebellum: The Link Between Movement and Learning

Neuroscience shows us that the brain is not a compartmentalized organ; rather, its regions interact with each other, in a way that links the motor function (i.e., movement) with cognitive processes (i.e., learning).

One area of research demonstrating the benefit of employing movement in the classroom specifically evaluates the cerebellum, located at the base of the brain behind the brainstem and serving to coordinate our motor activity.

Research on the cerebellum over the past 30 years demonstrates this portion of the brain's influence on language, memory, and general cognition. Beyond

---

1   Friez, 1996.

> "When we physically move, the [parts of the brain linked with] cognition are ignited."

enabling smooth and coordinated movements, the cerebellum, storehouse to almost half of the brain's neurons, communicates with key cognitive areas of the brain.[2] One study concludes succinctly that "when we physically move, the [parts of the brain linked with] cognition are ignited."[3]

When initiating a physical movement, the cerebellum does not simply send a message to perform a physical act. It also fires off directives to the parts of the brain underlying cognition, amplifying learning capacity and memory. On a cellular level, physical or kinetic action "moves" neurons to bind together via synapses, the cellular structures underlying learning and memory.[4]

Existing Educational Studies Linking Movement and Learning

In light of this perceived link between movement and cognition, neuroscientific studies (primarily in elementary education but with relevance to secondary) have explored the relationship between movement and learning.

Several elementary school-level studies indicate that designing lessons to include physical activity can enhance the brain's learning capacity.[5] When teachers consciously incorporate some movement aligned with a cognitive task, they ultimately energize the brain in more productive ways than if the physical component were absent. Both math and language arts students who participated in physical activity during their lessons outperformed their peers in the control group who merely sat at their desks and listened to instruction.

More recently, a review of 54 research studies involving 29,460 elementary students left no doubt that movement increases the effectiveness of academic learning.[6]

There are also several research studies conducted on college-level students

---

2   Stoodley CJ, 2012; Ivry, R.. & Fiez, J. 2000; Schmahmann JD, 2019; Friez, J., 1996.
3   Diedrichsen J., 2019; Middleton, F. & Strick P., 1994.
4   van Praag & Christie, 2015; Schmahmann, 2019; Rogge AK, Röder B, Zech A, et al., 2018.
5   Norris, E., 2019; *On Achievement in Math:* Fredens, K., 2018; Mavilidi, M.F., Drew, R, et al., 2019; *In Language Arts:* Mavilidi, M. F., Lubans, D. R., et al., 2018.
6   Petrigna, 2022.

demonstrating enhancement in learning and skill acquisition when movement is incorporated into the educational curriculum.

One study compared two methods of instruction in basic library concepts for first year college students at Saint Leo University.[7] The class was randomly separated into two groups. The control group received standard library instructions, while the experimental group received instructions augmented by a physical demonstration, a kinesthetic exercise, and a visual model. The experimental group demonstrated enhanced understanding of library concepts based on their responses to questions at the end of instruction.

In another college-level study,[8] physics students physically engaged with an experiment testing the mechanical forces acting on a bicycle wheel, such as torque and angular momentum. Students were found to have enhanced activation of sensorimotor regions detected on brain imaging during the initial learning process and then later while applying what they learned. The "hands-on" students attained higher scores on a subject matter test compared to their desk-bound peers.

These studies outline the principle of embodied cognition, the idea that one's body or the interactions of one's body with the environment plays a role in, or actually gives rise to, cognition.

They also reinforce research in *Preventive Medicine* that documents the positive correlation between academic lessons infused with moderate physical activity and increased performance on standardized tests.[9]

Movement and Memory

Our memory function, too, becomes stimulated when we move. Several studies reinforce the link between memory and moderate physical activity,[10] some emphasizing how even slight movement or gestures of the body assist our ability to remember.[11] Memory, our ability to learn, the ability of our neurons to create stronger connections, and even our brain's ability to adapt to change all

---

7   Bryan & Karshmer, 2013.
8   Kontra et al., 2015.
9   Donnely, J.E. & Lambourne, K., 2011.
10 Raskin, 2017; Moriya M, 2016.
11 Madan, 2012.

advance when we move. Exercise triggers neurological responses that are unlike those while in stasis, even changing the gene expression in the brain's primary memory center, the hippocampus.[12]

Movement and Brain Chemistry

Physical movement also triggers the production of what John Ratey calls the "Miracle-Gro" for neurons, BDNF (brain-derived neurotrophic factor).

> Physical movement also triggers the production of what John Ratey calls the "Miracle-Gro" for neurons, BDNF (brain-derived neurotrophic factor).

This protein revitalizes current neurons and the connections between them, tiny junction points called synapses. It also stimulates the creation of new neurons, a process referred to as neurogenesis.

BDNF "gives the synapses the tools they need to take in information, process it, associate it, remember it, and put it in context." In the lab, researchers learned that, after adding BDNF to neurons, they "automatically sprouted new branches, producing the same structural growth required for learning—and causing me to think of BDNF as *Miracle-Gro* for the brain."[13]

As early as 1998, scientists began linking physical activity with the increased production of BDNF, which was found to produce a range of positive effects on the brain. BDNF promotes "neuron survival, enhances sprouting, protects neurons against insult, and may be involved in several aspects of learning and memory. Furthermore, behaviors such as physical activity and learning may help maintain and protect neurons at risk in aging and neurodegenerative disease via increased BDNF expression."[14]

In addition to stimulating the production of BDNF, movement also enhances several neurotransmitter (brain chemical messenger) systems, all of which facilitate learning and memory.

These include the dopamine system, which plays a central role in motivation; the

---

12   Tong, 2001.
13   Ratey, 2008.
14   Kesslak JP, 1998.

serotonin system, important to maintaining a state of well-being and positive emotions; and the norepinephrine system, which promotes attention, sensory perception, and motivation.[15]

Movement-based activities help the teacher establish a classroom that takes advantage of these chemicals in the brain. They inject an energetic, positive atmosphere in the classroom that can capture students' attention, strengthen their motivation to attend to the task, and elicit their intellectual effort. They can help those students, who normally might "hate" English or find reading boring, overcome their negative feelings about the subject matter, as they find the process of learning more exciting and engaging.

One reason for this is that such activities involve social engagement. While performing the activity, students relate with each other through eye contact, activating so-called "mirror neurons" that enable imitation and adoption of other people's movements and gesticulations, enhancing communication.

Additionally, during such moments, powerful neurochemicals secrete from the neuron: endorphins, which relieve pain and create a sense of well-being; oxytocin, which promotes social-bonding; and dopamine, which drives motivation through feelings of accomplishment and reward.[16]

> English teachers can also use movement-based activities to prevent certain brain chemicals from inhibiting student learning.

English teachers can also use movement-based activities to prevent certain brain chemicals from inhibiting student learning. Negative emotional states, such as stress, fear, or anger, inhibit the learning process. In such states, excessive levels of cortisol, norepinephrine, and dopamine are released,[17] and the amygdala (the fear center of the brain) blocks acquisition of new information by placing one's brain into a fight-or-flight state of mind.[18] Moreover, the prefrontal cortex shows particular susceptibility to stress-induced discharge

---

15   Doherty & Miravalles, 2019.

16   Willis, 2007.

17   While dopamine is typically associated with a positive sensation of reward, an excess level of dopamine in the brain has been linked to aggressive behavior and poor impulse control. Think of the agitation a child exhibits after "too much screen time": this is in part a result of excess dopamine.

18   Doherty & Miravalles, 2019; Willis, 2009.

of norepinephrine and cortisol, leading to dysfunction of higher level cognitive functions, including executive functions, attention, and working memory.[19]

English teachers can make strategic decisions in light of the brain's response to stress, either introducing it to elicit students' greater attention, concentration, and urgency, or moderating it to prevent students from disengaging and giving up.

In both cases, we are taking into account norepinephrine, which is triggered during moments of urgency, and helps the brain to focus on what it identifies as important and to ignore what is judged irrelevant.[20] This neurochemical can provide enhanced attention and focus to students who are given a clearly defined task and desired goal in a situation defined by urgency, such as timed writing activities or competitive games.

> Our brains are not fixed; neither are our students' potentials. Science verifies this.

However, if we fail to provide students with clarity about the task, the moves required to complete it, or the desired goal, or if the intellectual challenge we give them is not appropriate to their level, then an excess of stress response can have a negative impact on working memory.

In sum, our brains are not fixed; neither are our students' potentials. Science verifies this.

The Psychology of Expert Performance

In addition to research in neuroscience, the psychology of expert performance, a field traditionally considered separate from the language arts world, informs our thinking about secondary English instruction.

The insights from this field have led us to understand reading and writing as intellectual "movements" analogous to the physical movements trained in athletics and the arts. Adopting this paradigm, we have re-envisioned the classroom as a practice space where we help our students internalize a "playbook" of these movements.

---

19 Birnbaum et al. 1999; Liston, McEwen, & Casey, 2009.
20 O'Donnell et al., 2012.

This section will introduce the key principles from this field that have influenced our idea of movement in its figurative application.

Deliberate Practice

Primarily, our figurative understanding of movement is grounded in the work of psychologist K. Anders Ericsson at Florida State University, leading voice in the science of expert performance. Subsequent work by Geoff Colvin and Daniel Coyle has built upon the work of Ericsson.[21]

> Expert performers are not born; they are made. And "deliberate practice" is the process.

This research has concluded that notable achievement occurs not because of innate characteristics or natural talent, but because of "deliberate practice," a specific method of training. In other words, expert performers are not born; they are made. And "deliberate practice" is the process.

Its key principles, used by great coaches, music teachers, and others, shape a "playbook" for distinct achievement:[22]

1. **Motivation:** You must be motivated to attend to the task, fully engaging and paying attention, exerting effort to improve. Expert performers are deliberate, and they select a training regimen specifically designed to give them the skills they need. They are always thinking about their performance and trying to improve it.

2. **Comfort zone:** The most effective training takes place outside your comfort zone; you must willfully push yourself.

3. **Pre-existing knowledge & clarity:** The design of the task should take into account your pre-existing knowledge so that the task can be correctly understood after a *brief* period of instruction.

4. **Feedback:** You should receive immediate informative feedback about the results of your performance. Great coaches know how to pinpoint exactly the areas an athlete must improve. Likewise, the best athletes receive feedback often and use it to modify their performance.

5. **Repetition:** Repeatedly performing the same or similar tasks will rewire your brain for faster processing, and will also allow you to "automate"

---

21 Colvin, 2010; Coyle, 2009.
22 Ericsson, Krampe, & Tesch-Romer, 1993; Ericsson & Pool, 2016.

functions, so that you can perform certain tasks without thinking. Count only good repetitions, though: whatever you do repeatedly, you will encode.

6   **Chunking:** Expert performers know how to chunk: they slow it down, break it up, go over the target performance again and again. Breaking down more complex movements into shorter sequences allows your brain to learn them faster. Doing this also provides greater clarity about the elements of the target performance.

7   **Developing Memory Networks:** Intricate neural networks explain why the best football players, jazz musicians, and chessmasters can respond effectively to a given situation without thinking: their brains have integrated massive amounts of data into meaningful frameworks (what Ericsson calls "mental representations") and stored this information in long-term memory. Deliberate practice depends on developing these memory networks so that the brain can run more efficiently. It enables the brain to quickly process large amounts of information without coming up against the restrictions of short-term memory. Sophisticated memory networks enable the top performers to automate their skills, freeing their minds to focus on strategic execution.

The principles of deliberate practice have branched outward from the psychological community, taking root in other fields. In the sports world, they influence how the best coaches and athletes think about training. Music teachers apply these principles to refining musicianship, and entrepreneurs adopt them in their approach to business.[23]

More recently, the principles of deliberate practice have also begun to find their way into the classroom. The work of Robin Fogarty, Gene Kerns, and Brian Pete applies Ericsson's thinking to general education; similarly, Doug Lemov outlines teaching techniques informed by Ericsson's work.[24]

It is time that secondary English teachers started listening, too. While the direct application of Ericsson's principles to the classroom may have certain limits, we would be foolish to ignore them, especially if it means denying our students a pathway towards greater achievement and mastery of complex skills they need to be successful in the world.

---

23   Kyska, 2012; Barr, (n.d.).
24   Fogarty et al., 2018; Lemov, 2010; Lemov, 2012.

For English teachers, the import of Ericsson's work is two-fold:

First, it encourages us to abandon counterproductive beliefs about our students' potential.

> Ericsson and others debunk the popular notion that "talent plays a major, even determining, role in how accomplished a person can become."

Ericsson and others debunk the popular notion that "talent plays a major, even determining, role in how accomplished a person can become."[25] Their findings imply that we are mistaken to think that "you can't teach writing," that it's a "gift," that a student is innately "a math person," or that one who writes "how he talks" cannot be taught the proper vocabulary, grammar, and style.

The research affirms that, rather than being predetermined or fixed by genetic differences, our students' potential is *plastic*. They can change, move, and grow; we can shape them. It is important for us to believe this as teachers. If we believe otherwise, we will limit our students' learning. Not only must we believe it, we must also communicate this reality to them, that their capabilities in English, in all school subjects, and in all areas of life are not fixed.

Second, Ericsson's principles tell us how we must design our classrooms if we wish to enable students to achieve.

The challenge we face is that the majority of our students do not seek expert performance in English. Our students, along with the majority of human beings, do not naturally emulate the would-be expert, but the amateur or the mediocre performer, who engages not in deliberate but in "naive" practice, who *just* plays the song, shoots the ball, runs around.

Likewise, in school, most students do not behave deliberately. They focus on "getting homework done," "turning it in," and "getting the grade" with minimal effort, and minimal attention paid to the process.

To slow down, to "embrace struggle," to concentrate on the diction of a poem,

---

25   Ericsson & Pool, 2016.

for example, is much more difficult for them, something many will not choose to do on their own.[26]

Ericsson acknowledges this difference between students in the classroom and individuals who have purposefully chosen to pursue excellence in a field:

> Teachers in the general education system are at a disadvantage . . . when compared with sports coaches and teachers of music or dance, whose charges have generally **chosen to participate** in these activities and **presumably had some initial interest**. By contrast, a classroom teacher must help every child improve their performance and start building skills, no matter how little motivation they may have or what abilities they may bring to the classroom.[27]

While we know that most students will not choose by themselves to step onto the pathway towards excellence in English, we also know that it is up to us to design lessons that have them take those crucial steps. You walk before you know you are walking.

In other words, in a classroom where "deliberate practice" occurs, the teacher has to take on the role of the motivated individual, and design lessons that engage Ericsson's methodologies.

The Profile of the English Coach

To this end, Ericsson's thinking points to teaching strategies that mirror those of the coach who trains athletes by deliberate practice. They allow us to envision the profile of an English "coach," an individual "familiar with the abilities of expert performers" in reading and writing "and with how those abilities can best be developed."[28]

- **The English Coach clearly delineates a training program that allows students to see the path to higher achievement in their field.**

To be shaped into expert performers in English, our students need a training program with well-defined, specific goals, similar to the ones coaches use to train their athletes. Our instruction should chart a path toward the target

---

26 Kyska, 2012; Coyle, cited in Fogarty et al., 2018.
27 Foreword to Fogarty et al., 2018, emphasis added.
28 Ericsson & Pool, 2016.

performance that we aim to develop in our students' reading and writing.

Our daily lessons, like the coach's plan, should break down this overall objective into smaller ones. Each day we focus on "improving some aspect of the target performance." Each lesson constitutes a step in "a series of small changes that will add up to the desired larger change" of developing our students into critical readers and writers.[29]

- **The English Coach creates a playbook for students to practice, helping them visualize and understand the key elements of the target performance.**

In any field, the expert performers have highly detailed and sophisticated "mental representations" for the actions they regularly perform.

A mental representation is the mental picture created when we think about an object, action, or concept. Take, for example, the experienced cab driver's mental map of New York City. The pictures in Lionel Messi's brain of ways to dribble the soccer ball around defenders are another.

Untrained students do not possess these pictures: they do not have a clear, detailed sense of English performance.

Some look at a paragraph and simply see a block of text, their eyes scanning over it without recognizing moments of transition or understanding the logical relationship between sentences. Asked to define a paragraph, they might only mention that it must contain a certain number of sentences.

> We must remove all abstract, vague ideas our students have about reading and writing, and replace these with specific, concrete moves they can make.

As teachers, we must remove all abstract, vague ideas our students have about reading and writing, and replace these with specific, concrete moves they can make. We must give them a playbook to help them visualize how the skilled readers and writers move.

To create a well-written paragraph, for example, requires doing several smaller things right. We identify these movements: the topic

---

29   Ericsson & Pool, 2016.

sentence, blended textual evidence supporting it, elaboration of one's ideas, logical transitions, etc. We develop a common language to identify them. And in our lessons, we regularly point students back to them.

- **The English Coach engages students in daily practice designed to help them internalize the playbook, that is, to develop their memory networks related to reading and writing movements.**

Practicing the movements of reading and writing must become the focus of class time. Coaches in athletics do not spend most of practice time talking about performance; their trainees begin to practice the skills "after a brief period of instruction."[30] Following this example dictates that we talk about reading and writing only in the context of how our students can execute them. Nor do we delay students' practice until after they have mastered the knowledge, placing all moments of action or assessment at the end of a class period or the end of a unit.

Instead, after a brief period of teaching new content, we must require students to use this new information in practice. Engaging them in this way provides a relevant context for their knowledge, so that students know why it is useful and how it may be applied.

Ericsson explains that balancing brief instruction with student practice is crucial, because it aligns with the brain's natural memory function:

> If you teach a student facts, concepts, and rules, those things go into long-term memory as individual pieces, and if a student then wishes to do something with them—use them to solve a problem, reason with them to answer a question, or organize and analyze them to come up with a theme or a hypothesis—the limitations of attention and short-term memory kick in. The student must keep all these different, unconnected pieces in mind while working with them toward a solution. However, if this information is assimilated as part of building mental representations aimed at doing something, the individual pieces become part of an interconnected pattern that provides context and meaning to the information, making it easier [for the brain] to work with.[31]

In brief, what Ericsson is telling English teachers is, you need to weave the content you want students to learn

---

30   Ericsson, Krampe, & Tesch-Romer, 1993.
31   Ericsson & Pool, 2016.

- about literary genres,
- about literary devices like allusion, archetype, and metaphor,
- about the rules of punctuation,
- about sentence structures, and
- about paragraphing

into activities that engage them in practicing the movements you want them to be able to perform, such as

- commenting on the tragic nature of a scene in the literary text,
- explaining how the author's use of allusion, archetype, or metaphor establishes a larger idea,
- writing an essay that contains no errors in punctuation,
- developing a writing style that employs a variety of sentence structures, or
- writing effective expository paragraphs.

> If you delay the moment when students have to move intellectually, you also delay the moment when they will begin acquiring mastery.

Trying to first give them all of the knowledge and then have them do something with it later can actually inhibit student performance and *waste class time*, because the neurons encoding the knowledge remain isolated from the neurons related to close-reading or composition.

The English Coach understands that if you delay the moment when students have to move intellectually, you also delay the moment when they will begin acquiring mastery.

- **The English Coach uses repetition deliberately, enabling students to automate their skills.**

Like the coach, we also should have our pupils "repeatedly perform the same or similar tasks," repetition being a powerful engine for developing and internalizing skill.[32] Research underscores how repetition anchored in

---

32 Ericsson, Krampe, & Tesch-Romer, 1993.

classroom instructional design physically alters our students' brains for better performance.

The brain's fundamentally adaptive nature should inform our thinking about teaching. Daniel Coyle shows that our students' skills are directly related to the function of the neural circuits in their brains, for these circuits "dictate the precise strength and timing of each muscle contraction, the shape and content of each thought."[33]

Repetition improves the function of these circuits because it facilitates the production of myelin, a whitish fatty coating that wraps around the axons of nerve cells and increases the speed of electrical signals that travel through them. This increased velocity leads to faster execution of the physical or mental movement.

Once a neural circuit reaches a certain velocity, the related skill becomes *automatic*; the more our brains fire a particular circuit, the less we are aware of it. Where at first great concentration and effort were required, the movement is now unconscious, as if it were innate. This "automaticity" is what world-class athletes and musicians acquire through deliberate practice. It enables them to respond fluidly, rapidly, even creatively in their performance.

The direct relationship between repetition and neurological development ultimately suggests that "the brain really is like a muscle," and that the "dynamics of practice" in the cognitive realm are parallel to those in the physical.

In *Unlocking Student Talent*, Robin J. Fogarty and her colleagues even recommend "exploring deliberate practice [in the classroom] through a gym-based analogy," viewing the lesson as a "workout" for the brain to build more myelin along the neural pathways related to the essential academic skills.[34]

---

33 Coyle, 2009.
34 Fogarty et al., 2018.

> Whatever our students do repeatedly will cause their brains to adapt, so that they may do it more quickly. Conversely, what they do not repeatedly practice, they will not internalize.

Whatever our students do repeatedly will cause their brains to adapt, so that they may do it more quickly. Conversely, what they do not repeatedly practice, they will not internalize.

Note that the repetition required by deliberate practice is distinct from the mentality of "drill and kill."

Rather than solely focusing on rote memorization of the parts of speech, or regurgitation of facts, the repetition of deliberate practice focuses on refining specific aspects of the target performance.

- **The English Coach understands that struggle and failure are a necessary part of training.**

The research about repetition and skill should also influence the way we think about our students' mistakes. If students perform reading or writing skills at a mediocre level, we should understand that this does not indicate inability or intellectual stasis. On the contrary, their neural circuits are not firing optimally, as Coyle points out:

> So there's the picture in a nutshell: each time we deeply practice a nine-iron swing or a guitar chord or a chess opening, we are slowly installing broadband in our circuitry. We are firing a signal that those tiny green tentacles sense; they react by reaching toward the nerve fibers. They grasp, they squish, and they make another wrap, thickening the sheath. They build a little more insulation along the wire, which adds a bit more bandwidth and precision to the skill circuit, which translates into an infinitesimal bit more skill and speed. **Struggle is not optional—it's neurologically required: in order to get your skill circuit to fire optimally, you must by definition fire the circuit suboptimally; you must make mistakes and pay attention to those mistakes; you must slowly teach your circuit.** You must also keep firing that circuit—i.e., practicing—in order to keep myelin functioning properly.[35]

The implicit reminder: students are *plastic* individuals; their potential is not fixed or limited by intellectual struggle. We want our weaker students to fire those

---

35 Coyle, 2009, emphasis added.

"suboptimal" skill circuits under our guidance as often as possible. If "struggling in certain targeted ways—operating at the edges of your ability, where you make mistakes—makes you smarter," our lessons must create this "targeted," planned challenge.

Change the way we think about failure. Struggle as a neurological requirement means that we have to change the way we think about failure. The way the brain learns should encourage us not to avoid or delay skills practice until knowledge has been fully acquired and students are "ready" for it (i.e., won't make any mistakes).

We actually want students to make mistakes so that we may guide them. The longer we delay the practice of an essential movement, we are also delaying their mastery of it. If the movement appears too complex for them to handle, perhaps we need to do some further chunking, breaking that movement down into something students can do today.

Let us remember that the majority of students will certainly not embrace struggle and "slowly teach [their] circuit[s]"; we as teachers—coaches in the classroom—take on that role. Our lessons therefore must aim to generate the high number of repetitions needed to strengthen the related neural connections.

- **The English Coach gives immediate feedback to students about their performance.**

Finally, one last trait of Ericsson's ideal coach that we should notice is that this coach does not stop with the repetition of the movement, but provides the performer with "immediate feedback" and intervenes to modify the performance.

Less of a "sage on the stage," the English Coach uses his or her expertise to observe and intervene, preventing students from mindlessly going through the motions, instead focusing them on specific aspects of their performance, and communicating strategies to modify their behavior and address problems with it.

Athletic Coaching

A third field, athletic coaching, offers English teachers still more insights about how to design their classrooms to enable student achievement.

Due to the intersection of the psychology of expert performance with the world of athletics, several relevant coaching principles, like feedback, have already been mentioned in the previous section. For the sake of clarity, we will not be repeating these principles where this intersection occurs.

Look like the Game

An overarching idea that guides coaches' decisions is to make practice "look like the game," to focus in training on the essential movements that a player must use in a live performance. Specifically, we invite teachers to consider two coaching applications of this larger idea: the SAID principle and the use of scrimmage.

The SAID Principle - Specific Adaptation To Imposed Demands

"One of the most basic concepts in sports science," the SAID principle stands for Specific Adaptation to Imposed Demands: "when the body is placed under some form of stress, it starts to make adaptations that will allow the body to get better at withstanding that specific form of stress in the future." In other words, the body specifically adapts to the demands placed upon it in training.[36] Or as Coach Charlie DeLong puts it in the foreword to this book: "You get [in the game] what you train for [in practice]."

Applying the SAID principle means, first, understanding that "every sport poses its own unique demands and that, in order to improve skills unique to a particular sport, it's best to practice the moves used in that sport."[37]

> Effective coaches break the game down and isolate the various movements necessary for successful performance.

Effective coaches, therefore, break the game down and isolate the various movements necessary for successful performance. Then, they design practices that specifically train each of these movements. These practices impose demands on their players' bodies and minds that mirror the demands of the game, forcing the players to adapt in ways that will improve their performances.

Basketball coaches, for example, break down the game of basketball into its smaller movements: shooting free-throws, dribbling around defenders, running down the court,

---

36   Hargrove, 2009; Pearson et al., 2000.
37   "What is the SAID Principle?", 2013.

blocking shots, getting rebounds, etc. They think carefully about the demands a game imposes on players trying to complete these movements successfully, and they design practices to prepare their players for this tension.

In a game, players not only have to be able to shoot the ball accurately, they have to be able to do so quickly, from many different positions, and most often with opposing players trying to block their shots. A shooting drill informed by the SAID principle would not have players simply hold the ball and shoot whenever, wherever, or however they like. Instead, the training exercise would seek to recreate the demands of the game, giving the player the ball in different areas, limiting the amount of time the player has to shoot, or adding defenders in the player's way. These demands would increase incrementally, practicing in a 1-on-1 situation, then a 3-on-3, and finally a 5-on-5 play. In this way, a coach applying the SAID principle gradually augments the complexity and tension of the training environment until it looks like the game.

As good coaches understand, players need to experience what it feels like to execute the movements of the sport in game-like situations; such training is the best way to prepare them to perform in a real game.

This principle also holds true for the secondary English classroom.

In the classroom, we are not conditioning the physical body, but the brain, which adapts to the specific *mental* demands placed upon it, rewiring its neurons to become more efficient at the intellectual movements it repeatedly performs. Our instructional time, then, devotes itself to training the different movements required in our academic field's game.

The game for English students is often a timed performance that requires critical, analytical reading and expository or persuasive writing (or speech). Taking place on the figurative field of the literary text and the written page, this game involves specific movements, like isolating evidence inside the text, linking evidence with an interpretive claim, constructing coherent sentences and paragraphs, and so on.

The English game also imposes demands that make executing these movements challenging: the difficult syntax or vocabulary of the literary author, the time limit of the reading or writing exercise, the student's familiarity with the passage being analyzed, the changing shape of a verbal discussion, and other demands.

The SAID principle affirms that English students need to train for this game's specific movements in our classrooms, not merely hear us talk about them.

> English students need to train for this game's specific movements in our classrooms, not merely hear us talk about them.

A teacher reading information about thesis statements off of a set of slides gives students no direct experience of this movement or the tension that arises when trying to execute it in a game. Executing a lesson plan in this manner delays the actual practice of the movement.

By contrast, a teacher employing the SAID principle might briefly discuss a few sample thesis statements, but would also involve students in the practice of creating one in a demanding environment.

For example, this teacher might give students ten minutes to draft on the board thesis statements that model one of the provided samples and develop a claim about a passage in the text. The teacher might gradually increase the demands on students by having them create a thesis statement for a passage they have not seen before, giving them less time, or requiring them not only to develop a thesis statement but also two topic sentences supporting it. This is how a teacher would train a specific aspect of the English game, which will require students to draft multi-paragraph essays (including a thesis statement) in a limited amount of time.

Additionally, this coaching principle calls secondary English teachers to rethink what a drill is. Often, in our academic field, we have understood "drill" to mean the isolation of a skill and a mechanical repetition of a movement until it is internalized.

> Rethink what a drill is.

With grammar, for example, we might "drill" the participle phrase with our students: doing a worksheet together that requires them to identify the participle phrase within a sentence, fill in the blank with a participle phrase, write ten sentences containing participle phrases, etc.

The SAID principle tells us that a drill can—and must—be more than this. It's training for the game.

A SAID-inspired drill would train the participle phrase skill by "practicing [it] in a game-like situation,"³⁸ such as imitating a model sentence that contains this structure, or creating a sentence that uses this structure to introduce the writer's interpretive voice before a piece of evidence.

Practicing the skill in game-like situations like these requires students both to use the new skill and relate it with others (e.g., the skills of recognizing subject and verb, of writing compound sentences, of creating parallel structures). It also allows them to begin understanding the application of the skill in the larger context of the game, when and why and how to use it, "matching the right techniques to the right moments" in a game.³⁹

Helping them to experience this application is critical. A student who only drills a sentence structure in isolation will not automatically start employing this structure in the more complex situation of writing an essay in a timed situation. He will not suddenly come upon a blank in his own sentence that demands a participle phrase.

> "If they can't see the application of something you're doing in practice, *they won't use it* in a game."

As Chris Hill, head basketball coach at Jesuit College Preparatory School, explains, "You *need* to help [the players] see the application. If they can't see the application of something you're doing in practice, *they won't use it* in a game."⁴⁰ His words align with what research tells us about the brain, that it naturally filters out and discards information that it does not recognize as relevant to a given context or task.⁴¹

Like athletic coaches, English teachers will "get [from their students] what they train [them] for [in class]," and this reality requires us to think carefully about how we use our instructional time.

- Which movements of the game are we training?

- What demands are we imposing during the practice of this movement?

- Does our practice look like the game, or is it delaying students' experience of it?

---

38   DeLong, 2022.
39   Lemov, Woolway, & Yezzi, 2012.
40   Hill, 2022.
41   For more details about this topic, see "Behavioral Relevance" and "Developing Memory Networks" in chapter 2.

Scrimmage

Another useful concept in athletic coaching that falls within the larger category of "Look like the Game" is the scrimmage.

After training players with the SAID principle, honing individual movements in incrementally more demanding and complex situations, coaches often move into scrimmage (a practice game) to assess whether players have internalized the sport's movements, understand their proper application, and are ready to combine them in an actual performance.

In scrimmage, the training environment increases in complexity to simulate actual gameplay as closely as possible. It is no longer a shooting or passing or sprinting exercise; all of the movements and variables are in play. Good coaches know that players need to spend some of their practice time here. If they only train their skills in isolation, or in an oversimplified environment, they may be unable to perform them on game day.

While the players scrimmage, coaches step back and take on a facilitator role. Occasionally, they may interrupt the scrimmage to provide feedback or question their players about what the scrimmage is revealing.[42]

For the most part, though, scrimmage is a time for coaches to observe, not intervene. It tells them what the team still needs to work on, while it gives the players the freedom to play, test themselves, see what they can do on their own, and learn from the game itself. After the scrimmage, the team can transition back into the SAID stage of training, working on individual movements that the players did not perform effectively in the scrimmage.

This continual back-and-forth between drills (informed by the SAID principle) and scrimmages is the strategy that emerges from the coaching world, and this strategy aligns with neuroscience and psychology research about how the brain learns.[43]

The coach uses the drill to train a neural skill circuit in their players' brains: the neurons related to passing the ball, for instance. The coach then uses the

---

[42] For more on the use of inductive questioning and dialogue as tools to develop players' metacognitive abilities, see "Guided Discovery" later in this section.

[43] See "What Teachers Need to Know About the Brain" in Chapter 2 of this book, specifically, the categories of Behavioral Relevance, Inductive-Predictive Instruction, Recognizing Patterns, and Developing Memory Networks.

scrimmage to connect these neurons to a larger memory network of what the game is like, a network that includes other skills, tactical knowledge, memories of specific game situations, and other information.

This rhythm of practice, drill and scrimmage combined, has produced competent athletes for decades, but we have only recently begun to understand the neurological reasons explaining its effectiveness.

English Scrimmage

Seeing its application in athletics, we propose that scrimmage is a useful strategy for the English classroom and an important moment for the English learner.

For our purposes, we will define the scrimmage in English as a major classroom activity that involves multiple skills used in the actual game and allows the teacher to assess students' mastery of them.

Chapter Four of this book provides several examples. In *The Discussion Quiz*, typically occurring at the end of a unit, students sit in a circle and discuss a series of questions about the literary text. This discussion provides the teacher with a vehicle to assess students' abilities to develop a claim; identify relevant diction, detail, and imagery in the text to support a claim; pair logical interpretive associations with a piece of textual evidence; and elaborate on an existing claim by providing additional textual support. Similarly, *The Tournament of Scholars* facilitates a scrimmage combining reading, writing, and speaking skills in a timed competition.

In Chapter Four, *The Paragraph Chart*, a graphic organizer used to identify and structure a paragraph's several components, provides another framework for class scrimmage. In a given class period, it can become the field on which students play the game, drafting as much of a paragraph as they can in the allotted time. While they work, the teacher watches and gathers valuable data about student performance.

The idea of applying scrimmage to the English classroom through activities like these may appear impractical or daunting.

"My students are not ready for that yet."

"That would never work in my class."

"This activity would be such a mess with my kids."

An essential lesson from the world of athletics is that reactions like these get in the way of our students' development.

> Coaches do not wait for their players to master a skill before letting them practice it.

Coaches do not wait for their players to master a skill before letting them practice it. They understand that using the skill in a game-like environment is an important part of the journey *towards* mastering it.

Scrimmage implies *lots* of failure. But this failure signals neither the coach's incompetence nor a player's hopelessness of ever achieving success. Scrimmage simply reveals areas that still need improvement, while giving the players an important opportunity to apply their skills in a game-like environment.

This does not mean, of course, that we should stop all use of activities that, like drills, focus on individual skills in isolation. Such activities remain useful refining tools.

We should question, though, what motivates our desire to rely solely on these smaller activities and delay putting students into the larger game until we deem they are all fully "ready" for it. This impulse to only let students "play the game" when they are sure to be successful runs contrary to what neuroscience, psychology, and coaching have to say about performance. If we want to train our students properly, moments of scrimmage are vital.

Guided Discovery

In addition to designing practices that look like the game, coaches seek to develop players' awareness and understanding of the game's movements.

Ultimately, good coaches do not want players to need their instructions to know what to do in a game; on the contrary, US Youth Soccer Coaching Director Sam Snow writes, "Every coach's dream is to have 'self-thinking players' who can make their own decisions on the field, easily learn from mistakes, and take ownership of their development even with limited instruction from the coach."[44]

---

44   Snow, 2015.

Guided discovery is one method coaches use to develop such players. The defining characteristic of this technique is the use of inductive questioning, instead of explicit directives, as a teaching tool. The coach "never tells [players] the answer" to a problem posed by the game, but leads them with questions to discover it for themselves.[45]

To provide a simple example, one soccer coach might say, "Kick through the laces!" But the coach using Guided Discovery would ask, "Which part of the foot should you use to strike the ball? Why?" In the first case, players receive instructions without having to think; in the second, they must find answers, "understand the why," before the practice continues.[46]

In this way, Guided Discovery pushes the players to become aware of their own thought processes and decision-making; in other words, it facilitates "metacognitive activity," a concept we will explain further in the next chapter's section on the brain.

Using this technique has other benefits, too. Questioning conveys to the players that the coach believes they have valuable answers to give, an important role in what happens at practice, and a responsibility for their own development. Requiring their answers also requires their attention, actively engaging them in the learning process.[47]

Additionally, this method of coaching through questions aligns with how the brain learns, appealing to its instinctive impulse to make predictions and recognize patterns.[48]

Finally, it provides coaches with valuable information about their players, which aids them in their planning.

As Chris Hill explains, "In practice, I try to only ask questions. Because when you ask the players questions, that will tell you what they don't know, and *that* will tell you where you have to go next."[49] Guided Discovery not only guides the players, then. The coach, always one step ahead, uses players' answers to shape future training sessions.

---

45   Mosston, 1966; Germain, 2013.
46   Germain, 2013; Barber, 2015.
47   Germain, 2013.
48   See "What Teachers Need to Know About the Brain" in Chapter 2 of this book.
49   Hill, 2022.

Cultivating this awareness of how to move, and why, is equally vital for the game of reading and writing. Our students must discover how to play this game for themselves, become aware of their own decision-making, and develop their understanding of the movements we practice with them.

Discovery in the English Classroom

Here is an example of guided discovery applied to the English classroom.[50]

First, the teacher identifies a fundamental movement to practice, and students perform this movement while the teacher observes and evaluates their current skill level. For instance, the teacher might choose to practice the skill of blending textual evidence in a sentence. The teacher divides the students into pairs and defines the task.

- "You and your partner have five minutes to write a sentence that contains a quotation from the passage we read, along with your own words."

Following this initial practice, the teacher asks a series of questions and leads students inductively toward discoveries about the movement.

- "When you're trying to use a quotation inside the sentence – what sometimes happens?"
- "Read this one out loud. What's wrong here? What do we have to do to fix this?"

As students respond to these questions, the teacher draws the class' attention to the ideal answers they offer, introduces cues that become part of the class playbook, and identifies common mistakes:

- "What Noah said was excellent – so, when we want to use a piece of evidence in our sentence, what do we have to do? We have to *blend* it."
- "Okay, take a look at these three models. Which ones have evidence *blended* with the writer's own words?"
- "What did this pair do wrong? What can we do to *blend* this one correctly?"

---

50   Drost & Todorovich (2013, cited in Germain, 2013) outline the application of this technique in a physical education context. Here, we have adapted their outline to an example from English.

After this discussion, the class practices the movement again. But this time, students begin to incorporate through directed practice a newly discovered concept (i.e., blending) and they "practice with a purpose."[51]

Clearly, guided discovery differs greatly from deductive methods commonly seen in the English classroom, where the teacher prepares a presentation about using textual evidence, tells students the rules, and reads examples to them, using a significant amount of class time to relay information, thus delaying the time when students will have to think and act on their own.

The deductive approach attracts many teachers because it seems easier and more effective in the short term. Telling students what to do is easy.

"Don't use a piece of evidence in a topic sentence."

Pushing them to discover the proper application of a skill requires more planning, energy, and class time. Simply imagine if, instead of giving the brief command above, the teacher guides students to discover this rule through a series of questions:

- Teacher: "What is a topic sentence? What does it do?"
- "I like how Casey put that. It's sort of like your 'main point.' What else?"
- "'What the paragraph is about.' 'What you're trying to prove.' – I like those answers. When you're trying to 'prove' something, what do you have to do first?"
- "What comes next?"
- "Where does evidence go in a paragraph, then?"
- "After the topic sentence – that's right. Why?"
- "What happens if I put evidence before my topic sentence? Or inside it?"
- "Why would I not want to do this?"

Too often, however, the above process doesn't occur. Instead, the teacher works deductively, desiring more control over whether or not the class "gets through" the lesson within the class period.

---

51 Germain, 2013.

> *Students who have not discovered "the why" require the teacher to explain again and again how to move.*

Yet while telling students how to perform a particular movement and "getting through" the lesson saves time in the short term, it wastes it in the long term, delaying the process of integrating new skills into the brain's long-term memory. Students who have not discovered "the why" require the teacher to explain again and again how to move.

Neuroscience has now made clear the significant limitations of deductive methods.

What we now know about the brain confirms that we are wasting instructional time when we are talking and our students are not having to move intellectually on their own.

This neurological reality challenges us to set aside our own wishes to control what students think or hear them repeat our own thoughts back to us. Our true role in the classroom is to coach our students how to think, not to think for them. Ultimately, when the coin toss cues the start of the game, we'll be on the bench observing the results of all our training sessions.

We are not saying that coaches *never* tell their players what to do. But the best coaches are mindful of the difference between "self-thinking" players and those who can only respond to a coach's directives. If we seek to help students to become like the former, we must avoid designing lessons that do not force them to think and move on their own.

We have to watch what we say.

Silence

"That's where the gold is–when I shut up."[52]

Basketball coach Chris Hill intentionally limits the amount of time he talks during practice. "I get one minute to intro a drill. During a drill, I get 30 seconds to stop it and talk. Coach Alexander knows that I can go on and on, so now, if I talk too long, he just turns the music back up and I have to stop."

---

52   Hill, 2022.

> Their movement needs to predominate far more than the movement of our mouths.

Hill's words remind us of the appropriate relationship between teacher talk and student movement: their movement needs to predominate far more than the movement of our mouths. Effective coaches know this and strategically adopt silence as part of their coaching practice. Some coaches will even record themselves during a practice session and listen later to evaluate how effectively or excessively they spoke.[53]

Silence allows coaches to stop focusing on what they are saying and pay attention to what their players are communicating through their words and actions.[54]

- Do they understand why we're doing this?
- Is the task clear to them?
- How do they think I want them to execute this particular skill?

Coaches who stop talking and get their players moving receive valuable information about their players' performance and their practice design.

Silence also allows the players to play the game without having their minds crowded by endless instructions. They need enough silence to forget the coach and focus on their performance.

Obviously, this is not to say that a good coach is one who rarely speaks. As Nathan Barber affirms, "A coach has great instructional information to give his players. Players need to hear what their coach has to say about their strengths and weaknesses, how to improve, and how to prepare for the next match. Players need to hear their coaches' vision and expectations."[55]

> Good coaches recognize the right moment (when they should speak) and the right content (what is useful to say).

Good coaches, though, recognize the right moment (when they should speak) and the right content (what is useful to say).

---

53   DeLong, 2022.
54   Cushion, 2010; Barber, 2015.
55   Barber, 2014.

There are a few key "right moments" for the coach to speak:

- when briefly explaining the day's training exercises at the beginning of practice;
- when giving brief instructions at the introduction of a drill;
- when intervening with short, simple cues to direct or correct the players' movement during a drill;
- when giving feedback or questioning players after a drill.

In none of these moments is it helpful for the coach to pontificate about the game, digress into personal anecdotes, or lecture at length about the art of the dribble.

Neuroscience documents that players' brains will not know what to do with this information, and will therefore filter it out. It is more useful to give players actionable information related to their performance; coaches' verbal interventions should be short, simple, and quick.

The example of celebrated basketball coach John Wooden illustrates this point. Researchers studying his coaching technique observed Wooden's "economy of talk": "His [modeling] demonstrations are rarely longer than five seconds, but they are of such clarity as to leave an image in memory much like a textbook sketch."[56]

His exquisite feedback skills depended in part upon his use of silence. Wooden understood that his players needed to hear specific, essential information, and then needed to get back to playing the game.

English teachers need to incorporate this concept of silence into our understanding of what happens instructionally. We must become aware of our own behavior in the classroom.

- What percentage of class time am I using to talk?
- What percentage of class time engages students in moving intellectually?
- When I intervene in the middle of an activity, how long does this take?

---

56   Gallimore & Tharp, 1976.

- How much time elapses between the moment I ask a question and the moment I start talking again?
- If students do not answer my question, do I answer it for them and keep talking?

We must develop a set of brief, efficient cues that refer to specific plays, a "common language" that allows us to quickly direct students' movement:[57]

- "I'm not seeing any L2 in this sentence."
- "Your L2 and your L1 don't match."
- "Look at your topic strings. Which string has no L2 in it?"
- "Highlight the L1 in your paragraph. Read it out loud to me. Which L1 does not prove your Topic Sentence?"

It takes time for students to learn the teacher's cues, and it requires self-awareness and effort for the teacher to practice this economy of speech. Yet this balance of efficient speech and intentional silence ultimately benefits students' learning. It allows them to focus on their own performance during an exercise, and it draws their attention to what most needs improvement with clear, direct feedback.

Neuroscience, Psychology, and Coaching: Application

While the education world has begun to take note of research in neuroscience, psychology, and coaching, specific instructional applications for the secondary English classroom have yet to take shape.[58]

Our book fills this gap, for it is designed to help secondary English teachers visualize how these three fields can direct their instructional choices as they build their own playbook.

In the following chapters, we apply the research in these fields to the design of a secondary English playbook for the classroom. We then present movement-based activities that train the core plays.

---

57 Lemov, Woolway, & Yezzi, 2012. In Chapter 3, we explain these cues as we define the core plays in our playbook.
58 Barber, 2014; Fogarty et al., 2018; Lemov, 2014; Lemov, Woolway, & Yezzi, 2012.

02

WHAT WE NEED TO KNOW ABOUT THE BRAIN

The Athletic Paradigm

Great coaching programs produce great playbooks—a carefully constructed set of movements for players to execute during game time. Each play is triggered by a simple language cue that directs a player toward a precise behavior. The entire coaching staff works from this playbook. Players learn and memorize the movements, and field practice allows players to internalize these moves so that they instinctively respond to game-time stimuli.

After players internalize the correct movement of each play, the ultimate goal of consistent practice is—as Craig Simmons writes—to "perform the technique without thinking about it, allowing attention to be devoted to strategic and tactical aspects of performance."[59]

English teachers need to borrow this paradigm, and now brain research demonstrates that we must see our classrooms as a field to practice the intellectual movements that help ensure all students experience success.

Designing a playbook for the English student begins with core questions:

- What skills must the English student internalize in order to read complex texts?

- What skills assist the student with crafting an essay within a timed situation?

- How can we break these movements into smaller parts so that our weakest students can practice them?

- How can we design language cues that correspond to precise movements in writing and reading?

The playbook demystifies the expert performance of the ideal reader and writer. For students who think they can't write well or can't interpret poems convincingly or can't do grammar, the playbook reveals they can and shows them how.

---

[59] "Skill Acquisition in Football 8 to 16 Year Olds." (N.D.)

Because the playbook contains precise movements that students can understand and then execute, it opens a pathway to academic achievement for all students.

As English teachers, we often forget that the majority of our students have not magically internalized the skills of interpretive reading and analytical writing that spurred us to major in English. Too often we fail to realize that students will not acquire these skills unless we as teachers stimulate their acquisition through coherent strategies. Simply running a glorified book club in class, waxing philosophical with a few gifted students during fifty minutes, pretending a Socratic dialogue is occurring while the weakest students sit passively wondering how Michele decided that the image of the spider reflects the psychological entrapment employed by Miss Havisham—none of these manifest effective instruction.

We would scoff at a coach who used the majority of practice time to talk *at* his players. But we have lauded the sages on the stage. Science proves, though, that the teacher-centered model stymies the impulses of the brain.

With neuroscience and the psychology of expert performance, the English teacher is equipped to craft a playbook that will indeed win championships.

What Teachers Need to Know About the Brain

Our brains continue to grow and respond to stimuli in a process called **neuroplasticity**; our brains are not static but dynamic. Our instructional decisions ought to stimulate the neuroplastic energy that fuels learning and memory. These decisions expedite physical changes that make our students' brains work more efficiently.[60]

Learning, in fact, is the primary way in which our brains grow and change; our brain's strength is not marked by the presence of newly created neurons, but marked rather by the formation of new connections between existing neurons, forming new **memory networks**.[61]

---

60   McTighe & Willis, 2009.
61   Owens, 2017.

As the brain begins to learn, it becomes more effective if it absorbs stimuli from a variety of modalities—auditory, visual, physical.[62] In this basic process, information and new learning gets prioritized and sifted, either discarded for lack of relevance or incorporated into previous or emerging circuits of memory.[63]

> Our goal as instructors is to direct new learning so that it becomes part of longer term memory.

Our goal as instructors is to direct new learning so that it becomes part of longer term memory.

The good news—teacher choices can positively influence each stage of this intricate process, providing all students the opportunity to achieve.

The brain possesses several basic impulses that should direct our instructional choices. The brain

- is dynamic and changing, continuing to grow through a process of neuroplasticity;[64]

- strengthens memory networks that are stimulated frequently;[65]

- possesses a survival instinct that derives pleasure from predicting outcomes based on seeking patterns;[66]

- processes a limited amount of new information: its filtering system will quickly discard information not used or connected to existing memory networks;[67]

- must be connected to larger long term circuits;[68]

- requires breaks between new learning to rehearse and review information just entered into the short term memory;[69]

- strengthens memory circuits when learning occurs through multiple

---

62 Schneider, et al., 2018; van den Heuval, et al., 2009.
63 Eichenbaum, H. 2017.
64 Jensen & McConchie, 2020; McTighe & Willis, 2009.
65 Sanes, J., & Lichtman, J., 2001; Jensen, 2005.
66 McTighe & Willis, 2009.
67 Thalmann, Soua, & Oberauer, 2018.
68 Luiten, Ames, & Ackerson, 1980.
69 Smolen, Ahang, & Byrnem, 2016.

modalities—auditory, visual, motor.[70]

15 Principles

The English Coach's playbook, the core design of repeated movements throughout the year and throughout the vertical team, incorporates and reflects the following fifteen principles informed by our knowledge of how the brain functions. We've noted in brackets the corresponding coaching and expert performance categories mentioned in Chapter 1 that are related to the brain category.

> When we fail to show students why the learning is significant to them, that doorway to the brain remains closed and no learning of significance will take place.

1. Behavioral Relevance [Look like the game, SAID]

Beginning a new unit requires a hook to entice students to engage with learning, to secure that "buy in." This intuitive practice reflects a principle of the brain: the hook is like the porter opening a doorway to the brain, creating what researchers call "behavior relevance." When we fail to show students why the learning is significant to them, that doorway to the brain remains closed and no learning of significance will take place.[71] But when the porter opens that doorway (achieving behavioral relevance), the brain activity begins and "the chances of its being learned, remembered, and internalized increases."[72]

2. Brain Breaks

Research once thought that evening sleep provided the only time for our brains to replay the learning that occurred in the day, a time to strengthen some of the newly formed neural networks. But this natural brain instinct—that

---

70   Pashler, et al., 2008; van de Hueval, et al., 2009; Schneider, et al., 2018; Cassidy, 2004.
71   Kilgard & Merzenich, 1998; Jenson and McConchie, 2020.
72   O'Keefe & Linnenbrink-Garcia, 2014.

reviews the lesson and reinforces memory—can be triggered during our class periods in a manner of seconds, providing the brain relief from information overload or from the dissonance emerging whenever students struggle with the task.[73] The brain break, ideally for high school students, occurs after thirty minutes of a learning activity, the moment when the amygdala, the brain's filtering system, closes down. Shifting the brain away from its complex cognitive task provides that particular neural network resting time, an opportunity to recharge while the brain moves to another area.[74]

Brain breaks lead students to a separate, already-rested area of the brain.

These breaks can engage students with additional physical movement or social interaction prompting positive emotions—joy, calmness, belonging, fellowship. Reading humorous poems without accompanying interpretation; playing musical chairs to switch groups or partners; playing a requested song or video clip; writing on the board a favorite hobby, sport, musician, movie; viewing artwork that connects to a current reading unit.

After the break, students return to the more challenging task with a refreshed brain, ultimately strengthening the long-term memory circuit connected to the lesson's goal.[75]

3. Chunking [SAID]

Chunking involves breaking down complex tasks into manageable parts. This essential technique for expert performance recognizes the brain's ability to manage only a finite number of learning tasks at a time.[76] Researchers have found that we can take in only three-to-seven chunks of information before we overload and begin to miss new incoming data.[77]

Teachers need to avoid "too much content, too fast" because it "is unlikely to get processed correctly and saved accurately."[78]

---

73   Terrada, 2022.
74   Willis, 2016.
75   Buch, E. R., et al., 2021; Robertson, E.M., 2019; Kelley, P. & Whatson, T., 2013; McTighe, J. & Willis, J. 2019; Smolen, Ahang, & Byrne, 2016.
76   Thalmann, Souza, & Oberauer, 2018; Jenson & McConchie, 2020.
77   Linden et al., 2003; Jensen, 2005.
78   Schacter, Guerin, & Jacques, 2011; Paas, & Ayres, 2014.

Chunking also increases the efficiency of classroom feedback because a single movement or two from the playbook can be quickly assessed by the teacher.[79] For example, a lesson focusing on one sentence incorporating quoted material practices a smaller movement inside the more complex movements of the paragraph.

4. Clarity [SAID]

> The brain dislikes chaos. Its natural filtering mechanism discards information that it cannot clearly connect to a current memory network.

The brain dislikes chaos. Its natural filtering mechanism discards information that it cannot clearly connect to a current memory network, information that is confusing, and information that lacks immediate relevance.[80] Learning tasks, then, need to be clear, understandable and actionable. An actionable task is one the student can immediately implement after receiving direction, a task that corresponds to a precise observable movement (i.e. writing a sentence with an opening absolute phrase). The goal must also be within student developmental reach, and classroom instruction should provide apt models that visualize for students both what to do and what the ideal product should look like.[81] A coherent and understandable playbook with actionable movements provides the ideal clarity necessary for successful learning.[82]

5. Feedback [Guided Discovery, Silence]

One of the most effective lessons from the athletic world involves providing actionable, timely, clear, and specific feedback.[83] Ideal feedback activates the students to correct[84] their incomplete or flawed understanding of a movement from the playbook. The timeliness of feedback increases the likelihood that the

---

79   Owens, 2017; Gobet, 2001.
80   Eichenbaum, 2017.
81   McTighe & Willis, 2019.
82   Hattie, J. 2013; 2008; 1992.
83   Wiggins, G., & McTighe, J. 2012; Hattie & Timperley, 2007.
84   Kopp, B., & Wolff, M., 2000.

skill becomes part of a permanent long-term memory.[85] While, for instance, students are doing sentence work in class, the teacher pinpoints the need for more textual evidence in a particular sentence, or suggests the use of an absolute phrase to reduce wordiness.

> A well-designed playbook also aids teachers in refining their feedback skills so they can communicate effectively what students need to do.

The dynamic aspects of feedback animate the primary cognitive parts of the brain significantly, activity not observed during teacher-centered models.[86] Because each movement in the playbook has its own precise definition followed by clear samples of its ideal form, teachers can more efficiently and successfully deliver feedback quickly. (Elements of the playbook will be discussed in the next chapter.) A well-designed playbook also aids teachers in refining their feedback skills so they can communicate effectively what students need to do in order to move closer to mastery of each skill. The ideal brain experience occurs when the students' trial and error movements are quickly corrected and redirected, allowing that memory circuit to embed itself more forcefully into long-term memory.[87]

6. Graphic Organizers [SAID, Guided Discovery]

Graphic organizers respond to the brain's interest in order and clarity, for they transform chaotic thinking and writing processes into visible parts, manageable sections, reducing the potential strain on the brain to juggle too much data at one time.[88] Organizers possess several benefits for which the brain responds well:

- help students "link new content to what they already know";[89]

- provide a framework for reinforcing metacognitive skills, forcing students to consciously think about several "plays" effective for paragraphing and

---

85 Black & William 1998; McTighe & Willis, 2019.
86 Hiebert et al., 2014; Peters et al., 2014.
87 Bangert-Downs, R., Kulick, C., Kulick, J., & Morgan, M. 1991; Peters, S., Braams, B., Raijmakers, M., Cedric, P., Koolschijn, M. & Rone, E. 2014; Owens 2017; Roediger & Butler, 2011.
88 McTighe & Willis, 2019.
89 Luiten, Ames, & Ackerson, 1980.

plays core to the process of close reading;

- create opportunities to break down complex skills into manageable chunks—because graphic organizers often contain multiple "plays," (the paragraph chart, for instance, contains four distinct movements), teachers can isolate one or two skills within sections of the organizers;

- allow students to reinforce their memory networks dedicated to the movements of the playbook.[90]

7. Inductive-Predictive Instruction [Guided Discovery, Silence]

As a general principle, teachers should think of their instructional choices *inductively* rather than deductively, because a deductive classroom approach focuses on the teacher, the "sage on the stage," before whom students sit passively absorbing information.

Induction, however, asks students to mine through data, recognizing patterns and drawing conclusions, a predictive task the mind instinctively knows, a basic survival impulse.[91] Inductive classroom teachers understand that students learn by doing, engaging in mental manipulation[92]—activities where the teacher refrains from supplying answers. Teachers carefully align sets of variables that allow students to predict an outcome, to discover a conclusion on their own.[93] In Chapter 4, for example, the activity focusing on difficult texts lists partial phrases from a poem students have never seen. They are to reflect on the fragments of the poem to predict some of its key ideas before seeing the complete text.

---

90 Matthews, R.C., 1977; McDaniel, Waddell, & Einstein, 1988; Owens, 2017; Nesbit & Adesope, 2006; Allen & Tanner, 2003.
91 McTighe & Willis 2019; Richard et al., 2013.
92 Wiggins & McTighe, 2012.
93 Sanes & Lichtman, 2001; Silver, Strong, & Perini, 2007; Beyer, 1997.

8. Intellectual Challenge [SAID, Guided Discovery]

When students engage in complex and challenging tasks, more cerebellar activity ignites, more neurons start firing and fusing into emerging networks. Less challenging tasks and learning objectives, situations where objectives require little cognitive effort, result in static brain activity.[94] For instance, simply asking students to recall a fact from their reading is less challenging than asking students to locate a detail, image, or words that reflect a repeated thematic idea.

Teachers often need to decide the nature of the challenge students can appropriately undertake without so much anxiety that they disengage. In order to establish parameters to evaluate appropriate intellectual challenge, the Russian psychologist Lev Vygotsky argues for placing students in the zone of proximal development (ZPD).

ZPD is "the distance between the actual developmental level . . . and the level of potential development . . . under adult guidance, or in collaboration with more capable peers."[95] In the classroom, while some students may be able to construct multiple sentences supporting a topic sentence, for others, such a task needs to be narrowed further. The teacher might, therefore, provide the topic sentence and ask students to create the first sentence that would support it with textual evidence.

Students navigate the intellectual discomfort of challenge when the clarity of the task is clear, immediate teacher feedback occurs, and students have models that aid their visualization of the ideal result.

Learning situations that challenge students to link prior knowledge to new situations and applications fire up memory networks and reinforce them.[96] For instance, on Monday, students learn how to use an absolute phrase as an efficient tool to extend the elaboration of a claim in a sentence. Later in the week, when drafting multiple sentences for a body paragraph, the teacher can suggest at the very moment of a student's sentence construction the apt location for the absolute phrase. This reinforcement strengthens the memory of what might otherwise be grammatical knowledge in isolation.

---

94 Ivry R., 1997; Black, Isaacs, Anderson, Alcantara, & Greenough, 1990; Hochanadel & Finamore, 2015; Rosenthal & Jacobson, 1969.
95 Vygotsky, 1978.
96 Baeten, M., Kyndt, E., Struyven, K., Dochy, F., 2010.

9. Metacognitive Activities [Guided Discovery, Silence]

Metacognition broadly refers to students' abilities to consciously reflect on a learning task and its components:

- What are the challenges of this task for me?
- How should I go about achieving success, selecting which strategies I've learned to overcome each challenge?
- How will I respond to failure?

Neuroscience now confirms that these metacognitive skills not only trigger a specific neural network in the brain, but their very activity also assists other cognitive functions.[97]

The English teacher's playbook maps out a framework for explicitly teaching and modeling metacognitive skills: each play, once learned, invites students to reflect on its strategic use. For instance, *I know how to use verbal phrases to combine sentences and remove wordiness; where in my paragraph do unnecessary words delay the reader from understanding my key idea? And where can a verbal phrase increase my conciseness?* As teachers use class time to model, practice, and provide swift feedback regarding flaws and the apt application of each play, students' metacognitive skills increase.[98] These students demonstrate higher academic performance than those students who lack metacognitive awareness.[99]

Explicit modeling instruction clearly reinforces for students why a specific strategy is effective and how it can be instrumental in their success,[100] ultimately leading students to the intuitive and strategic use of the play.

These activities also allow students to talk about their understanding and use of the plays, which reinforces the neural network in which it is stored.[101] Discussing with a partner the elements of the paragraph chart or the presence of word and logic glue anchors new information to previous learning, causing the

---

[97] Vacarro, 2018.
[98] Stanton JD, Sebesta AJ, Dunlosky J., 2021.
[99] Clements 2016; Lin et al. 2007; McCutchen 2006; Saddler & Graham 2007; Harris, S. 2010; Karlen 2017; Graham & Harrison 2000; Wang, et.al 1990.
[100] Tanner, 2021.
[101] Sekeres et al., 2016.

new information to shift out of short-term memory and attach itself to a long-term memory network.[102]

Metacognitive activity in the classroom provides opportunities to explore, identify, and seek solutions that diminish confusion about the nature of any movement in the playbook. These trial-and-error moments manifested by students during class practice provide the teacher an opportunity to strengthen the internalization of the play.[103]

10. Movement [SAID, Scrimmage, Guided Discovery]

Once thought only to control our physical movements, the cerebellum actually directs messages to the cognitive areas of the brain. In fact, the majority of neural circuits in the cerebellum, triggered by even low intensity movement, point outward, enhancing memory and the learning functions of the brain.[104]

> Once thought only to control our physical movements, the cerebellum actually directs messages to the cognitive areas of the brain.

The cerebellum is intimately linked to the learning and cognitive modalities of the brain.[105] When movement involves shifting partners or groups, the brain typically releases dopamine in response to positive social interaction, the result motivating students to learn.

The brain also responds to the movement of handwriting, which triggers[106] neural activity involving memory and learning, activity not seen when working on a computer.[107] Overall, drafting on white boards, on desks, taking notes in journals, and writing out sentence imitations increases oxygen flow to the brain, which triggers neurons to fire off connecting signals, strengthening memory networks.[108]

---

102   Posner et al., 1982.
103   Tanner, 2012.
104   Middleton & Strick, 1994; Chen, Zhu, Yan, & Yin, 2016.
105   Jensen, 2005.
106   Plebanek D. & James K, 2022.
107   Li, J. X., & James, K. H. 2016; Smoker, T. J., Murphy, C. E., & Rockwell, A. K. 2009.
108   Vinci-Booher, S. A., James, K. H. 2017; Midling, A. S. 2020; Ose Askvik, E., van der Weel, F. R. & van der Meer, A. L. H., 2020.

11. Repetition [SAID, Scrimmage, Guided Discovery]

Repetition, the cornerstone of expert performance, is linked to brain research.[109] What occurs during the repeated practice of the playbook movements is the strengthening of our memory circuits, triggered by the thickening of myelin, the insulation surrounding a linked network of neurons.

Repetition stimulates neuroplasticity by continually engaging with emerging and already established memory networks.[110]

A playbook guides classroom activity that maintains the key movements of critical reading and writing, designed instruction that requires multiple repetitions to become a habit.[111]

12. Recognizing Patterns [Guided Discovery, SAID]

> Actively teaching students to look for and recognize relationships provides the fuel needed for the brain to engage in neuroplasticity.

Pattern formation is the brain's organizational method for creating order out of disorder. Data is grouped together by similarity, difference, degree, classification, causality, etc.[112] This neural movement allows the brain to then begin linking the organized information to previous memory networks, ultimately transferring short term memory to long term.[113]

Helping students understand this fundamental trait of the brain to recognize patterns further increases their ability to glue new information or unconnected knowledge quickly to larger networks already forged in their brains. Disparate facts become linked to larger concepts, facts that would otherwise drift away and be discarded by the brain. Actively teaching students to look for and recognize relationships provides the fuel needed for the brain to engage in the process of neuroplasticity.[114]

---

109   Lally, P., van Jaarsveld, C. H. M., Potts, H. W. W., & Wardle, J. 2010; Sanes & Lichtman, 2001; Kilgard & Merzenich, 1998; Owens, 2017.
110   McTighe & Willis, 2019.
111   Jenson & McConchie, 2020.
112   Haystead & Marzano, 2009.
113   Marzano, Pickering, & Pollock, 2001; Marshall & Bredy, 2016.
114   McTighe & Willis, 2019.

13. Retrieval Activities [SAID, Scrimmage]

Retrieval activities ask students to recall details about a learning task from memory, without the aid of notes or discussion. Routine retrieval activities help the brain activate the neural networks where a learning task is stored. The more the brain retrieves the remembered task, the stronger and more efficient it becomes, a key feature of neuroplasticity.[115]

Retrieval activities are considerably more effective than studying notes.[116] As soon as the bell rings, the teacher asks students to write two ideas that appear repeatedly in the novel they are currently reading. Or they define the components of the body paragraph. Later, the teacher interrupts classroom activities to record student understanding—in a Google Form, a sheet of paper, a list on the board, or a partner share. This data provides useful feedback for the teacher when deciding which areas of the playbook need strengthening.[117]

14. Understanding Neurotransmitters & Proteins [Guided Discovery]

Neurotransmitters are protein chemicals in the brain. Over 100 protein chemicals exist. These neurotransmitters carry messages between neurons, passing through synapses as they do so. These messages strengthen memory and create new memory circuits.[118]

Because neurotransmitters affect how we learn, knowing a few of these chemicals provides useful information for teachers making instructional choices:

- **Dopamine** enhances learning, focus, motivation, and memory. It is released during social interactions and other moments of reward (when students experience praise, make accurate predictions);

- **Acetylcholine** supports memory, learning, and neuroplasticity. It is released during instructional moments of surprise, novelty, and problem solving;

---

115 McTighe & Willis, 2019.
116 Jensen & McConchie, 2020.
117 Owens 2017; Roediger & Butler, 2011.
118 Cleveland Clinic, 2022.

- **Norepinephrine** increases focus and learning and assists in memory and neuroplasticity. It is triggered by movement and activities developing urgency (timed writing, timed competitions, timed group work). The release of norepinephrine is effective when the learning objective is clear and the models assist students in reaching the ideal product. If students cannot visualize the goal clearly and see it within grasp, the release of the norepinephrine will frustrate students and the brain will be unable to learn effectively.

- **Serotonin** aids cognitive focus and motivation, preparing students to learn. It is released in the brain during moments of security, confidence in the environment, and calmness, stabilizing positive emotions.

- **BDNF** strengthens the circuitry of memory networks and enhances overall learning. It is a protein or "Miracle-Gro for the brain"[119] released by physical movement, which stimulates the growth and effectiveness of new brain cells.[120]

- **Cortisol** is a potential threat to learning. It is released in high doses during moments of anxiety and interferes with learning and memory function. The goal in the classroom is to monitor the potential elevation of cortisol and shift to activities that reduce it—activities that break down complex tasks for weaker students. Instead of requiring an entire paragraph, some students may need a sample topic sentence to model, followed by one or two sentences to begin their work.

A teacher aware of these six neurotransmitters will provide a classroom environment that maximizes learning potential.[121]

15. Developing Memory Networks [SAID]

To build and strengthen memory networks, the brain must recognize where to attach new information it receives. If the knowledge being taught exists in isolation and it possesses no recognizable connection to a larger network,

---

[119] Ratey, 2008.

[120] Cunha, C, Brambilla, R, & Thomas, K.L., 2010.

[121] Cleveland Clinic, 2022; Owens & Tanner, 2017; Sukel, 2019; Huang, et al. 2022; Jensen, 2013; Zull, 2002; Cozolino, 2010; Baram, et al. 2008; Yan et al., 2011.

> This "worksheet" method of teaching is often futile when done in isolation and not simultaneously connected to real movements or patterns of the "game."

the brain will filter it out.[122] For example, in English, an enduring method of teaching grammar revolves around "drill and kill," a series of grammar worksheets that require students to correctly identify or reproduce a particular grammar structure several times.

However, this "worksheet" method of teaching is often futile when done in isolation and not simultaneously connected to real movements or patterns of the "game," such as sentence creation, combination, or imitation within the context of drafting an essay. Great coaches know that a new or emerging skill must quickly be used on the field, tested by the stimuli the player may encounter during competition.

Chapter 3 explores the definitions of the core plays of our playbook.

---

122 Thalmann, Soua, & Oberauer, 2018; Luiten, Ames, & Ackerson, 1980.

03

DEFINING THE CORE PLAYS

THE READING *Plays*

- L1 — Identify evidence to support a claim
- L2 — Make associations
- L3 — Identify relationships between L1 and L2

THE WRITING *Plays*

- Thesis statement
- Topic sentence
- Topic string
- Word & logic glue
- Organizing L1
- L2-L1-L2 syntax
- Modified L1
- To the right

L1, L2, L3 Plays

The Playbook's Core—the writer's analytical voice

The Reading Plays Chart, pictured at the right, introduces to students three core plays for reading and writing about texts.

Flannery O'Connor, one of America's finest writers of fiction in the twentieth century, asserts an essential task of the teacher of English, a task that is the focus of this chapter: providing the student with "tools to understand a story or a novel." These tools ultimately become woven into the voice of the student as writer, a writer's voice that contains a particular interpretive point of view, a writer's voice that explains how ideas emerge from the diction, details, and imagery in the chapter of a novel, the verses of a poem, or the paragraphs of an essay.[123]

---

[123] Sections of this chapter are excerpts from *Crafting Expository Argument* by Michael Degen.

The Reading Plays Chart

Level One [L1 Play]

Identify the evidence observed by you, the reader.

- Details: What's the setting? Who are the characters? What is the situation?
- Diction: What types of words are used or repeated?
- Imagery: How is the image created? What are its parts? What senses are provoked?

Level Two [L2 Play]

Identify the conceptual associations [ideas, qualities, conditions] that emerge from the details, diction, and imagery of the literary work you are reading.

Examples of concepts that might be associated with pieces of evidence include, but are certainly not limited to, the following:

- Fear. Excitement. Joy. Love. Disdain.
- Violence. Chaos. Control. Order. Arrogance.
- Submission. Humility. Confidence. Authority. Wisdom.
- Confinement. Freedom. Tyranny. Benevolence. Refinement.
- Skepticism. Faith. Greed. Penury. Parsimony.

Level Three [L3 Play]

Identify the relationships among the associations linked to details, diction, and imagery in the text.

- Repetition [similarity, analogy, recurrence, echo, parallelism]
- Contrast [incongruity, antithesis, opposition, tension]
- Juxtaposition [contiguity, adjacency, proximity]
- Shift [turn, transformation, alteration].

To develop such a voice can be a challenge for student-writers. This voice does more than merely re-create or summarize the details in a work of literature the students have observed; it requires the ability to analyze.

An ability to analyze a work of literature is a learned behavior. It entails a way of "seeing" what student-writers are reading. That way of "seeing" is primarily a method, or strategy, for thinking about the work as students read it. Such a strategy of thinking allows student-writers to "see" beyond the mere diction, details, and imagery of the plot or poem and, instead, guides them toward a discoverable claim or argument about the text they have been reading.

Understanding the Plays — L1, L2, L3

The literary work under consideration may be a poem, a novel, a short story, an essay, a play, a speech—for any aesthetic form, the process, or way of "seeing," is the same.

To demonstrate this process of thinking about literature, we will first provide a discussion of each level of the Reading Plays chart. Afterwards, we will examine two passages—one fiction and one nonfiction.

- As we discuss each passage, we will consider separately each level of thinking so that the concept of each stage is clear.

- After skills increase, students will notice themselves simultaneously blending two or more of the levels as they read.

- Once students begin to write about the passages they have read, what they write will contain all three levels simultaneously.

Now let's examine the Reading Plays bookmark and its components.

THE L1 Play

Identify the evidence observed by you, the reader

Level One of the Reading Plays directs student-readers to observe carefully the passage's diction, details, and imagery, the evidence that will later become part of a written argument. What often distinguishes effective arguments from mediocre ones is the writer's ability to point out evidence another reader may not have noticed.

Details

First, what are the details—or facts—contained in the text?

- What is the setting: the city? the countryside? the schoolyard?
- Who are the characters: a parent and child? a teacher and student? two friends? two enemies?
- What is the situation: a Christmas dinner? an interrogation? a carriage ride to the country? A fist fight?

Diction

Diction refers to the words used by the author, words that come in a variety of types, which the careful reader observes:

- Are these words concrete, abstract, colloquial, formal, informal, jargon, figurative, foreign?
- Do any of the words belong to a specific category (words related to religion, to education, to finance, to sports, to medicine, to the law, to marriage, to war, etc.)?

Imagery

Finally, the careful reader will also want to notice how collections of words form mental pictures, images that allow the reader to see more clearly a setting, a character, an action or situation.

- How is the image formed?
- What components or parts of the image seem prominent or significant?

For example, many images of a broken-down car can be created by an author: one image may focus on a mangled hubcap dangling off the rim by one rusty screw; another image may center on the three-inch diameter dent in the driver's side door, the flakes of burgundy paint falling to the dirt.

All of these observations will influence what student-writers ultimately say—their interpretative perspective—about the specific work of literature they are reading.

Identify the conceptual associations [ideas, qualities, conditions] that emerge from the diction, details, and imagery of the literary work you are reading

The next level of thinking, Level Two of the Reading Plays chart, involves attaching associations to the diction, details, and imagery we isolated above.

Conceptual associations

So what are associations? As students read, they interact with details, images, and words, their minds making conceptual associations. The image of an infant may cause student-readers to think of abstract concepts such as innocence or vulnerability. The repeated use of the word "red" may cause them to associate its use with the idea of death or destruction. The specific details involving a major character's living arrangements—that the character lives in a mansion with fifty rooms and drives a different sports car for each day of the week—will likely produce associations related to wealth, power, and extravagance.

Well-crafted speeches are often rich with conceptual associations. Patrick Henry, in his famous speech to the Virginia Convention in March 1775, spoke of the "insidious smile" of the British monarch in response to the colonists' pleas for a respectful resolution of their claims. "Trust it not, sir; it will prove a snare to your feet. Suffer not yourselves to be betrayed *with a kiss*." Certainly, the word "snare" evokes ideas of treachery, entrapment, and deception, as does the phrase "betrayed with a kiss," a phrase that reminds those hearing—or reading—Henry's speech of the betrayal of Christ by Judas.

The logic of conceptual associations for the student-writer

When students write about any work of literature, they want to move beyond plot summary—which is the mere re-telling of what happens in the story, poem, play, essay, or speech.

How do students do this?

They explain what concepts, or ideas, are anchored in—associated with—the words, details, and images found in the text. These details and language provide the evidence for the written argument being made about the work of literature.

Not all conceptual associations are equal in value as not all such associations will make logical sense in the context of the work of literature the student is reading and about which the student is thinking.

That's why the student writing about a work of literature must make decisions, must, in other words, select associations to attach to the evidence in the text. Once the students begin the process of selecting certain associations rather than others, they then begin to develop an *analytical voice*, a way of seeing the evidence (diction, detail, imagery), a perspective about the work of literature under consideration.

No student will want to attach an associative concept to an image that doesn't make logical sense. That image of an infant's foot is not associated with the concept of evil or violence simply because a student asserts it or because some evil act was committed against a child. While there are many ways to talk about a text, and many possible associative words a writer can use, these assertions must be grounded within the logical associations of its words, details, and images. Attaching conceptual associations to textual evidence is not a random or arbitrary activity.

Writing about conceptual associations with precision

Student-writers want to consider the precision of their associative word choices when they write their compositions analyzing a work of literature.

Just as an author chooses specific words to form distinct images and to elaborate individual details, students want to use appropriate diction to explain any of these images or details in the passage under consideration. For example, Lady Macbeth's conversations with her husband about pursuing the throne of Scotland by murdering King Duncan may be considered "bad," "cruel," "heartless," or "ugly"; but more precise language would describe her conversation as "shrewd," "manipulative," or "conniving." The "crazy" arguments she puts forth to persuade her husband might be described more aptly as "hyperbolic" and "fallacious."

An additional task of student-writers, then, is to broaden their storehouse of vocabulary used while engaged in composing.

Selecting appropriate conceptual associations

Whenever students begin attaching various associations to parts of the text, some may later be discarded while others may be used to formulate the larger structure of their argument—a thesis statement or its topic sentences.

What associations would be disregarded and why? Imagine an image of a stone wall. Students may consider multiple and contradictory associations with such an image. On the one hand, walls may be associated with positive ideas such as security, stability, order, protection; on the other hand, they may be associated with negative attributes such as entrapment, concealment, restriction, imprisonment.

Which associations are more reasonable? The answer is to examine the other details, images, and words contained in the text. Are more pieces of evidence positive or negative? Perhaps white light shines on the wall, whose stone is intricately and beautifully designed. Within the area encompassed by the wall sits a gentleman comfortably relaxing in a chair, his face reflective and at ease, gazing upon a child who is playing in the grass, smiling and gleeful. These additional details direct the tone of the wall's description and surroundings toward our positive list, particularly if no other details or images are negative.

Some students may realize that those negative associations regarding a stone wall can be discarded, that the text they are reading contains positive conceptual associative elements. However, others may notice that the actual design on the stone wall, although aesthetically pleasing, is of a flowering rose bush. The blooms are lush, the petals open toward the sun, but each stem is notably thorny. While details may at first glance seem entirely positive, these may be, on a closer look, details that cause doubt or cast a shadow.

The general reading principle here directs students to examine all other pieces of evidence in the text: the entire collection of images and details should guide a consistent and plausible reading. If no details of the text point to a negative tone, students can disregard those associations that are negative. However, if the details embrace both associations, the student-writer will want to consider how both associations play out in the story.

Elaborate direct quotations with conceptual associations

These conceptual associations will be used to elaborate the directly quoted material cited inside the body's analytical paragraphs. Many beginning writers often wonder *"What do I say next?"* after having used a direct quotation from the literary work being analyzed.

Discuss those associative ideas that are linked to the evidence they have directly quoted. A student might comment on the significance of a single word, image, or phrase within that direct quotation, showing how the idea associated with it relates to other aspects of the literary work: the protagonist's character traits, or a general theme of the work, or how it establishes a specific contrast or similarity with another character or situation in the tale.

Many direct quotations will, of course, have more than one such word, image, or phrase whose conceptual associations call for thoughtful elaboration.

Identify the relationships among the associations linked to diction, detail, and imagery in the text

Level Three of the Reading Plays chart concerns the language of relationships, which work as "tools," as Flannery O'Connor says, for students to employ as they "operate inside the work" of literature.

Student-readers must learn to observe the relationships among words and images and details, for these relationships are what form associative ideas into specific claims about the work of literature being examined.

Four general relationships (and their synonyms) appear on the Reading Plays bookmark: repetition, contrast, juxtaposition, and shift. Under each of these categories in the chart, we have placed various synonyms that, as writers, students may use to avoid the potential monotony of repeating the same words. We'll explore what these relationships mean in order.

Repetition
similarity, analogy, recurrence, echo, parallelism

The most important relationship in a text is repetition, which signals to the reader the key ideas of the passage and the entire work, ideas pertaining to theme, character, setting, and point of view. As the attentive reader becomes aware of repetition in a literary work, patterns emerge. Student-writers make a stronger written argument about a literary work whenever they identify various repetitions and, therefore, convincingly demonstrate that any such patterns exist.

When we notice repetition, we notice not simply that sometimes exact words or images are repeated, but that similar associations attached to different words or images or details continue to surface throughout the passage.

An example of the repetition of similar associations attached to different details and language is found in this short nonfiction excerpt from Virginia Woolf's essay, "A Room of One's Own." Here, Woolf describes her meal at one of the male colleges at Oxford. She writes that

> ...the college cook had spread a counterpane of the whitest cream,.... After that came the partridges, but if this suggests a couple of bald, brown birds on a plate you are mistaken. The partridges, many and various, came with all their retinue of sauces and salads, the sharp and the sweet, each in its order; their potatoes, thin as coins but not so hard; their sprouts, foliated as rosebuds but more succulent.... Meanwhile the wine glasses had flushed yellow and flushed crimson; had been emptied; had been filled. (10-11)

The details and language of the situation repeat the associative ideas of plenty and abundance: "the partridges, many and various," the "retinue of sauces and salads," the wine glasses "flushed" and "emptied" and "filled." The idea of consummate beauty recurs as well: "the whitest cream," the sprouts "foliated as rosebuds." All these different words and images, used collectively in this passage, reinforce the associative idea of luxury or opulence.

Contrast
incongruity, antithesis, opposition, tension

Another important relationship for the careful reader to observe is contrast. Contrast in a literary text sends the reader a signal: it indicates the presence of an essential situation—tension, conflict, opposition, difference—a situation that may add a significant complication, require an eventual resolution, or reflect a serious universal idea.

A teacher must guide student-readers to the discovery of contrast. As readers, we often notice first the concrete presence of contrast: one character barks, "Bah humbug," while another character responds, "Merry Christmas"; one setting is marked by a dilapidated house, windows broken and paint flaking off the siding, while the other setting is marked by a house freshly painted, daisies lining its sidewalk. The contrast observed in each of these examples is both concrete and associative. For instance, the comments of the two aforementioned characters reflect a distinction between a pessimistic, or surly, outlook and one that is optimistic or genial; the characteristics of the two houses reveal a contrast between decay and vibrancy.

A student-writer wants to communicate to the reader these associative contrasts anchored in the concrete references to the text.

Let's explore a further example. In the opening chapter of Charles Dickens' *Great Expectations*, we read of a convict who has escaped prison. Dickens presents two distinctly contrasting images of the convict. The first image is one of a dangerously violent aggressor, a man furtively grabbing the young eight-year-old Pip, exhorting, "Keep still, you little devil, or I'll cut your throat," a character clearly ominous and threatening to Pip. Near the end of this chapter, however, Dickens provides a quite different image of the convict, one in apparent opposition to his initial belligerence. Here, he is a man slipping away from Pip while mumbling, "I wish I were a frog or an eel," as "he hugged his shuddering body in both his arms—clasping himself, as if to hold himself together—and limped towards the low church wall." Both the sentiment and the visualization turn the initial combative image into one of vulnerability and weakness.

What then is the function of this contrast or difference in characterization?

Contrast allows the author, in this case Dickens, to create a character more complex than the monstrous figure whom Pip—and the reader—at first appear to encounter. If this contrast were absent, the convict would be a static one-dimensional character, our perception of him likewise limited. In addition, the distinct presence of contrast in the novel's first chapter alerts the reader to ideas that may become more prominent as the story progresses: the differences between appearance and reality, the faulty nature of first impressions, the forces of deception present in the landscape of the work.

Juxtaposition

contiguity, adjacency, proximity, nearness

A third relationship, juxtaposition, reveals that which might otherwise remain hidden. By placing two items (two details, images, words) in close proximity, or alignment, a new idea is produced, one that would otherwise remain unobserved were the elements located further apart from each other.

Let's imagine some simple advertisements. First, visualize an image of four red Toyota Corollas linked together on a bright yellow roller coaster. Though such a depiction seems unrealistic and fantastic, by juxtaposing the Corollas with the roller coaster, Toyota fashions a new idea about the Corolla, one the viewer would not have conjured if the car were, in the context of its advertisement, merely placed in a suburban driveway. This juxtaposition, however, envisions ideas associated with the joys and thrills of an amusement park smiling twenty-year-olds, multiple hands boldly extended into the sunshine—in an advertisement featuring vibrant primary colors. It communicates to consumers that the Corolla inherently possesses youthful power and exhilaration. It reinforces the idea that purchasing the Corolla will produce a sensational experience not possible with other automobiles.

In another advertisement, The Coca-Cola Company uses juxtaposition to produce a new idea about Diet Coke. The ad contains a sleek black background; in the center a Diet Coke can floats upside down, the silvery can with its bold red and black logo dappled with beads of moisture. Directly above the can are the words "yoga class." In the proximity of "yoga class" with such a Diet Coke can, a new idea about this soft drink emerges. The soft drink, the ad suggests, produces benefits similar to those a yoga class delivers—meditative relaxation, self-discipline, flexibility, an overall health linking the mind and body—benefits that heretofore have not customarily been associated with Diet Coke.

Let's consider a few literary examples of juxtaposition. In Charles Dickens' *Great Expectations*, the main character, Pip, visits the house of Miss Havisham. Inside the house, Pip enters a room and encounters a strange sight, a table set for a wedding feast, an image typically associated with joy, yet across the tablecloth run "spiders" and "black beetles," creatures commonly associated with something evil, sinister, or corrupting. Miss Havisham then explains that the strange object on the table Pip cannot recognize is her "bride-cake." Placed side-by-side, the juxtaposed details of the wedding cake and the tiny creatures that infest it figuratively reveal a truth about Miss Havisham. She is a woman whose heart has been deeply wounded by betrayal; an evil has warped her sense of life's goodness and joys. This condition later leads Pip to suffer, too, as she seeks to avenge past heartbreak by inflicting it on him.

The opening passage of Cormac McCarthy's *All the Pretty Horses* provides another example of juxtaposition. With the novel's first words McCarthy introduces the image of a candle burning and flickering in a room as a young man enters it. A few sentences later, McCarthy writes that the young man looks at the face of his deceased grandfather, the owner of the family ranch, lying in his funeral casket. On the next page, the young man stands out on the plain and watches a train passing swiftly in the darkness. The train's light has a specific visual effect on the darkened landscape, illuminating the ranch fenceline and carrying it away into the darkness as the train passes. In the juxtaposition of the candle-flame, the body lying in repose, the passing train, and the ranch's fence, a new idea emerges about the nature of the world and human existence within it. Life, McCarthy suggests, is fleeting, as easily extinguished as a candle-flame, as transient as a swiftly passing train. Moreover, the proximity of the dead man's face and the image of the disappearing ranch fenceline suggests that not only a man's life, but also his achievements, dissolve within the grand scope of time.

Shift
turn, transformation, alteration

The final relationship, shift, signals a movement away from one idea and a turn toward a different associative idea. The purpose of the advertisements regarding Toyota's Corolla and Diet Coke is to shift our notion of these products. In the Corolla ad, Toyota transforms the audience's previous impression of a vehicle that is sedate and lackluster into one possessing energy, zest, and youthfulness. Likewise, the Diet Coke ad alters the idea of a potentially bland-tasting soft drink severely reduced in calorie content by connecting it to physical, mental, and spiritual health.

Our recognition of such a shift, or turn, directs us to a central issue or purpose in any text we are reading.

In poetry, for example, this turn is a primary source of the poem's intellectual energy. The structural fulcrum of Shakespeare's sonnets resides in the altered perspective shaped by the turn, as in Sonnet 29.

> When, in disgrace with fortune and men's eyes,
> I all alone beweep my outcast state
> And trouble deaf heaven with my bootless cries
> And look upon myself and curse my fate,
> Wishing me like to one more rich in hope,
> Featured like him, like him with friends possess'd,
> Desiring this man's art and that man's scope,
> With what I most enjoy contented least;
> Yet in these thoughts myself almost despising,
> Haply I think on thee, and then my state,
> Like to the lark at break of day arising
> From sullen earth, sings hymns at heaven's gate;
> For thy sweet love remember'd such wealth brings
> That then I scorn to change my state with kings.

In the first two quatrains of the sonnet, the speaker, "in disgrace with fortune and men's eyes," laments his "outcast state" with "bootless cries." Cursing his "fate," he pines to be someone other than himself: "like to one more rich in hope," with different features, surrounded by friends, "desiring this man's art and that man's scope." The speaker appears the epitome of someone in the midst of despair and bottomless self-pity.

Yet there is that "yet," and it is that very word—a conjunction indicating contrast—that initiates the third quatrain and signals the shift in the sonnet, an alteration that is typical in the structure of the Shakespearean sonnet. With this single word, the speaker juxtaposes the previous quatrains' "thoughts myself almost despising" with his new "state," a transformed mental and spiritual condition, one that occurs when "haply I think on thee." This shift from interior self-loathing to an exterior joy, then, occurs when he who was "in disgrace with fortune" fortunately—"haply"—*turns* his thoughts to another and recalls "thy sweet love," a recollection anchored in the intimacy of a genuine relationship. This sudden remembrance is so fortunate—bringing "such wealth"—that, his emotional state similar to a "lark at break of day arising from sullen earth," the speaker now "scorn(s) to change my state with kings."

The transformation from misery to exultation becomes the central issue of the sonnet, one that causes the reader to ask how and why the change occurs. In the case of Shakespeare's sonnet, a potential thesis statement might suggest that a person's happiness comes not from coveting attributes others possess but from the loving relationships that we nurture.

The careful reader of any work of literature will want to observe diction, details, or images suggesting a shift. Any such turn is likely to become a significant part of an analysis of the work.

Overview of the Three Plays — L1, L2, L3

Heretofore, our focus has centered on the specific "plays" of the Reading Plays bookmark.

- First, the student monitors the evidence provided in the text, the evidence being the literary work's concrete details and language (diction and imagery).

- Second, students attach conceptual associations to the evidence found in the text.

- Third, students recognize that relationships among the associations linked to the pieces of evidence—relationships of repetition, contrast, juxtaposition, and shift—bring about meaning in a literary work, thus allowing the writer to provide an interpretative perspective, a claim, about the work in a subsequent essay.

This inductive reading process—the movement from observing the evidence in a literary work to drawing associative conclusions about the evidence—is a manner of thinking about the literature, a way of "seeing" as students read, that provides the basis for a thoughtful written analysis.

Applying the L1, L2, and L3 plays to a passage from a novel

Now let's apply this strategy to a short passage from a novel, *A Tale of Two Cities* by Charles Dickens.

> *Monseigneur, one of the great lords in power at the Court, held his fortnightly reception in his grand hotel in Paris. Monseigneur was in his inner room, his sanctuary of sanctuaries, the Holiest of Holiests to the crowd of worshippers in the suite of rooms without. Monseigneur was about to take his chocolate. Monseigneur could swallow a great many things with ease, and was by some few sullen minds supposed to be rather rapidly swallowing France; but, his morning's chocolate could not so much as get into the throat of Monseigneur, without the aid of four strong men besides the Cook.*
>
> *Yes. It took four men, all four ablaze with gorgeous decoration, and the Chief of them unable to exist with fewer than two gold watches in his pocket, emulative of the noble and chaste fashion set by Monseigneur, to conduct the happy chocolate to Monseigneur's lips. One lacquey carried the chocolate-pot into the sacred presence; a second, milled and frothed the chocolate with the little instrument he bore for that function; a third, presented the favoured napkin; a fourth (he of the two gold watches), poured the chocolate out. It was impossible for Monseigneur to dispense with one of these attendants on the chocolate and hold his high place under the admiring Heavens. Deep would have been the blot upon his escutcheon if his chocolate had been ignobly waited on by only three men; he must have died of two.*

Identify the evidence observed by you, the reader

Now let us explore L1 observations in the passage above–the details, diction, and imagery.

First, the reader can observe several **details**, or facts:

- The setting is a "grand hotel in Paris" and the main character is "Monseigneur, one of the great lords in power at the Court."

- Monseigneur is "in his inner room."

- The worshippers are in a different location outside the "inner room"

- "Monseigneur" is about to eat his morning chocolate.

- Monseigneur swallows things with ease.

- Monseigneur is swallowing France quickly.
- It takes four men to serve this chocolate to him.
- He cannot manage going without a single servant.
- The "Chief" servant could not execute his responsibilities (note the phrase "unable to exist") without a minimum of "two gold watches in his pocket."
- Each servant has a single task—one to carry the pot, one to stir the chocolate with a prescribed tool, one to open the napkin (note it is "favoured"), and one to pour the chocolate.

The reader may observe that the author has employed specific words, or **diction**, to create the details in the scene:

- The words "great" and "power" and "grand" are used when describing Monseigneur's reception at the Paris hotel.
- The ritual of the Monseigneur being served his chocolate is described using the following words: "sanctuary," "Holiest," "worshippers," and "the sacred presence."
- "swallow"
- "to conduct"
- "lacquey"
- "impossible"
- "noble," "ignobly," "chaste"
- "favoured"
- "blot"

Finally, the reader may notice **imagery** that the author creates:

- The Monseigneur "rapidly swallowing France."
- The Monseigneur holds a "high place among the admiring heavens"
- "The throat of Monseigneur"
- The servants "ablaze with gorgeous decoration"

Identify the conceptual associations that emerge from the diction, imagery, and details of the literary work you are reading

Once readers have noticed several pieces of L1 [diction, detail, and imagery], they are ready to apply the L2 play to the passage. Remember that the L2 play involves creating associations (interpretive words), for each piece of L1 they have found. Here's a selection of what might be listed.

L1 Evidence *diction, detail, imagery*	L2 Associations
"great lords," "power"; "court"	majesty, prestige, nobility
"his inner room" = "the sanctuary of sanctuaries, the Holiest of Holiests"	sacred, religious atmosphere, divine, superlative form, hallowed
worshippers in separate rooms	religious service, isolated, set apart
"about to take"	as if preparing for communion
eating chocolate	trivial activity, personal pleasure, appetite
could swallow many things with ease	appetite = colossal, effortless
rapidly swallowing France	metaphor of conquering, unrestrained appetite for power, devouring, France = a possession or commodity
four strong men required — ablaze with gorgeous decoration, gold watches	excessive, wasteful, profligate, ironic vulnerability and weakness of the Monseigneur
milled and frothed the chocolate with the little instrument, lacquey carried the chocolate-pot into the sacred presence	ceremony, ritual being made of the trivial
to conduct	a performance carefully designed, formality, orchestrated
sacred presence	religious atmosphere
chaste	sacred, holy obligation of restraint, prudence

Identify the relationships that form between associations linked to details, diction, and imagery in the text

Now let's examine L3 relationships, noting that several relationships become apparent and hence significant—specifically, the functions of repetition, contrast, and juxtaposition.

In both paragraphs of the novel, two repetitions emerge. Several words, details, and images in the passage suggest the sacred, religious atmosphere surrounding the Monseigneur's morning ritual, while others evoke the trivial, superficial nature of this ritual, which serves to gratify the man's natural appetite. We have highlighted these two repetitions in the chart below:

L1 Evidence *diction, detail, imagery*	L2 Associations	L3 Relationships *repetition, contrast, juxtaposition, shift*
his inner room = the sanctuary of sanctuaries, the Holiest of Holiests	sacred, religious, divine, hallowed	repetition of a sacred, religious atmosphere
worshippers in separate rooms	religious service, isolated, set apart	
about to take	as if preparing for communion	
chaste	sacred, restraint, holy	
the lacquey carried ... into the sacred presence	like an altar server or priest	
eating chocolate	trivial activity, personal pleasure, appetite	repetition of the trivial, the superficial, the natural, the gratification of the appetite
swallow	eating, everyday, ordinary action	
into the throat	consuming, natural, instinct, appetite	
poured the chocolate out	gratifying the appetite, natural, not spiritual	

The primary structure of the passage relies on juxtaposing these two sets of details, diction, and imagery—to contrasting effect. We have highlighted a few examples of juxtaposition and contrast in the table below. Evidence from the first paragraph is grouped together in white, while evidence from the second paragraph is color-coded in light blue.

L1 Evidence diction, detail, imagery	L2 Associations	L3 Relationships repetition, contrast, juxtaposition, shift
Holiest of Holiests	sacred, religious, divine, hallowed	juxtaposition of contrasting associations: a sacred, religious atmosphere vs. the desire, appetite, material excess of the Monseigneur
about to take	as if preparing for communion	
drinking chocolate	appetite, personal pleasure, trivial	
swallow...with ease	appetite, excess, devouring	
the lacquey carried...into the sacred presence	like an altar server or priest, holy, religious	juxtaposition of contrasting associations: the hallowed, serious, dignified ceremony vs. its trivial, superficial purpose
the chocolate-pot	appetite, consuming, pleasure, trivial	
ablaze with glorious decoration	ornamentation, ceremony	
to conduct	performance carefully designed, formality	
among the admiring heavens	hallowed, divine, elevated	

What is the result of such a juxtaposition, an incongruity established by describing so reverently an act so inconsequential? Certainly, the reader senses the absurdity, that something is out of kilter—reflections that point to irony, a disparity between our expectations and the actual reality. In this case, we expect, because of the serious diction, the Monseigneur to be engaged in an equally serious act, but he is not. The incongruities recurrent throughout the passage are particularly embellished and exaggerated, which marks the nature of satire and a sarcastic voice, techniques intended to ridicule or criticize someone or some situation. In this case, the Monseigneur is the object of the ridicule.

Executing Additional Writing Plays

Placing L2 to the left *and* to the right of L1 allows the writer to assertively communicate an interpretive point of view. This syntactic pattern produces a sentence with the most forceful voice.

In the following samples, we have bolded the writer's L2 and colored in blue the L1 quoted from the text.

Such a **sacred** *setting is then juxtaposed to the* **trivial** *detail that* "Monseigneur was about to take his chocolate," *a detail not simply* **trivial but also one marked by physical pleasure and personal privilege**.

Even the physical descriptions of the attendants contribute to the **ostentation** *of the event, for they are* "ablaze with gorgeous decoration," *the foremost of the four having not one but* "two gold watches in his pocket," *as they proceed* "to conduct the happy chocolate to the Monseigneur's lips," *the infinitive* "to conduct" **evoking not only a form of guidance or conveyance but also the idea of performance being staged**.

This play is not simply placing L2 to the right of the L1, but placing L2 so specific to the L1, that the interpretive assertion cannot be attached to another piece of evidence elsewhere in the paragraph.

Such an ordinary task as "taking his chocolate," a daily occurrence, requires "the aid of four strong men beside the cook," the adjective "strong" **amplifying the ridiculous nature of the situation**.

Even the physical descriptions of the attendants contribute to the ostentation of the event, for they are "ablaze with gorgeous decoration," the foremost of the four having not one but "two gold watches in his pocket," as they proceed "to conduct the happy chocolate to the Monseigneur's lips," the infinitive "to conduct" **evoking not only a form of guidance or conveyance but also the idea of performance being staged**.

In this play, the writer defines an L1 as a particular type of evidence—diction, detail, or imagery—and modifies this term with an L2. The play allows the writer not only to communicate an additional L2 but also classify the type of evidence being discussed.

Such a sacred setting is then juxtaposed to the trivial detail that "Monseigneur was about to take his chocolate," **a detail not simply trivial but also one marked by physical pleasure and personal privilege**.

This idea of desire and appetite continues as the narrator notes the "ease" with which this noble can consume not merely his chocolate but all of France, the present participle "swallowing" reinforcing the excessive nature of his appetite, that he devours all those around him, an **image of comprehensive power**.

Student Sample Compositions

Here are several examples of what it looks like to combine all three levels of the Reading Plays chart to make a claim about the passage from *A Tale of Two Cities*. Within each sample, we have labeled evidence (L1) in blue and bolded all of the writer's associations (L2). We have also noted in brackets selected instances where the writer uses other plays like L3, modified L1, and to the right.

Sample #1

Beginning with imagery of a **lavish** and **gluttonous** lifestyle, the narrator portrays a Monseigneur in a **negative** light, **ironically mocking his greed and voracity**. **Repeatedly [L3]** using **godly** diction to diminish Monseigneur's character, the narrator appears to be **acrimoniously critiquing** the **lavishness** of his lifestyle. Initially, the narrator makes a **mockery** of Monseigneur's **lavish** lifestyle through the **repeated diction of divinity [modified L1]** as he **compares [L3]** his room to a "sanctuary," the "Holiest of Holiests," **patronizing** Monseigneur's lifestyle for being **profligate** and **immoral**. Furthermore, the narrator's precise use of the word "worshipers" when describing those who are **envious** of Monseigneur contributes to the **spurious praise** of the narrator with his **divine language** describing **immorality**. With his **opulent** and gaudy lifestyle, the Monseigneur "could swallow a great many things with ease," illustrating his **gluttonous** and **pampered** views of the world. Alongside his **gluttony**, the Monseigneur remains "unable to exist with fewer than two gold watches in his pocket," portraying a man **consumed by greed** and **flawed natures**, natures that the narrator places in **contrast** [L3] to **ironically mock** them. As the Monseigneur continuously grows **desperate** for the **lavish** things like gold watches and rivers of chocolate, the narrator **derides** the lifestyle more and more. **Hyperbolically critiquing his neediness**, the narrator claims that "if his chocolate had been ignobly waited on by only three men; he must have died of two," **ironically** exaggerating his **dramatic dependence on luxury** to the point of death **[to the right]**. The narrator derides the **gluttony** and **desperation** the Monseigneur exudes through his **gaudy** and **superfluous** demands of those who attend to him. **Hyperbolizing unsatisfactory service** to the point of fatality, the narrator conveys an attitude of **disgust** and **abhorrence** to the **insatiable demands** of the Monseigneur.

Sample #2

Dickens utilizes the seemingly **gluttonous** and **divine** Monseigneur as well as his reception to properly explicate the **lavishness** and **excess** of the French aristocracy, his life and setting **compared [L3]** to "the Holiest of Holies" and the **affluent** guests "worshippers in the suite", a **Biblical allusion** revealing the aristocrats **distorted** notion of themselves believing they are **higher than god [to the right]**. This **warped** viewpoint further reveals the **inherent self-absorption** and **greed disfiguring the hearts and minds of the wealthy** within French society. Moreover, the necessity of "gorgeous decorations" and the inability to "exist with fewer than two gold watches" **ironically** places the "noble," thinking of themselves in "chaste fashion," as **profligate** individuals who **consume superfluous material objects** "with ease," augmenting the state of **corruption** in association with the nobility. Furthermore, with **glamor** revealing itself at the center of the **tumultuous** lives of the aristocracy, so does **a lust for extravagance** convey **a false facade** for the rich. A consumption of the temporary allure and enchantment produced from material pleasures reveals the **malignant** nature of the nobility to place **material lust** over the **strife of the insignificant** and **petty** state. Finally, his **nobility** and **privileges prized** over common sense, the **gluttonous** Monseigneur fears a "[deep] blot upon his escutcheon if his chocolate had been ignobly waited on by only three men," the **stained image [modified L1]** of a "blot upon his escutcheon" repeating his need to keep his **wealthy reputation stable** and **untainted**. Including this **irrational** and **self-centered worry**, Dickens emphasizes the **nonsensical extravagance** the plutocracy demands for themselves. Further embodying this **sanctimonious** yet **gluttonous** nature, the Monseigneur claims "he must have died [if only two]" men "ignobly" served him, the **gravity** of death associated with a **distorted shame** in his mind, as anything less than extreme **lavishness** indicates **shame worse than death**. By displaying the **self-centered** representative of the French aristocracy as such, Dickens portrays the **incongruity[L3]** between the **overly lavish** and the masses **struggling in poverty**.

Sample #3

In the second half of the excerpt, the Monseigneur displays his **absurdly pampered** character, mirroring the aristocracy's **looming doom** due to the government's **irrationality**. First, the Monseigneur displays his **apathetic disregard for the lower classes** as he permits only those "ablaze with gorgeous decoration" to assist him, a **pompous** requirement that displays the **haughty** aristocrat's **absolute detachment from the common man**. **Contrarily,[L3]** the Monseigneur alleges his **purity**, with a prerequisite that the assistants must "emulat(e) the noble and chaste fashion set by Monseigneur," the **modest diction [modified L1]** of "chaste" juxtaposing the **contrastingly pompous [L3]** requirements, a **clash [L3]** further exposing the **incongruence** of the aristocracy's function. Advancing the **fatuity** of the situation, if the Monseigneur chooses to "dispense with one of these attendants" he loses his "high place under the admiring Heavens," which serves as an **egotistic** example of the aristocrat's **obsession with his own divine status** rather than the **well-being** of his **malnourished** constituents. Furthermore, the Monseigneur reveals the **coddled** nature of his character through the absurd assertion that if "ignobly waited on by only three men," he would have a "blot upon his escutcheon," a **trivially blemished image** displaying how the aristocrat demands such **preposterously consummate perfection** that he needs an entire person to combat spills. Finally, the Monseigneur intensifies his **spoiled**

dependency through a **peremptory** declaration that "he must of died two," the **mortal diction** of "died" emphasizing how the four helpers supersede **frivolous** assistants and instead represent the **decrepit** aristocracy's anchoring in **nonsensical** practices for its survival **[to the right]**.

Scan to see more student samples.

Applying the Plays L1, L2, L3 to a nonfiction passage

Here we will proceed to an application of the Reading Plays bookmark to a literary work of nonfiction, in this case a passage from "Living Like Weasels," the opening essay from Annie Dillard's *Teaching a Stone to Talk*.

Twenty minutes from my house, through the woods by the quarry and across the highway, is Hollins Pond, a remarkable piece of shallowness, where I like to go at sunset and sit on a tree trunk. Hollins Pond is also called Murray's Pond; it covers two acres of bottomland near Tinker Creek with six inches of water and six thousand lily pads. In winter, brown-and-white steers stand in the middle of it, merely dampening their hooves; from the distant shore they look like miracle itself, complete with miracle's nonchalance. Now, in summer, the steers are gone. The water lilies have blossomed and spread to a green horizontal plane that is terra firma to plodding blackbirds, and tremulous ceiling to black leeches, crayfish, and carp.

This, mind you, suburbia. It is a five-minute walk in three directions to rows of houses, though none is visible here. There's a 55 mph highway at one end of the pond, and a nesting pair of wood ducks at the other. Under every bush is a muskrat hole or a beer can. The far end is an alternating series of fields and woods, fields and woods, threaded everywhere with motorcycle tracks—in whose bare clay wild turtles lay eggs.

Identify the evidence observed by you, the reader

In this Annie Dillard passage, let us follow the same process, observing the evidence as we did with the fictional excerpt by Charles Dickens.

First, some **details** that the reader may notice within the passage include::

- The pond is two minutes from Dillard's house
- It's across a highway and next to a quarry, a place where stone is made
- The water is shallow, only six inches deep
- Dillard goes to the pond at sunset to sit on a tree trunk
- The pond has six thousand lilypads in it
- In winter, there are steers
- The presence of wildlife: blackbirds, black leeches, crayfish, carp, turtles, ducks, muskrat
- The pond is located in the suburbs
- The seasons mentioned in the passage: winter, spring, summer
- Under every bush is a muskrat hole or a beer can

The **diction** the writer uses in creating this scene include words like:

- miracle
- nonchalance
- blossomed
- spread
- plodding
- tremulous
- everywhere / every

And finally, the **imagery** Dillard creates within her description of the pond:

- six inches of water and six thousand lily pads
- brown-and-white steers stand dampening their hooves
- water lilies blossomed and spread to a green horizontal plane
- The plodding blackbirds
- Tremulous ceiling to black leeches, crayfish, and carp
- Nesting pair of wood ducks
- Under bush is a muskrat hole or a beer can
- Threaded with motorcycle tracks
- Bare clay wild turtles lay eggs inside motorcycle tracks

Identify the conceptual associations that emerge from the details, diction, and imagery of the literary work you are reading

And here are some of the associative ideas that emerge from the diction, details, and imagery found in the passage:

L1 Evidence diction, detail, imagery	L2 Associations
sunset, lily pads, blackbirds, steers	wonder of the natural world, natural beauty, abundance and vibrant life
miracle	extraordinary, improbable, inspires awe, amazement
55 mph highway, beer can, motorcycle tracks	man-made creations, desires
beer can	waste, ephemeral desire
blossomed, spread	growth, vibrancy, transformation
plodding, tremulous	steady movement, consistent energy
pond is 2 minutes from house	man encroaching on nature
everywhere	ubiquitous, widespread

L1 Evidence *diction, detail, imagery*	L2 Associations
houses not visible from within the pond	humanity concealed, nature isolated
muskrat hole	natural habit, haven
threaded	connected, woven, intertwined, linked, embedded
field of woods threaded with motorcycle tracks	vastness of nature intertwined with human desire, freedom
wild turtles lay eggs inside motorcycle tracks	growth and potential of nature embedded into the human world

Identify the relationships that form between associations linked to details, diction, and imagery in the text

Both the evidence we as readers observe in the Dillard passage and the conceptual associations we are making with that evidence provide a further opportunity for the reader to recognize relationships as they gradually emerge from a literary work.

Clearly, Dillard juxtaposes the proximity of human and nonhuman worlds, but it is especially interesting to observe how she does it. Notice that in the first paragraph, the only human involved in this natural setting is the author herself. It therefore appears, at first glance, that humans may come close to but not actually involve themselves that much in the peaceful world of Hollins Pond. The one person who does enter and stay sits on a tree trunk and remains the passive observer.

However, after she closes this paragraph with images of summertime tranquility, an abrupt shift occurs at the beginning of the next paragraph, a shift breaking the illusion of nature's detachment from the world of man.

The chart on the next page begins to organize for the reader and writer these emerging ideas.

L1 Evidence *diction, detail, imagery*	L2 Associations	L3 Relationships *repetition, contrast, juxtaposition, shift*
twenty minutes from my house…is Hollins Pond	separation between human and natural world	Details of human life Juxtaposition of human and natural world Repetition of nature's beauty and wonder
Hollins Pond..by the quarry..across the highway	outside the natural world, those closer relationship between human and natural	
Dillard goes there to sit on a tree trunk	solitude, lone human presence in nature	
in winter…now in summer	movement in time, the transformation of the seasons of growth	
water lilies blossomed.. plodding blackbirds and tremulous ceiling…	tranquility of summer, growth, abundance, fecundity	
This, mind you, suburbia.	human community, order, establishment	shift away from natural beauty to the human world
55 mph highway	encroaching human world, speed, a life ungoverned by nature	repeated juxtaposition of the human world with the natural world contrast between natural life and human consumption, encroachment, and waste
nesting pair of wood ducks	peaceful, safety, natural habitat	
beer can	intrusion of the human world, waste, ephemeral desire	
muskrat hole	natural habitat, haven, refuge	

Blending the L1, L2, and L3 plays when crafting a composition

So let's look at a short composition concerning this passage from Dillard that, as with the analysis of Dickens, fuses all three levels of the Reading Plays bookmark to make a claim. Again, you will notice that we have combined several statements we have previously written in our consideration of each level of thinking. As before, we will bold selected examples of the plays.

Sample Composition

Dillard suggests not only that the human and natural world are **intricately intertwined**, but also that the natural world's **beauty**, though it remains **viscerally poignant**, is **in jeopardy** amidst the **civilizing impulses** of man. The **image of nature's serene, harmonious grandeur [modified L1]** that occupies the first paragraph is shattered in the subsequent paragraph by the **imagery of human civilization besieging the natural world**.

The reader's first exposure to Hollins Pond reveals the landscape as a **sanctuary**, or **refuge**, for the author. Her journey "twenty minutes from [her] house" leads her into the **meditative solitude** of the pond, where "I like to go at sunset and sit on a tree trunk." The reader enters the pond as the author does, **leaving behind the markers of civilization**, traversing "through the woods by the quarry and across the highway."

The **marvels** of nature await the narrator—and the reader—in "a remarkable piece of shallowness" that "covers two acres of bottomland near Tinker Creek with six inches of water and six thousand lily pads." It is here that the reader, along with Dillard, revels in "miracle's nonchalance": the steers that stand **passively** in the pond during winter, their hooves "merely dampening." The cattle, she tells us, "are gone" now that it is summer. The **tranquil** silence of winter has been replaced by summer's **steady pulse**, the water lilies that "have blossomed and spread" reminding the reader of the **vibrancy** that accompanies **spring's transformations**. Now the **methodical certainties of summer** present "a green horizontal plane that is terra firma to plodding blackbirds, and tremulous ceiling to black leeches, crayfish, and carp," all created with the **ease** and "nonchalance" of **miracle**. The narrator's **movement through the seasons <u>anchors her—and her reader—in a world thoroughly natural [to the right]</u>**.

At this **peaceful** moment in the reader's encounter with the **natural** world of Hollins Pond, Dillard **shifts abruptly [L3]** from the **wonder of nature** to the **perilous encroachment** of human civilization upon nature's **splendor**. Directly addressing the reader, the stark voice of the narrator breaks the illusion heretofore created: "This, mind you, suburbia." Even the syntax of Dillard's sentences **shift** from the **balance** and **poetry** of the opening paragraph to sentences that, in the subsequent paragraph, are more **barren**, **merely cataloging** a series of **sharp contrasts [L3]**. The image of the **tranquil** pond is replaced by a landscape already **trapped** on three sides by "rows of houses."

Images of nature, previously **harmonious**, now align with the **pernicious** elements of man's world: muskrats and wood ducks evoke images of trappers and hunters, and the "55 mph highway at one end of the pond" conjures up the **discord** of suburban traffic, noise, exhaust, and road kill. Beer cans are as **predominant** under bushes as muskrat holes, and the series of woods and fields are "threaded everywhere with motorcycle tracks—in whose bare clay wild turtles lay eggs." This final **haunting** image brings to the fore the **imminent danger that threatens** all of Hollins Pond, the past participle "threaded" indicating the **inescapable entanglement of human beings in the natural world [to the right]**.

The idea of wild turtle eggs splattered by motorcyclists reminds the careful reader of a **potential warning** residing in Dillard's previous paragraph. There is, in the first paragraph, one sentence that, because of its brevity, stands apart: "Now, in summer, the steers are gone." As the reader contemplates what is happening in Dillard's **sanctuary**, it is a sentence that is worth a return. Since the steers could only come and go by way of the one side of Hollins Pond that is not bounded by "rows of houses," it seems likely, considering the scale of the **human invasion**, that this last portal is **in danger** as suburbia continues its **restless expansion**. The steers that are gone in summer may, within a few years, be gone for good. Without cattle in winter, a **major source of fertilization** for the pond and its wildlife will be removed. What Dillard has revealed in two paragraphs is the process of **extinction** as the **human community overwhelms the natural world**.

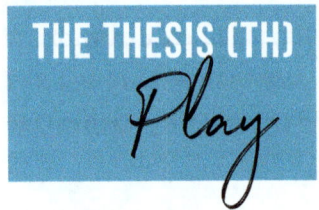

Once the student understands the L1 and L2 Plays, understanding a thesis statement becomes clearer.

A thesis statement = a topic [L1] + L2

A thesis statement presents the writer's approach (L2) toward, or insight concerning, the topic—the details, diction, and imagery found in the text (L1). In any expository argument, it expresses an opinion that is open to dispute and must, therefore, be argued with evidence logically constructed from the literary text.

A thesis statement referencing L1 without the writer's L2 does not move beyond plot summary.

Examples of thesis statements without L2

- Ebenezer Scrooge is forced to remember events of the past.

- Huck and Jim experience several conflicts during their travel down the river.

- There are many symbols in the book.

- Dickens repeats images of "hands" throughout the novel.

- Matthew Arnold uses a metaphor involving the sea in his poem.

A thesis statement that asserts L2, however, activates the writer's interpretive voice.

Examples of thesis statements with L2

- Scrooge's encounters with ghosts depict **memory's transformative power**.

- Huck and Jim's path toward **friendship moves through three stages: the meeting, the challenge to survive, and love**.

- The archetype of clothing mirrors Huck's **desire for individuality**.

- In *Great Expectations* the hands motif indicates Pip's location in the **journey toward maturity**.

- The sea metaphor allows Matthew Arnold to develop **a political commentary on the Victorian Age, a time in which man is isolated and void of religious conviction, a situation that can only be rectified by human love**.

- The diction and imagery Twain uses in relaying Huck's story reveals his **personal struggle with freedom and civilization**.

Paragraph Plays: Topic Sentence, Topic String, Glue, Organization

The plays establish for the student the inductive process of discovering what to write about after reading a text—what to say about character, setting, atmosphere, theme. Students need regular reminders that ideas (L2) emerge out of the reflection on evidence (L1) and the relationships among the associations linked to pieces of evidence (L3).

Students can't write a thesis statement and its topic sentences without reflecting on the L2-L1 pairings they've collected—a thesis statement and the topic sentences that support it develop as students begin noticing the patterns (L3) among the evidence. Students need to understand that arguments don't drop down from the sky neatly packaged; they are embedded, hidden, and lurking inside all the evidence that has been gathered, evidence at first appearing incoherent, chaotic, messy.

The process is not quick or immediate; it demands intellectual patience and regular practice.

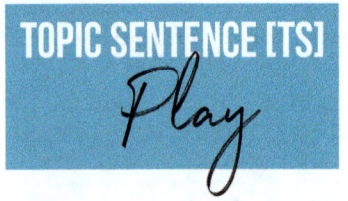

To explore the topic sentence play, we'll examine the character Joe Gargery from Dickens' *Great Expectations*. Understanding how to arrive at a topic sentence emerges from the application of the **L1, L2, and L3 Plays.** Students first assemble pieces of evidence inside a chart, shown on the opposite page. The chart will contain L1—the diction, details, and imagery gathered from the text—about Joe, along with L2 for each L1. Finally, the chart will contain L3—the relationships that form between the L2. Once gathered, students want to select some of the similar L2 in the chart to use to build a topic sentence.

To build the topic sentence, students learn, through an inductive process, to notice the most significant L2 that were generated with the L1 in the above chart. Students select some of the exact L2 from the chart to build the topic sentence. The topic sentence must contain L2 (formatted in bold in the example on the next page)—otherwise, it merely provides plot summary and no interpretive claim.

Topic sentence

Pip's **surrogate father**, Joe, frequently **safeguards** Pip when **in desperate need**, demonstrating the **servant's active participation in restoring community**.

A Joe Gargery Evidence-Association Chart

L1	L2	L3
1) "quietly fenced me up there with his great leg."	strength, **fatherly**, **guards** Pip	
2) Pip's sister "brought [him] up by hand."	punishment, abuse, unideal parenting, **in need**	
3) Joe says, "I wish there warn't no Tickler for you, old chap; I wish I could take it all on myself."	sacrifice, comforts, care, wants to **safeguard**, selfless	**Repetition** (1, 3, 6, 7): guarding or caring for Pip
4) Mr. Wopsle uses the word "swine" to describe Pip.	filth, attack, vulnerable boy **in need**	**Contrast** (3, 4): Wopsle attacks with words, Mrs. Joe punishes, Joe comforts

Repetition (2, 4): Situations where Pip is in need. |
5) "But he always aided and comforted me when he could, in some way of his own, and he always did so at dinner-time by giving me gravy."	surrogate **father**, loving, **caring**, **serving others**	
6) Joe gives Pip "more gravy" after each insult by Mrs. Joe or the dinner guests	healing, **protection**, deliberate choice to restore, **servant** to one in need	
7) Joe leaves the forge to go to London to help Pip convalesce after his illness.	devotion, selfless, sacrifice, taking action to **serve** Pip, healing	**Repetition** (6, 7): actively serving
8) "O God bless this gentle Christian man!"	Pip acknowledges the pain he has caused Joe, goodness	

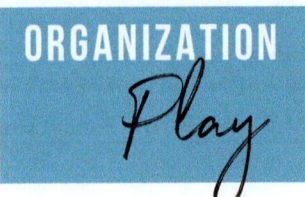

ORGANIZATION Play

The next decision involves the logical sequencing of evidence within the paragraph. Evidence can be organized by **Time**, by **Place**, or by **Idea**—and often, we might blend at least two of these methods or strategies. Once students have internalized these strategies, they can more quickly analyze their collection of evidence, knowing what patterns to look for.

Returning to the Joe Gargery Chart on the previous page, students see that the L1 in the chart appears both in different scenes (kitchen, Christmas dinner, London) and in chronological order—**place** and **time**. Students learn through the creation of a chart to shape a paragraph, that practicing the skill of observing both L1 and L2 determines two plays—Topic Sentence and Organization.

After writers choose an organizational strategy, they select transition words associated with that organizing method.

Transitional words or phrases—connected to time, place, or idea—appear at the beginning of each chunk (the chunk being *a collection of similar pieces of evidence, linked by an idea, a place, or a time*). These transitions before each L1 chunk help the reader understand how evidence is sequenced inside the paragraph.

On the next page is a Paragraph Chart, a helpful graphic organizer for students as they internalize the paragraphing plays, with its Organization Play column filled in.

Note that the paragraph contains three chunks (three groupings of evidence from three different parts of the novel). The sentence beginning each chunk uses an introductory phrase that contains a time word (In the **opening**) and a place word (**kitchen** scene); in the first chunk, sentences two, three, and four all occur in the kitchen, hence an "X" is placed in the two boxes in the organization column below the phrase "in the opening kitchen scene." Sentence five, then, begins a new chunk, its evidence all located in time (**Later**) and place (**Christmas dinner**). Sentence seven begins a third chunk with a transitional phrase indicating, again, the organization of evidence by time (**Finally**) and place (**in London**).

A student might ask, "How many chunks do I need in my paragraph?" The answer is to return to the chart and its collection of L1, L2, and L3. How many chunks does the chart suggest? How is the L1 grouping—by place, time, or idea or some combination?

A Joe Gargery Paragraph Chart				
TS: Pip's surrogate father, Joe, frequently **safeguards** Pip when he is in **desperate need**, demonstrating throughout the story that a **servant** must be an **active participant in restoring community.**	**L2 in the TS:** Joe = surrogate father, safeguards Pip, desperate need, servant, restoring community	X	X	This paragraph is organized by <u>Time</u> and <u>Place</u>.
Sentences in the Paragraph	**Topic Strings** (the initial 5-8 words of the sentence)	**Logic Glue**	**Word Glue**	**Organization Words**
2) In the opening kitchen scene, "gentle" Joe guards a vulnerable Pip "with his great leg" from an enraged Mrs. Joe and her tickler.				In the opening kitchen scene
3) Here he actively attempts to shield Pip from being raised "by hand."				X
4) In fact, Joe protectively tells Pip he "wish there warn't no" beatings for him.				X
5) Later, at the Christmas dinner, Joe again alleviates the attacks on Pip from the holiday guests, who torment him and compare him to "swine."				Later, at the Christmas dinner
6) With each insult, Joe gives Pip "more gravy," demonstrating that small getures can help ease the grief of individuals and help the community move closer toward love.				X
7) Finally, in London, Joe helps Pip convalesce after his illness.				Finally, in London
8) Joe has chosen to leave the forge, his means of employment, to serve Pip, who eventually recognizes the pain he has caused both Joe and Biddy.				X

Having students create a chart to collect L1, L2, and L3 before they even consider creating a topic sentence redirects their thinking to the inductive approach—jump inside the evidence and look about before making decisions. The pieces of evidence (L1) the writer finds, the associations (L2) the writer links to them, and the relationships (L3) that emerge between these associations will naturally suggest a topic sentence and paragraph chunks.

Below are some additional samples of how to organize paragraphs.

Organizing Method One: Time

Organize according to chronology—the order of the narrative's plot, for instance, or the order of major details or images occurring in the poem. When organizing by Time, writers place the evidence in the order in which it appears in the text or in the order in which events in the protagonist's life happens. The use of various transitions will assist the reader in following the sequence of events. Such words include *first, second, next, later, after, afterward, at first, as, before, finally, immediately, now, previously, soon, then.*

> The speaker in the poem from *Songs of Innocence* responds to the bleakness of child labor by producing hopeful images of heaven and redemption. **Opening** with a desolate image of a helpless child whose "father sold [him]" (3), the poem establishes the malevolent nature of life as a chimney sweeper, magnified in bleakness by the failure of the father to protect and provide for his child. **Then, in line 5**, the abandoned child destined to the squalid fate of sleeping "in soot" (5) suffers even in his time of rest, sleep no longer the archetype of rejuvenation and, as Macbeth says, "the balm of hurt minds." The most salient image, **in stanza three**, of desolation—"thousands of sweepers/... were all of them lock'd up in coffins of black" (12-13)—hyperbolically captures the universality of this suffering and identifies the gravity of their misery as death.

Organizing Method Two: Place

When writers organize by Place, they group evidence by locations or settings within the story. Some details or events in *Great Expectations* all occur at Miss Havisham's house, while others happen in London; additional pieces of evidence are from scenes at the Gargery's house. Writers may also employ transitional words referencing place that assist the reader: *above, ahead, among, beyond, down, elsewhere, farther, here, in front of, in the background, near, nearby, next to, there.*

First, Simon often helps those in need, paralleling Christ in his selflessness. This concern for others occurs with both the smaller children and the older ones. For example, **in the jungle** struggling to find food to preserve his own life, Simon assists the littluns by "finding for them the fruit that they could not reach, pulling off the choicest from up in the foliage, and passing them back down to the endless, outstretched hands" (56; ch.3). Because Simon supplies nourishment for the littluns in a time of need, they "cry out unintelligibly" (56; ch.3) for him to become their provider, just as Jesus' followers intuitively sought his assistance in times of distress. In addition, **at a campfire** Simon demonstrates his willingness to put aside his own needs in order to provide for others by graciously sharing with Piggy. For instance, while Jack denies Piggy a piece of meat "as an assertion of power" (73; ch.3), Simon provides for him by "shoving his piece of meat over the rocks to Piggy" (73; ch.3). Here Simon shows his ability to put aside his needs for someone outcast, much like Christ did, serving and dining with the poor and ostracized.

Organizing Method Three: Idea Divided into its Specific Components

Organize according to the ideas (associations) introduced in the topic sentence, possibly dividing the main associative idea into various parts. This organizational method may allow the writer to highlight different aspects of a definition; draw an analogy, a comparison, or a contrast; classify specific categories; delineate a cause-effect relationship or define scenes, settings, or characters as contraries.

The paragraph below, based upon *The Canterbury Tales*, defines a "virtuous pilgrim." Each chunk focuses on a different aspect of the virtuous pilgrim—one who respects others, demonstrates humility, and practices spirituality.

> Chaucer depicts the knight as a virtuous pilgrim, a person who fights for the Church, rejects extravagance in exchange for humility, and treats those around him with respect. **Respecting others** means refraining from insults, a habit many others indulge. The Knight, however, "never yet a boorish thing had said / In all his life to any, come what might." It is this courtesy that people from other countries recognize and revere: "He often sat at table in the chair / Of honour, above all nations, when in Prussia." The Knight's **respect is juxtaposed with his humility**, his lack of desire to flaunt wealth extravagantly: "He possessed / Fine horses, but he was not gaily dressed." In fact, not only does he avoid "fine" clothes, but he does not care about trivial aspects of his appearance, arriving at the pilgrimage "with smudges where his armour had left marks." This pilgrimage ranks higher than any worldly concern. For the Knight is most concerned with his **spiritual commitment**, his obligation to the Church. He takes this duty seriously, having "done nobly in his sovereign's war / And ridden into battle." Chaucer even reveals how often the Knight has battled successfully: "In fifteen

mortal battles he had been / And jousted for our faith at Tramissene." Indeed, these battles, as well as his appearance and behavior toward others, earn the Knight Chaucer's praise as "a most distinguished man."

TOPIC STRING Play

Within a paragraph, a writer's sentences must stay focused on the topic—the central idea—that appears in the paragraph's topic sentence. When the writer crafts a sentence that does not flow from the paragraph's stated or implied topic, such a change—or shift in topic—is likely to confuse the reader.

To prevent this shift in topic, craft the paragraph's supporting sentences so that whatever appears at the beginning of each supporting sentence maintains the reader's focus on the paragraph's central idea. Regardless of the type of sentence opening, the focus of each sentence's beginning words or phrases or subordinate clause ought to act as a tie, or connection, to the paragraph's topic. Such connections are known as the topic string.

To create a strong topic string, the writer uses a number of methods. Sometimes the key word or words from the topic are repeated. Other connecting possibilities include synonyms and pronouns for the topic's key words.

Since serious writers of expository prose vary the beginnings of their sentences, they strive to avoid monotony. These writers understand that sentences do not have to start with the subject, that quite often their sentences will open with an introductory phrase or an introductory subordinate clause.

In brief, a "topic string" emerges during the first half of a sentence within the writer's paragraph, often within the first 5-8 words. The simple directive we give students is to place associations (L2, bolded below) within their topic strings, making sure that these associations connect to words found in the topic sentence.

Original: The topic string breaks because the writer shifts topic focus.

In *Lord of the Flies*, Jack's **proud** nature leads to the **destruction of order and authority** on the island. The conflagration, representing the boys' only hope to leave the island, burns out due to his lack of supervision, a careless decision that commences the power struggle with Ralph. Ralph is the elected chief on the island and he complains about Jack hunting, even though Jack says that "we needed meat" (65; ch. 4), an action defying Ralph's authority and showing that Jack believes he knows what is best for the boys. Later at that night's assembly, the boys are **disorderly** and Ralph attempts to gain control. He even shouts at Jack, "you"re breaking the rules!" (84; ch. 5) to which Jack responds, "Who cares?" (84; ch. 5) clearly showing his apathy towards Ralph's power and his arrogance believing that he made the right decision.

Revision that maintains the topic string

In *Lord of the Flies*, Jack's **proud** nature leads to the **destruction of order and authority** on the island. Jack's **pride** first manifests itself when the conflagration, representing the boys' only hope to leave the island, burns out due to his lack of supervision, a careless decision that commences the power struggle with Ralph. In explaining his **rash** course of action, Jack tells Ralph that "we needed meat" (65; ch. 5), an action defying Ralph's authority and showing that Jack believes he knows what is best for the boys. In response to Jack's continued **rebellion**, Ralph, at a nightly assembly, shouts at Jack, "you"re breaking the rules!" (84; ch. 5) to which Jack responds, "Who cares?" (84; ch. 5) clearly showing his apathy towards Ralph's power and his arrogance as he believes that he made the right decision.

Let's return to our Joe Gargery Paragraph Chart (on the next page) and see the topic string column filled out. Note that the box directly to the right of the topic sentence contains the key L2 words from the topic sentence that we should see—either as exact repetitions or synonyms— when we look down the topic string column.

A Joe Gargery Paragraph Chart

TS: Pip's surrogate father, Joe, frequently **safeguards** Pip when he is in **desperate need,** demonstrating throughout the story that a **servant** must be an **active participant in restoring community.**	**L2 in the TS:** Joe = surrogate father, safeguards Pip, desperate need, servant, restoring community	X	X	This paragraph is organized by <u>Time</u> and <u>Place</u>.
Sentences in the Paragraph	**Topic Strings** (the initial 5-8 words of the sentence)	**Logic Glue**	**Word Glue**	**Organization Words**
2) In the opening kitchen scene, "gentle" Joe guards a vulnerable Pip "with his great leg" from an enraged Mrs. Joe and her tickler.	In the opening kitchen scene, **"gentle"** Joe **guards** a vulnerable Pip			In the opening kitchen scene
3) Here he actively attempts to shield Pip from being raised "by hand."	Here he **actively attempts to shield**			X
4) In fact, Joe protectively tells Pip he "wish there warn't no" beatings for him.	In fact, Joe **protectively** tells Pip			X
5) Later, at the Christmas dinner, Joe again alleviates the attacks on Pip from the holiday guests, who torment him and compare him to "swine."	Later, at the Christmas dinner, Joe again **alleviates**			Later, at the Christmas dinner
6) With each insult, Joe gives Pip "more gravy," demonstrating that small gestures can help ease the grief of individuals and help the community move closer toward love.	With each insult, Joe **gives** Pip **"more** gravy"			X
7) Finally, in London, Joe helps Pip convalesce after his illness.	Finally, in London, Joe **helps Pip convalesce**			Finally, in London
8) Joe has chosen to leave the forge, his means of employment, to serve Pip, who eventually recognizes the pain he has caused both Joe and Biddy.	Joe has **chosen** to leave the forge, his means of employment, to **serve Pip**			X

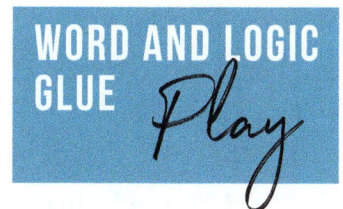

Word glue and logic glue act as transitions necessary to provide coherence for a paragraph. These transitions from one sentence to another help the reader understand how each sentence supports the topic.

Word Glue

Word glue is the actual diction a writer uses to tie, or blend, two sentences together so that the reader understands the writer's thinking process. Key words—including their synonyms—and pronouns can act as word glue, as can a large number of traditional transitional words and phrases.

Key words   The repetition of a word or words—either literal repetition or their synonyms— that tie a sentence to the previous sentence

Pronouns   Words such as *it, he, she, they, those, these, this, that used to refer to nouns in previous sentences*

Traditional transitional words and phrases

for example	furthermore, in addition, therefore
to illustrate	moreover, likewise, consequently
next	later, finally, that is
as a result	even though, for this reason first, second, etc.

Logic Glue

Logic glue represents the relationship between two sentences. This relationship is implied, rather than directly stated with transitional words.

When a subsequent sentence, for instance, continues the same idea of the previous sentence by adding new facts to elaborate that idea, then the implied logical relationship is an "and" relationship.

If a subsequent sentence illustrates the effect that is caused by the idea in the previous sentence, then the implied logical relationship is a "therefore" relationship.

Although these words—or synonyms for them—will not appear between the sentences, the reader recognizes that they represent the implied logical relationship between them. The following is a list of the types of implied logical relationships that occur between sentences.

and	continues the same idea with new facts
but/yet	a change in the idea of the previous sentence
or	an alternative for what is stated in the earlier sentence
that is	a definition or restatement of the idea in the earlier sentence
for example	an illustration of the idea in the earlier sentence
therefore	a conclusion or effect based on the earlier sentence
for	a reason or cause for what is stated in the earlier sentence

Finally, our paragraph chart is complete.

In the word glue column, student-writers enter more than one pair that glues two sentences together. And word glue can occur anywhere inside the sentence. When the student enters, for example, "safeguards - guards," the first word appears in the sentence above, in this case the topic sentence. The second word ("guards") appears in sentence two.

In the logic glue column, the student indicates which of the logic glue relationships (see above) join two sentences. When the student enters "for example," as in the first box underneath "Logic Glue," this indicates that sentence two provides an illustration of the idea in the Topic Sentence. In the next box, "and" indicates that sentence three elaborates upon the idea in sentence two, providing additional explanation and evidence.

The Paragraph Chart: Application

One function of the paragraph chart is to organize graphically several key **plays— topic sentence, topic strings, word glue, logic glue, and organization**. The chart serves as a metacognitive activity that reinforces for students the plays that create coherence and unity within a body paragraph.

Teachers may use the chart with students at any stage of the writing process: having students draft a paragraph inside the chart, or having them use the chart to examine a paragraph they have written previously.

A Joe Gargery Paragraph Chart				
TS: Pip's surrogate father, Joe, frequently **safeguards** Pip when he is in **desperate need**, demonstrating throughout the story that a **servant** must be an **active participant in restoring community**.	**L2 in the TS:** Joe = surrogate father, safeguards Pip, desperate need, servant, restoring community	X	X	This paragraph is organized by Time and Place.
Sentences in the Paragraph	**Topic Strings**	**Logic Glue**	**Word Glue**	**Organization Words**
2) In the opening kitchen scene, "gentle" Joe guards a vulnerable Pip "with his great leg" from an enraged Mrs. Joe and her tickler.	In the opening kitchen scene, **"gentle"** Joe **guards** a vulnerable Pip	for example	TS-#2: Joe-he / safeguards - guards	In the opening kitchen scene
3) Here he actively attempts to shield Pip from being raised "by hand."	Here he **actively attempts to shield**	and	#2-3: Joe-he / guards - shield	X
4) In fact, Joe protectively tells Pip he "wish there warn't no" beatings for him.	In fact, Joe **protectively** tells Pip	and	#3-4: shield - protectively	X
5) Later, at the Christmas dinner, Joe again alleviates the attacks on Pip from the holiday guests, who torment him and compare him to "swine."	Later, at the Christmas dinner, Joe again **alleviates**	for example	#4-5: Joe-Joe / protectively - alleviates	Later, at the Christmas dinner
6) With each insult, Joe gives Pip "more gravy," demonstrating that small getures can help ease the grief of individuals and help the community move closer toward love.	With each insult, Joe **gives** Pip **"more** gravy"	and	#5-6: Joe-Joe / alleviates - ease	X
7) Finally, in London, Joe helps Pip convalesce after his illness.	Finally, in London, Joe **helps Pip**	for example	#6-7: Joe-Joe / help-helps... convalesce	Finally, in London
8) Joe has chosen to leave the forge, his means of employment, to serve Pip, who eventually recognizes the pain he has caused both Joe and Biddy.	Joe has **chosen** to leave the forge, his means of employment, to **serve Pip**	that is	#7-8: Joe-Joe, he / helps-serve / Pip-Pip	X

04

DAILY PRACTICE
— THE FUNDAMENTALS —

Practicing the Plays

In this chapter, we will present several activities shaped by the principles of our playbook (outlined in the previous chapter), principles we have developed in light of what the fields of neuroscience, psychology, and coaching tell us.

These are the activities that we use regularly in our classrooms to train "the fundamentals" of reading and writing, our daily practice program to prepare students for the game that awaits them in English, the essay.

In the following chapter, "Putting the Plays Together," the reader will find activities designed to recreate game-like moments in which students must put all of the plays they have practiced to use.

For each activity, we specify the key plays students will practice.

We have also highlighted "Why It Works," explaining how a principle from neuroscience, psychology, or coaching applies. This section points back to research introduced in Chapter 1 and the 15 design principles outlined in Chapter 2. The teacher interested in the rationale for a particular activity may selectively refer back to the relevant principle(s) in these chapters for both a brief explanation and research references.

Scan here for more samples.

Scan here for video demonstrations.

Movement Variations for Any Unit

As mentioned at the beginning of this book, we believe the idea of movement, in both a physical and a figurative sense, offers teachers a helpful paradigm to think about the way they run their classes.

Before outlining several activities in detail, we would like first to present several ways that we incorporate movement into our skills practice. These variations are often both physical (students get up, walk around, swap desks) *and* figurative (they practice the mental movements of the reading and writing plays: selecting L1, refining L2, placing L2 in a topic string).

Every teacher's classroom is different: the number of desks, the amount of board space, the presence or absence of digital technology (digital large board at the front of the classroom, student laptops, etc). All of the activities in this book may be adapted to suit your classroom's needs, including some of the variations listed below.

Boardwork

Whether practicing a new sentence structure, reviewing the plot of the novel, recording what they can remember about a paragraph's structure, creating an evidence chart, writing a sentence blending textual evidence, or some other exercise, students stand up, discuss, and write at the large whiteboards hung around the classroom.

> **Don't have much whiteboard space?**
>
> Substitutes include but are not limited to the following: miniature whiteboards (purchase a classroom set, or several larger ones for groups to use), large-size Post-It sheets, poster board, and so on.

- For example, at the beginning of the class period, students stand up and go to the board. The teacher displays/writes a sentence on the board and reads it to students, before asking them to answer a series of grammar questions: What are the subject(s) and verb(s)? What type of sentence is this—simple, compound, complex, compound-complex? What kind of phrase is found at the beginning of the sentence? After students have time to answer these questions, they rotate, and mark another student's answers: "Move clockwise to the next student's workspace. Now listen for the correct answers to the questions I just asked you."

- In another example, the class reads a passage from the book they are reading together. Then, students pair up, move to their workspace (a station at the whiteboard, for example), and create an evidence-association chart, writing out quotations from the passage they read and making associations for these pieces of evidence.

Rotation—Individual, Partner, Triad, Large Group

Designing an activity to involve moments where students rotate between moments of collaboration and individual work.

- As one example, the teacher has students work together in partners or triads and switch to a new seat or table every ten minutes. After a few rounds, the whole class briefly discusses their ideas with each other. Then, working individually, all students must produce _____ (a sentence, all or part of a paragraph, a thesis, topic sentences, etc.) before the end of class.

- In another instance, students work individually for ten minutes, then shift to collaborate with a partner for ten minutes. After the first partner round, students shift to a second partner and work together for ten minutes to produce _____ (a sentence, all or part of a paragraph, thesis, topic sentences, etc.).

Gallery Walks

In this variation, students have a set amount of time to move around the room while performing a given intellectual task at the various specified stations. After this time period elapses, the teacher discusses the results of student work with the whole class.

- As one example, at each "station" (section of the board or wall) is a line or two from a text for students to record their associations.

- In another instance, at each station is the name of a character from the novel the class is reading. Underneath each character's name, students must write the details about the character that they can recall.

- In another instance, the teacher places at each station a sentence about the novel (a thesis statement, for example). These might be sentences produced by students in a previous activity, or model sentences created by the teacher. Students move about the room, scoring each sentence for a particular play ("I want you to read each sentence and evaluate the quality of its L2: Is it distinctive, mastery, progressing, or insufficient?") Each student indicates the score for each sentence on a sheet of paper or scorecard provided by the teacher.

Large Table Discussions w/ Student Moderators

In this variation, the teacher arranges the classroom desks/tables so that students may sit in groups of six to ten. With their groups, students discuss a passage from the reading, while one or two students in the group serve as moderators, recording notes on their peers' responses (see the **moderator tally sheet** on the next page). Here is one example of this strategy:

- Students begin at their original tables. They have ten minutes to re-read and annotate the passage individually before discussion begins.

- After prep time is up, a ten-minute period of discussion begins: students discuss their ideas with each other at their tables.

- After ten minutes, students switch groups/tables, and another round of discussion begins. The activity may continue for as many rounds as the teacher desires.

- During the rounds of discussion, the teacher can circulate between tables to listen and give feedback.
- At the end of the discussion rounds, the teacher asks moderators to write down their final comments in the Notes column of the tally sheet. What were the most insightful comments made during discussion? Which students had the best associations?
- The activity then concludes with a class discussion between all students and the teacher. The teacher may begin by asking moderators to share some of the best ideas they heard during the discussion rounds, and providing feedback on students' reading of the text.
- At the end of the activity, moderators hand in their tally sheets. The teacher can look at the datat collected to see if students are engaging with all of the plays, and if students are participating (It does not have to be taken for a grade).

Moderator Tally Sheet

Student Name	# of times student speaks	L1 Play (Tally # of times these words are used)	L2 Play (List the best associations)	L3 Play	Notes (Best comments made by student)
		diction: detail: imagery:			
		diction: detail: imagery:			
		diction: detail: imagery:			
		diction: detail: imagery:			

The Writing Journal

Most of our students will not choose on their own to adopt the behaviors of the perspicacious reader and interpretive writer. Knowing this, we must design our classroom in such a way that encourages them to do so and shows them how.

The writing journal is one way that we accomplish this.

For almost a decade, the physical or tactile has slowly ceded its place to the digital, as laptops and other devices have supplanted notebook paper as the primary tool used by students. Recently, however, we have returned to physical handwriting, recognizing its power to enhance the creation of long-term memory.

We have, therefore, incentivized the use of a writing journal in the following way: in our courses, all essays are written in class in timed situations (we call these "timed writes"). On these timed writes, students are often only allowed to use their books, the Reading and Writing Plays Charts (see pp. 270-271), and any notes recorded in their journals.

Learning Objectives

- Students will begin to understand how the behaviors of taking notes, listening actively, and paying attention to models directly relates to their performance on a timed write.
- Students will commit information to long-term memory more quickly.
- Students will create accessible, direct references to elements of the playbook in their notes.

WHY IT WORKS

The writing journal helps create an immediate link for students between taking notes and the benefits of this practice: the content written down in their journals can be used on major assessments. This enticement to learning, the "buy in," creates what researchers call **"behavior relevance."** When we fail to show students why a specific behavior or practice is significant to them, that doorway to the brain remains closed and no learning of significance will take place.[124] But when we open that doorway (achieving behavioral relevance), the brain activity begins and "the chances of [a behavior] being learned, remembered, and internalized increases."[125]

Suggested uses of the individual student journal

- Recording "data" from class activities:
    - A thesis statement / topic sentence / blended sentence provided by the teacher as a model
    - A sentence imitation
    - A sentence created during class and identified as a model of distinctive performance
- Record the best L1/L2 from a class discussion activity. Copy down evidence, associations, or sentences from in-class board work.
- Paste a small writing sample [paragraph chunk, introductory paragraph] or handout [notes on archetypes, or tragedy] into the journal.

---

124 Kilgard & Merzenich, 1998; Jenson & McConchie, 2020.
125 O'Keefe & Linnenbrink-Garcia, 2014.

The Brain Break

Research once thought that evening sleep provided the only time for our brains to replay the learning that occurred in the day, a time to strengthen some of the newly formed neural networks. But this natural brain instinct—that reviews the lesson and reinforces memory—can be triggered during our class periods in a manner of seconds, providing the brain relief from information overload or from the dissonance emerging whenever students struggle with the task.[126]

The brain break, ideally for high school students, occurs after 30 minutes of a learning activity, the moment when the amygdala, the brain's filtering system, closes down. Shifting the brain away from its complex cognitive task provides that particular neural network resting time, an opportunity to recharge while the brain moves to another area.[127]

Brain breaks lead students to a separate, already-rested area of the brain.

These breaks can engage students with additional physical movement or social interaction prompting positive emotions—joy, calmness, belonging, fellowship. Reading humorous poems without accompanying interpretation; playing musical chairs to switch groups or partners; playing a requested song or video clip; writing on the board a favorite hobby, sport, musician, movie; viewing artwork that connects to a current reading unit.

After the break, students return to the more challenging task with a refreshed brain, ultimately strengthening the long-term memory circuit connected to the lesson's goal.[128]

---

[126] Terrada, 2022.

[127] Willis, 2016.

[128] Buch, E. R., et al., 2021; Robertson, E.M., 2019; Kelley, P. & Whatson, T., 2013; McTighe, J. & Willis, J. 2019; Smolen, Ahang, & Byrne, 2016.

- Create brain break teams for an ongoing competition—board games (*Trivial pursuit*, *Wit's End*, *Chronology*), charades, or Grammar Dice.
- Make a playlist of your favorite songs, or of songs that relate thematically to the current unit.
- Read humorous or interesting poems without accompanying interpretation.
- Create a Google Form for Students to Submit a song/video clip (This way you can listen to or watch the requests before playing them in class).
- Hold a stretch break. For fun, pick a student to call out the moves for the group. Lunges? Quad stretches? Arm swings? Pushups?
- Teach students a new dance move (Ex. Pique student interest in the world of *The Great Gatsby* by watching a video on how to do the Charleston).
- Poll the class with a silly question: "Would you rather…"
- Use a "book of questions" and select one a week—i.e. *The Book of Questions*, Gregory Stock, Ph.D.; *4,000 Questions for Getting to Know Anyone and Everyone*, Barbara Ann Kipfer. "If you were a car, what type would you be?"
- Teach the class a new idiom, saying, or expression in English—its meaning and origin ("feather in her cap," "chip on his shoulder," etc.).
- Prepare a folder or document with visual art—painting, photography—which may or may not relate to the current unit.
- Play a quick round of musical chairs to switch partners.
- Make a personal item list on the board: Tell students to go to the board and write their favorite band/movie/sport/hobby/etc.
- Have students perform: ask a student musician to play a song; ask a drama student to perform a favorite monologue; ask a martial artist to demonstrate a specifc technique.

Ian's Brain Breaks – "Berry Live"

I have played songs on the guitar for years. In my classroom, I will often play during my brain breaks, selecting songs that pair well with the book my students are reading. For example, as they read Cormac McCarthy's *All the Pretty Horses*, I will play songs like Marty Robbins' "El Paso" and Hank Williams "I'm So Lonesome I Could Cry."

SCAN ME

Musical Chairs

In an activity divided into a series of timed rounds, students examine small quotations or passages from the novel. When the music plays, they must move to a different location, where they sit with a new partner or group to discuss a new quotation.

Core Plays Involved

Learning Objectives

- Link any reading content with the practice of the core reading and writing plays.

Procedure

- Arrange the classroom desks into table formations (e.g., four desks pushed together to make a table).

- The teacher selects ten important quotations from the novel (See pp. 120-121 for examples). These could be from a chapter the students have already read, or one they are about to begin reading.

- Print these quotations (number them, or indicate the page number) and place each one at a different table. During each round of Musical Chairs, students will sit at a different table and discuss a different quotation.

WHY IT WORKS

The musical chairs activity responds to considerable research that links physical activity and the cognitive parts of the brain. When initiating a **physical movement**, the cerebellum does not simply send a message to perform a physical act. It also fires off directives to the parts of the brain underlying cognition, amplifying learning capacity and memory. On a cellular level, physical or kinetic action "moves" neurons to bind together via synapses, the cellular structures underlying learning and memory.[1]

Our memory function, too, becomes stimulated when we move. Several studies reinforce the link between memory and moderate physical activity,[2] some emphasizing how even slight movement or gestures of the body assist our ability to remember.[3] Memory, our ability to learn, the ability of our neurons to create stronger connections, and even our brain's ability to adapt to change all advance when we move. Exercise triggers different neurological responses unlike those while in stasis, even changing the gene expression in the brain's primary memory center, the hippocampus.[4]

Of course, Musical Chairs also allows the teacher to introduce students to some great music and potential dance moves.

- Tell students to have their notebook/journal or a sheet of paper ready. Students need a place to record their associations (L2) from each round.

- Have a musical device ready (online playlist, vinyl record, actual musical instrument). The music is the cue for students to move.

---

1 van Praag & Christie 2015; Schmahmann 2019; Rogge AK, Röder B, Zech A, et al. 2018.
2 Raskin, 2017. Moriya M 2016.
3 Madan, 2012.
4 Tong, 2001.

Before the first round, tell students to find a seat and give initial instructions:

- "We're going to do several rounds of musical chairs today. In each round, you will have five minutes to re-read and discuss the quotation at your table."

> **Make It Fun**
> Announce a theme for the day's music ("It's the disco edition of musical chairs, everyone…") or allow students to make song requests.

- "I've put a different quotation at each table in the classroom. We're going to do four rounds of this activity today. That means you need to visit four different tables during this activity."

- "See that the quotation at your table is numbered. Write this number down (Quote #3, Quote #7, etc)."

- "While your group discusses the quotation, I want you to write all of the associations you come up with under this number."

As students discuss their table's quotation, the teacher circulates among the tables. Remind students who need it that you've asked them to write down their group's associations. "Everyone's gotta do it!"

When the teacher senses that it is time to move to a new quotation, he or she puts on the music. Students have to get up, move to a new seat, and repeat the process with a new quotation.

- "I want you to find a new desk and new partners. Make sure you are not moving to a table you've visited already."

After completing several rounds, the teacher plays the music and students move one last time. When students are seated, the teacher begins a brief discussion of the associations that the class gathered:

- "With Dimmesdale's character…what were the most important associations? Which ones kept showing up?"

- "Did you notice any patterns as you moved through the different quotations about Tom Buchanan's house?"

- "If you had to select one quotation from this chapter as the most important example of a shift in Pip's character, which one would it be, and why?"

This final discussion gives students the opportunity to hear about quotations that they did not see during the rounds, and write down the associations they hear from students with whom they did not work. *Optional:* If your classroom has space along the wall where students can write (whiteboards, butcher paper, etc.), or if you want to set up a Google Form, you can require a representative from each table to record the group's best associations at the end of each round. While the music plays, and other students move to find a new table, the representative from each table either goes to the board or wall to write the group's associations, or quickly types them into a Google Form.

Example Musical Chairs Google Form

Students' Names: Mauricio, Kevin

Quotation #: 5

Your Groups' Associations (L2) for this quotation: generous, welcoming, warm, kind

---

The goal behind collecting the best associations at the end of each round is for students to have access to them later. The teacher can also open the responses spreadsheet and highlight the most insightful or precise ideas that students have developed during the activity.

Scan to see a sample responses spreadsheet.

Musical Chairs: The Adventures of Huckleberry Finn

Here is a list of quotations for musical chairs from the opening pages of *The Adventures of Huckleberry Finn*:

1.

"The Widow Douglas, she took me for her son, and allowed she would sivilize me; but it was rough living in the house all the time, considering how dismal regular and decent the widow was in all her ways."

2.

"The widow she cried over me, and called me a poor lost lamb, and she called me a lot of other names, too, but she never meant no harm by it. She put me in them new clothes again, and I couldn't do nothing but sweat and sweat, and feel all cramped up." (6; ch. 1)

3.

"[Her sister, Miss Watson,] … told me all about the bad place [Hell], and I said I wished I was there. She got mad, then, but I didn't mean no harm. All I wanted was to go somewheres, all I wanted was a change, I warn't particular." (7; ch. 1)

4.

"Pretty soon I wanted to smoke, and asked the widow to let me. But she wouldn't. She said it was a mean practice and wasn't clean, and I must try not to do it any more. That is just the way with some people. They get down on a thing when they don't know nothing about it. [...] And she took snuff too; of course that was all right, because she done it herself." (6; ch. 1)

5.

"I felt so lonesome, I most wished I was dead. The stars was shining, and the leaves rustled in the woods ever so mournful; and I heard an owl, away off, who-whooing about somebody that was dead, and a whippowill and a dog crying about somebody that was going to die; and the wind was trying to whisper something to me and I couldn't make out what it was, and so it made the cold shivers run over me." (7; ch. 1)

6.

"Pap he hadn't been seen for more than a year, and that was comfortable for me; I didn't want to see him no more. He used to always whale me when he was sober and could get his hands on me; though I used to take to the woods most of the time when he was around." (17; ch. 3)

Musical Chairs: *The Great Gatsby*

The teacher can also play musical chairs to examine various characters throughout the literary work. Here is a set of quotations from *The Great Gatsby* that invites students to look at the minor characters in the novel:

1. Jordan Baker (Chapter 3)

"...suddenly I remembered the story about her that had eluded me that night at Daisy's. At her first big golf tournament there was a row that nearly reached the newspapers—a suggestion that she had moved her ball from a bad lie in the semi-final round."

2. Myrtle Wilson (Chapter 2)

"She had changed her dress to a brown figured muslin, which stretched tight over her rather wide hips as Tom helped her to the platform in New York. At the news-stand she bought a copy of *Town Tattle* and a moving-picture magazine, and in the station drug-store some cold cream and a small flask of perfume."

3. Meyer Wolfsheim (Chapter 4)

'Who is he, anyhow, an actor?'

'No.'

'A dentist?'

'Meyer Wolfsheim? No, he's a gambler." Gatsby hesitated, then added coolly: "He's the man who fixed the World's Series back in 1919.'

'Fixed the World's Series?' I repeated."

4. George Wilson (Chapter 2)

"He was a blond, spiritless man, anaemic, and faintly handsome. When he saw us a damp gleam of hope sprang into his light blue eyes.

'Hello, Wilson, old man,' said Tom, slapping him jovially on the shoulder. 'How's business?'

'I can't complain,' answered Wilson unconvincingly."

5. Tom (Chapter 1)

"Now he was a sturdy straw-haired man of thirty with a rather hard mouth and a supercilious manner. Two shining arrogant eyes had established dominance over his face and gave him the appearance of always leaning aggressively forward. Not even the effeminate swank of his riding clothes could hide the enormous power of that body—he seemed to fill those glistening boots until he strained the top lacing, and you could see a great pack of muscle shifting when his shoulder moved under his thin coat. It was a body capable of enormous leverage—a cruel body."

Giving Feedback

During class, as students draft on the board, talk with partners, or submit their ideas via digital submission, we want to provide immediate feedback as they execute a play.

Our goal is to teach students, through repetition, the mental movements involved in the reading plays: first, look at the text; second, make associations for just those specific words.

Students will refine their abilities to execute these plays if we can help them clearly see how and when they perform them improperly. Here are a few common errors we see and quickly provide feedback to correct. These examples illustrate a problem with the student's L1-L2 pairings.

- Can you factor this idea?

    - We teach students to think of associations as things we can break down and reduce to a prime form—the most specific the idea can be. We call this process factoring.

    - As one example, a student reading *Lord of the Flies* comes upon the line where Jack's tribe forms a "solid mass of menace," and writes down the association **evil**.

    - This association is too broad and general: evil has many different aspects or parts. The aspect of evil on display here is its **threatening** and **predatory** nature.

    - Rather than giving the student these words, we ask, "Can you factor this L2? What aspect of evil is this? What about evil is this quotation specifically showing us?"

- Which words in the text gave you that idea?

    This is the first question we ask students whose associations do not make sense. Usually, this question prompts them to reveal an underlying issue in the logic of their reading of the text. Here are three examples of underlying issues:

    - First, one student reading Chapter 1 of *The Adventures of Huckleberry Finn* notices "how dismal regular and decent the widow was in all her ways," and suggests the associations **abusive**, **cruel**, and **wants to escape**.

The student recognizes "dismal" as a word with a negative connotation, and develops the associations **abusive** and **cruel**. However, these associations are too negative (a greater degree than dismal suggests), and clash logically with other words in the text, "regular and decent," which suggest the Widow to be an **orderly, moral** figure.

- A second issue occurs when a student's idea is logical and appropriate to the literary work, but the piece of evidence chosen is not one that reveals it.

The student in the example above has developed a viable association for Huck, *wanting to escape*, but this L2 comes from other words on the page, "when I couldn't stand it no longer" / Student L2: **feeling trapped, confined, wants to escape**

- A third issue is one we call the cause-effect error. Often a student wants to explain why a character does or says something but the text provides no clear antecedent.

For instance, another student reading Twain's novel observes that Huck says he "felt so lonesome" and suggests this L2: **Huck has no friends**.

We want to direct the student to stay focused only on the associations with the words in front of him/her; in this case, Huck's response is **emotional**, "felt," rather than **logical**. And "lonesome" is a state of **separation**, **isolation**, a **lack of connection to something outside the self**.

How to Engage "Difficult" Texts

This activity is particularly useful for helping students practice the skills of close reading. Reading a poem or the opening of a difficult novel is a challenge for all growing minds, but the design of this activity empowers students to meet this challenge, and see close reading as a skill they can develop by practicing specific, smaller actions.

Core Plays Involved

Learning Objectives

- Students will engage with intellectually challenging material as the teacher provides initial access to a single part of the chosen text—individual words or phrases from either a poem, the opening of a novel or play, a section of a novel or play not yet read, or the opening of a nonfiction essay.

- Students will refine their abilities to observe nuances in L1.

- Students will improve their abilities to pair L1 (evidence) with L2 (associations) in a logical way.

- Students will strengthen their abilities to develop sophisticated, precise L2.

- Students will begin to learn that even if they do not understand every word or phrase of a complex text, they can still apply the basic "play" of attaching associations to ones they do understand, and they can pay attention to the relationships emerging between the pieces of evidence in the story.

> ## WHY IT WORKS
>
> The key to this activity is breaking a challenging text into pieces that are accessible to students. Musicians and athletes understand this essential concept of **deliberate practice:** they slow an arduous task down, break it up, go over the target performance again and again. Breaking down more complex movements into manageable parts allows the brain to learn them faster—in this situation a Shakespearean sonnet, for example, or the opening of a Dickens novel. This essential technique for expert performance recognizes the brain's ability to manage only a finite number of learning tasks at a time.[129] Researchers have found that we can take in only three to seven chunks of information before we overload and begin to miss new incoming data.[130]
>
> Teachers need to avoid "too much content, too fast," because it "is unlikely to get processed correctly and saved accurately."[131] And if a student can learn pieces of Sonnet 29, he can ultimately learn the entire poem or a subsequent one.

Procedure

- From a given poem, novel chapter, play opening, etc., select ten to fifteen short fragments from the text (L1). A fragment is an individual word, short phrase, or paraphrased detail to which the teacher wishes to draw students' attention. From Act 1, Scene 1 of *Macbeth*, for example, some possible fragments include *witches; thunder, lightning, and rain;* "*hurlyburly;*" "*the battle's lost, and won;*" *the setting sun;* "*fair;*" *and* "*foul.*"

- Write these quotations in order on the boards around the room. If board space is limited, print these fragments on sheets/slips of paper

---

[129] Thalmann, Souza, & Oberauer, 2018; Jenson & McConchie, 2020.
[130] Linden et al., 2003; Jensen 2005.
[131] Schacter, Guerin, & Jacques, 2011; Paas, & Ayres, 2014.

and paste them at different locations around the room. Alternatively, a Google Form may be created for students to input their associations (L2) for each L1.

- If an important idea in the text emerges through a particularly difficult piece of evidence, the teacher may manipulate the original text to make it more accessible to the students (they will read the original later).

  - For example, in "Sonnet 29," Shakespeare writes, "[I] trouble deaf heaven with my bootless cries."

  - The teacher writes on the board: Heaven is deaf.

- Prepare the class to read the fragments with a brief introduction. The teacher may ask a question prompting students to look for a particular idea that appears throughout the words and phrases posted around the classroom:

  - "In this chapter, we're going to encounter an important character, and here are some of the things he says and does."

  - "Here's our chance to get a sneak peek at some of the ways the community functions in Chapter 8."

  - "As we read a few fragments from the narrator's opening remarks, ask yourself, what sort of narrator is telling this story?"

- Read the fragments in order as a class, giving students a chance to begin noticing patterns, making predictions.

- After reading and some time for student reflection, the teacher may ask students if they have any initial observations or predictions:

  - "How would you describe the atmosphere and situation

> **Make It Fun**
>
> Sometimes, I announce that the author has agreed to loan the class pieces of the manuscript for the day: "These have just been transported over from the museum and positioned around the room. What an honor…"

introduced by these fragments?"

- "What is this a story about?"

• After brief initial discussion, it is time for students to go to the board. They have ___ minutes to circulate around the room, writing their best associations underneath each piece of evidence.

- Students may walk past a station of the board if they can't think of any associations for the evidence that appears there.

- Students should avoid repeating an association that is already listed.

- Students should write at least ___ associative words on the board.

• Once students have made an entry for each fragment, begin discussing the associative patterns that now emerge:

- What are the traits of the character or setting that seem to be repeated?

- What is the atmosphere/tone?

- Are there multiple associative ideas? What are they?

- Is there a conflict present? What makes this situation complex?

Additional Suggestions

Ask students to initial their first names next to their associations. This makes it easier for the teacher to give feedback, even calling it out across the room after a student has moved on to a different piece of evidence.

- "Oh, Raul, great L2 for this one over here—*cynical*."

- "Chad, I was looking through these and wanted to ask about this L2 you wrote here. Could you tell me which words in the quotation led you to this association?"

- Typically, some or many of the associations that appear do in fact reveal accurately the ideas of the text. If no accurate associations (L2) have been written on the wall for one or more quotations, the teacher may discuss these with the class to help students understand them. Occasionally, students' misinterpretation of a fragment might indicate that the teacher should modify the lesson plan for the future, choosing a different fragment or paraphrasing the text.

- Once the students begin to see how they have discovered and predicted accurately, show them the complete text.

- Several options exist at this point in the exercise—to extend it or move on to another activity.

- **Continuation option**: Brainstorm as a class or in partners a possible thesis statement for the text. Some thesis syntactical patterns might include the following:

    - The speaker (verb) _[L2]__. [The speaker successfully **reframes his despair into internal fortitude**.]

    - The main character shifts from_[L2]_to_[L2]__. [Pip shifts from **selfishness to selflessness**.]

    - The speaker (verb) with L2. [The speaker struggles with **societal expectations for wealth**.]

    - The [L2] atmosphere of the opening chapter… [The **bleak** atmosphere of the opening chapter reflects a world of entrapment.]

- **Continuation option**: Once some draft thesis statements are created, discuss how many paragraphs would be part of a short essay proving the thesis statement:

    - How would pieces of evidence be grouped together?

    - Once the groupings are decided, draft possible topic sentences.

- **Continuation option**: Pair up students and place them at individual pieces of evidence around the room. For the next activity, partners must write a sentence that blends the piece of evidence with the best associations recorded during the gallery walk. The syntax should look like this: L2—L1—L2 (See p. 82).

Sample - Sonnet 29

When, in disgrace with fortune and men's eyes,
I all alone beweep my outcast state,
And trouble deaf heaven with my bootless cries,
And look upon myself and curse my fate,
Wishing me like to one more rich in hope,
Featured like him, like him with friends possessed,
Desiring this man's art and that man's scope,
With what I most enjoy contented least;
Yet in these thoughts myself almost despising,
Haply I think on thee, and then my state,
(Like to the lark at break of day arising
From sullen earth) sings hymns at heaven's gate;
For thy sweet love remembered such wealth brings
That then I scorn to change my state with kings.

L1 / Fragments from Sonnet 29 to place on the board:
   1. In disgrace
   2. I all alone beweep
   3. I'm an outcast
   4. Heaven is deaf
   5. I look upon myself and curse my fate
   6. Yet…I think on thee
   7. Then my soul…like the lark at break of day
   8. sings hymns
   9. at heaven's gate
   10. Thy sweet love remembered such wealth brings

Sample Student Responses to Fragments of Sonnet 29

in disgrace with men's eyes	all alone	outcast	deaf heaven	curse my fate
disgraceful	abandon, alone, deserted, neglect	unorthodox	?	death, end of time, gone
disheartened, disgusted	desolate, empty,	alone, abandoned	hysterical	desperate
shameful, dishonored, doubt	abandoned, alienated, deserted	cut off, leave	silence, peaceful	dishonor, detest
shameful	abandoned	hypocritical, thrown out	abandoned by God	hateful
shame	abandoned	apathy	colorless	disparaging
disappointed, let down	desolate	isolated	deserted, neglect	bitter, submissive
indifferent	lost, hopeless	abandoned, forsaken	hearing loss	vexed
dishonor, shame, discredit	solo, solitary, abandoned, deserted	odd, weird	quiet	blasphemy, unlucky

Sample - The First Pages of *The Great Gatsby*

L1 / Fragments to place on the board:
1. In my younger and more vulnerable years
2. My father gave me some advice: "Whenever you feel like criticizing anyone," he told me, "just remember that all the people in this world haven't had the advantages that you've had."
3. I'm inclined to reserve all judgments of others, a habit that has opened up many to me, and sometimes made me a victim.
4. I went to New York in the spring of 1922
5. To get a job in investment banking
6. Life was full of the sunshine and great bursts of leaves growing on the trees
7. I came back from New York in autumn of 1922
8. I wanted no more glimpses into the human heart
9. Only Gatsby turned out alright in the end.
10. He had a heightened sensitivity to the promises of life –
11. But a foul dust floated in the wake of his dreams.

Scan here for more samples.

The Evidence-Association Chart [EAC]

Core Plays Involved

 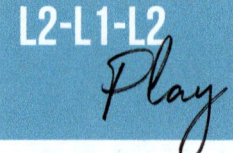 

Learning Objectives

- Students will practice applying the reading plays (L1, L2, and L3) to the literary text.

- Students will develop their abilities to make logical L1-L2 pairings and observe relationships between the details of the text.

- Students will practice moving inductively from reading the text towards writing about it, using the chart as a graphic organizer for their thoughts.

- Students will practice crafting interpretive sentences using content from the L1 and L2 columns of the chart.

See student samples and access charts to use in your classroom.

WHY IT WORKS

The EAC **graphic organizer** primarily appeals to the brain's desire for order, placing multiple parts into manageable spaces, reducing the potential strain on the brain to juggle too much data at one time.[132] Inside the chart, students can also more clearly **recognize patterns,** practicing the skills of **inductive** thinking, identifying relationships, which provides the fuel needed for the brain to engage in the wonder of "neuroplasticity," that is, the ability of the brain to adapt and change by forming new connections between neurons.[133] The EAC creates an ideal inductive lesson where students learn by doing, engaging in mental manipulation[134]—all while multiple "Plays" become reinforced in longer term memory—aligning L2 with L1, refining the quality of L2, practicing the L2-L1-L2 syntax play, writing topic sentences.

Procedure

When assigning an Evidence-Association Chart, the teacher decides how many entries must be completed, and how many columns must be filled out.

First, before considering different ways to use the chart, we would like to provide the basic instructions for completing it. An example of the chart may be found on p. 135.

- In the first column of the EAC, students gather evidence from the text (L1). Fill out this column by entering either direct quotations or paraphrased details/facts about the story (e.g., *The villain wears a mask* is a detail that does not require quoting the text).

---

132   McTighe & Willis, 2019.
133   McTighe & Willis, 2019.
134   Wiggins, G., & McTighe, J., 2012.

- In the second column of the chart, students indicate the type of evidence.

    - *diction* (the specific words the writer is using),
    - *detail* (the facts of the text–characters, setting, events–that do not require quoting its language), and
    - *imagery* (vivid, sensory images created by the writer's description).

- In the third column, students create associations (L2), the abstract ideas that emerge from the selected quotation.

- In the fourth column, they identify relationships (L3), the patterns emerging between the associations they are making: *repetition, contrast, juxtaposition,* and *shift*.

- Note: For a more detailed discussion of L1, L2, L3—the three Reading Plays—see Chapter 3.

- In column five, students practice the L2-L1-L2 writing play (see p. 82): They build sentences using the words in the first four columns of their charts. These sentences will blend pieces of evidence from the text (L1) with the writer's interpretive voice (L2 and L3).

- In column six, students create topic sentences to unify several pieces of evidence (L1). A topic sentence unifies several L1 when it contains associations (L2) linked with these L1.

Scan the QR code to see student samples
and access copies of the chart to
use in your classroom.

Sample Chart for the *Odyssey*

L1 Evidence	Type Diction, Detail, Imagery	L2 Associations	L3 repetition, contrast, juxtaposition, shift	L2 - L1 - L2 Sentence	Topic Sentence
1) Penelope "puts her husband to the proof." (23.203)	detail	clever, suspicion, testing, wary of deceit, protecting her marriage, virtue unorthodox,		**Virtuously protecting her marriage,** Penelope cleverly "puts [Odysseus] to the proof" when he returns home, **warily testing** him, not wanting to be **deceived** by a man who is not her true husband (23.203).	Once **reunited** with her husband, Penelope's **tireless** efforts to **preserve** her marriage are now fulfilled, and the family experiences long-awaited **joy** and **relief.**
2) Penelope "dissolve[s] into tears" when she realizes Odysseus has really returned (23.233)	detail	joyful reunion, recognition, relief, emotional release	shift from suspicion (evidence #1) to recognition repetition of Penelope's relief and joy		
3) "You've **conquered my heart,** my hard heart at last!" (23.258)	diction	heroic, masculine diction; overcome by love, sorrowful heart restored	repetition of Penelope's relief and joy contrast to Penelope's wary, defensive attitude (evidence #1)		

The Many Applications of the EAC

Students can complete the chart individually, with partners or groups, or as an entire class. A Google Form or writing journal are options for an EAC.

Teachers may use the EAC for one class day's exercise, or they may have students develop a larger evidence chart over the course of a unit.

- **Individual chart completed over the course of a unit**: During the class's reading of the novel, students complete their own charts, with an assigned # of required entries. The teacher may assign specific essay topics to different students; their chart entries would be pieces of evidence that support an answer to the assigned prompt.

- **At the board**: Partners or groups draw EAC charts on the whiteboards and complete them. This variation incorporates physical movement and engages multiple senses. It is great for channeling talkative, energetic students and encouraging quieter ones to verbalize their thoughts with their peers.

- **Rotation**: Partners or small groups rotate from their own charts to another one.

  - For example, a small group of students might have ten minutes to add L1 and L2 to their EAC at the board or at their table or desks. When the timer goes off, they will move to the right—to the next group's station—and add at least three L2 to that group's chart.

- **Quick guided reading of the text**: The teacher reads through a passage from the novel with the class, stopping at intervals to have students make an entry for the page just read.

  - Each time the teacher stops reading, students have to write on the board (or at their tables or desks if space is a problem) the L1 they think is most significant regarding character, setting, atmosphere.

  - At this point, the teacher can then direct the entire class' attention to a salient, single piece of evidence that has been chosen by students. All groups write this piece of evidence in their chart, and then make associations for it.

- The class discusses the significance of the quotation, and the best associations.

- The teacher may also highlight an important quotation in the passage that no one has noticed, and repeat the discussion movement.

- The teacher may repeat this cycle several more times, reading further in the text.

- **Class Digital Evidence Chart**: The teacher creates a Google Form, and the "Responses" spreadsheet functions as a class EAC.

    - Create a response box in the Google Form of each of the following:
        - L1
        - L1 type (multiple choice): diction, detail, imagery
        - L2
        - L3 (multiple choice): repetition, contrast, juxtaposition, shift
        - L2-L1-L2 sentence
        - Topic Sentence

    - Note: Students do not have to complete all columns of the chart each time—a student's response might only include L1, L1 type, and L2.

    - The teacher may select a series of pages or lines that students will chart throughout the activity. For instance, the teacher may select a longer passage from *Beowulf*, divide it into smaller groups of lines, and have students chart with them in a series of short, five-minute rounds.

> **Exploring *Beowulf*, lines 456-661, with the EAC**
>
> Submit one L1-L2 pairing to the class EAC each round
>
> - Round 1: lines 456-472 — 5 minutes
> - Round 2: lines 499-528 — 5 mins
> - Round 3: lines 530-606 — 5 mins
> - Round 4: lines 655-661 — 5 mins

- Students may work on their own, with a partner, or in groups to submit the required number of responses to the Google Form.

- While students complete their entries at their own pace, the teacher can observe online the changing class chart (the Form "Responses" spreadsheet) and provide feedback on how well students are executing the Reading and Writing Plays.

- This feedback offers students an instantaneous reward or gratification that can further motivate them in the next round. Give students dopamine rewards for a chart well done!

- The feedback period can also provide a moment at the end of the round when all students can add the best entries to their own books/journals/individual evidence charts.

Sample Class EAC Responses for *Beowulf*

Line #	L1	L1 Type	L2	L3	L2-L1-L2 Sentence
1724	"It is a great wonder how Almighty God in His magnificence favours our race with rank and scope and the gift of wisdom."	diction	wise, god-like, power	contrast	Hrothgar, speaking on the **dangers of power** says how it is a "great wonder how Almighty God...favours our race with rank and scope," a notion stating that Hrothgar does not understand why God would give mankind the "gift of wisdom" to **be used at their own expense.**
1855	"My liking for you deepens with time, dear Beowulf."	diction	continuation, fondness, affection	juxtaposition	Hrothgar speaking **fondly** to Beowulf after the battle says affectionately, "My liking for you deepens with time, dear Beowulf," issuing a true and honest belief of Beowulf's **significance** and **sacrifice** to bring together the two enemies and plant **peace** throughout.
1853	"Do not give way to pride. For a brief while your strength is in bloom but it fades quickly."	diction	fortitude, wisdom	repetition	Wise Beowulf **heeds the kings' wisdom** of "not [giving] way to pride," a commitment to **the value of *sapientia*, a wisdom that seeks to suppress the ego.**

Paragraph Chart

Core Plays Involved

| TOPIC SENTENCE [TS] *Play* | WORD AND LOGIC GLUE *Play* | ORGANIZATION *Play* | TOPIC STRING *Play* |

Learning Objectives

- Students will understand the core plays involved in writing paragraphs.[135]
- Students will use topic strings, word & logic glue, and organization strategies with increasing skill.

WHY IT WORKS

This **graphic organizer** works as a primary metacognitive exercise, asking students to consciously reflect on core writing plays—the topic string, glue, organization. Neuroscience now confirms that not only do these **metacognitive skills** trigger a specific neural network in the brain, but also their very activity assists other cognitive functions.[136] As the chart helps students "link new content to what they already know,"[137] students strengthen **memory networks** because the brain recognizes where to attach new information it receives. The chart takes previously learned information (a topic string, for instance) out of isolation and it connects it to a larger task of a student's actual paragraph draft.[138]

---

135 For a more detailed explanation of these plays, see pp. 94-105.
136 Vacarro, 2018.
137 Luiten, Ames, & Ackerson, 1980.
138 Thalmann, Soua, & Oberauer, 2018; Luiten, Ames, & Ackerson, 1980.

Procedure

The Paragraph Chart is a graphic organizer that facilitates student practice of various writing plays. This chart may be used as a tool to examine and revise an already-written paragraph, or a student may draft a new paragraph within the chart, completing the different columns as the paragraph develops.

- Provide students with, or have them create, a copy of the *Paragraph Chart*. Students may work individually, in partners, or groups.
- The teacher may wish to create a class Paragraph Chart in Google Sheets, in which each student is given a separate tab with his/her own chart. This allows the teacher to have one spreadsheet open on the digital board and click between individual students' charts. (It also circumvents the issue of "Undo," where a student clicking this button on one large shared Google Sheet can undo another student's work. If given separate tabs, this problem does not occur).
- Column 1: Sentences. Type or paste the sentences of the paragraph into the first column of the chart, one sentence per row.
- Column 2: Topic Strings (see p. 100). Type the interpretive associations (L2) that appear in the Topic Sentence in the first box of this column. In every box beneath this one, the writer pastes the first 5-8 words of the sentence on that row of the chart (Or, for your math students, the words to the left of the midpoint in the sentence).
- Column 3: Word Glue (see p. 103). The writer identifies the words that link pairs of sentences within the paragraph.
- Column 4: Logic Glue (see p. 103). The writer identifies the logical relationships that exist between sentences in the paragraph.
- Column 5: Organization (see p. 96). The writer types the organization words/phrases that signal the transitions in the paragraph. Additionally, at the top of this column, the writer identifies the organizational method indicated by these words/phrases: Time, Place, Idea, or some combination of these three.
- It is helpful to color-code the chunks of the paragraph (see our example on the next page). This action helps the student see how much/how little they are devoting to a section of the argument.

Sample Chart on Joe Gargery (*Great Expectations*)

Paragraph Chart				
TS: Pip's surrogate father, Joe, frequently safeguards Pip when he is in desperate need, demonstrating throughout the story that a servant must be an active participant in restoring community.	**L2 in the TS:** Joe = surrogate father, safeguards Pip, desperate need, servant, restoring community	X	X	This paragraph is organized by Time <u>and</u> Place.
Sentences in the Paragraph	Topic Strings (the initial 5-8 words of the sentence)	Word Glue	Logic Glue	Organization Words
2) In the opening kitchen scene, "gentle" Joe guards a young Pip "with his great leg" (14; ch. 2) from an enraged Mrs. Joe and her tickler.	In the opening kitchen scene, "gentle" Joe **guards**	#TS-2: safeguards - guards	for example	**In the opening kitchen scene**
3) Here he actively attempts to shield Pip from being raised "by hand."	Here he actively attempts to **shield**	S#2-3: guards - shield	and	X
4) In fact, Joe protectively tells Pip he "wish there warn't no" (43; ch. 7) beatings for him.	In fact, Joe **protectively** tells Pip	S#3-4: shield - protectively	and	X
5) Later, at the Christmas dinner, Joe again alleviates the attacks on Pip from the holiday guests, who torment him and compare him to "swine."	Later, at the Christmas dinner, Joe again **alleviates**	S#4-5: protectively - alleviates	for example	**Later, at the Christmas dinner**

Note: In column two above, the writer has bolded the association words that connect to the associations found in the topic sentence: guard, shield, and protectively all link with the word safeguards. In column three, the writer lists the words that connect each pair of sentences together (sentence two and three, three and four, etc.).

The paragraph continues on the next page.

Sentences in the Paragraph	Topic Strings (the initial 5-8 words of the sentence)	Word Glue	Logic Glue	Organization Words
6) With each insult, Joe gives Pip "more gravy," demonstrating that small gestures can help ease the grief of individuals and help the community move closer toward love.	With each insult, Joe **gives** Pip "**more**	S#5-6: Joe - Joe / alleviates - ease	and	X
7) Finally, in London, Joe helps Pip convalesce after his illness.	Finally, in London, Joe **helps** Pip convalesce	S#6-7: help - convalesce	for example	**Finally, in London**
8) Joe has selflessly chosen to leave the forge, his means of employment, to serve Pip, who eventually recognizes the pain he has caused both Joe and Biddy.	Joe has **selflessly** chosen to leave the forge	S#7-8: helps Pip - serve Pip	that is	X
9) Moreover, Pip sees Joe as a servant, the true "gentle man," who has helped him become a more loving member of the community.	Moreover, Pip sees Joe as a **servant**	S#8-9 Joe- Joe/ serve - servant	therefore	X

Teacher Feedback Opportunities

- Column 1: Point out when a student's sentences lack evidence or associations, or when the pairing of evidence and associations does not make sense.

- Column 2: Point out when students' strings lack association words, or when these L2 do not link to the topic sentence.

- Column 3: Point out when students' sentences are not linked by any associations (ex. The only words linking two sentences are *Joe* and *he*).

- Column 4: Point out when two sentences are not logically linked. Occasionally, this issue can be resolved by adding a transition word or phrase to the paragraph.

- Column 5: Point out when a student's chunk lacks organizational language. Remind them that they need to select a method (Time, Place, Idea) and use transition words for this method.

Teaching Aristotle's Topics of Invention
Definition, Classification, Comparison, Relationship

Core Plays Involved

THE THESIS (TH) Play **TOPIC SENTENCE (TS) Play** **ORGANIZATION Play**

Learning Objectives

- Students will develop a strategy for generating a thesis for an essay that includes an interpretive point of view regarding an entire literary work.

- Students will recognize patterns among evidence, both literary and non-literary.

- Students will develop strategies for paragraph organization.

WHY IT WORKS

While the brain naturally likes patterns, teaching students the Topics further assists their brains in knowing what possible arrangements they can use to organize information. One of the key functions of the brain is to **identify patterns,** to organize data, recognizing their similarities and differences, degrees of distinction and creating classifications. When we engage students in the deliberate practice of these skills of making patterns, they improve the efficiency of their memory circuits.[139]

---

139 Haystead & Marzano, 2009; McTighe & Willis, 2019.

Aristotle's Topics

Aristotle created the Topics[140] as a resource to help students find and structure their arguments, regardless of the subject. In other words, the four Topics discussed in this activity are different types of thesis statements, and each type additionally suggests a method for organizing paragraphs (This becomes clearer when looking at the samples, starting on p. 147). Knowing and understanding each of these topics provides students with a strategy to find something to say about any text under consideration.

For our purposes here, Aristotle's Topics are limited to the following four categories:

- Argument by Definition
- Argument by Classification
- Argument by Comparison
    - comparison of similarity
    - comparison of differences
    - comparison by degrees
- Argument by Relationship
    - the relationship of contraries
    - the relationship of cause and effect

Once students understand the topics, teachers can modify discussion questions during class—Roger Chillingworth appears to fit the definition of what archetypal character? When comparing Hester Prynne and Arthur Dimmesdale's method of penance, which is more effective? How can the reader classify the different types of predators Pip must battle? How do Madame Defarge and Lucy Mannette function as contraries?

---

140 For a more thorough discussion, see *Classical Rhetoric for the Modern Student* (1965) by Edward P.J. Corbett and Robert J. Connors.

Procedure

- The general lesson process, which may take more than one day, involves introducing one *Topic* (definition, for example); then, asking students to generate definition thesis statements based upon the current unit or previous units studied. After student creation and teacher feedback, move on to the second *Topic* (classification, for example).

- First, introduce the first category—typically "Definition arguments"—and, moving inductively, ask students to predict what comprises a definition argument.

- When their predictions are completed, which will probably identify key parts of the official definition, define this Topic or type of thesis formally—up on the screen as part of a powerpoint, for instance. The teacher might use examples from popular culture to serve as illustrations—film actors, athletes, musicians, or video game characters.

- Second, have students begin [alone, in partners, in triads, etc] creating possible ideas or drafts for definition thesis statement ideas based upon a familiar work of literature. Provide them with a sample of this type of thesis from pp. 148-150.

- Repeat the process for the remaining Topics.

- **Continuation option**: If desired, after providing feedback on student thesis statements for one of the Topics, the teacher may require students to create the topic sentences to support their thesis statements.

- The teacher may use a Google Form to collect the class' responses for each of the Topics. See p. 161 for a sample chart of student thesis ideas for *Twelve Angry Men*.

Thesis and Topic Sentence Samples for Each Topic

With each explanation of one of the categories of Aristotle's Topics, at least two examples have been provided. Each example consists of a possible thesis statement as well as the topic sentences for only two of the potential body paragraphs supporting each thesis statement. Clearly, to be conscientiously argued, many of these thesis statements would require additional body paragraphs based on other topic sentences.

Because the strategies for making an expository argument based upon a work of literature apply as well to other courses and fields of study, which also require expository writing by students, some of the following examples using categories of Aristotle's Topics have been applied to thesis statements not drawn from literary works.

Definition

When writers argue by Definition, they assert that the details of the text, or the details of a contemporary or historical situation, provide examples for the definition of a concept (such concepts may, for instance, be justice, fatherhood, decision-making, evil, or friendship). Each concept contains multiple aspects, each aspect, then, serving as the central idea for each body paragraph's topic sentence.

Definition Arguments from a literary work

Thesis: In Nathaniel Hawthorne's *The Scarlet Letter*, Roger Chillingworth mirrors various characteristics of evil.

[The writer will use each topic sentence to define a single quality of evil.]

Topic Sentence: Chillingworth practices deception, the attribute of evil that conceals its identity.

[The writer will show multiple examples of how Chillingworth deceives by concealing his identity.]

Topic Sentence: Chillingworth, like evil, manipulates the most vulnerable human characteristic—the heart.

[The writer will show multiple examples of how Chillingworth manipulates the emotions of others.]

TH: In the poem "Mending Wall," the poet Robert Frost creates a specific situation that reveals the paradoxical nature of barriers in human relationships: what separates human beings physically is what allows us to live together amicably.

[Here, the writer will be defining the paradox of "the wall" in the poem by examining its apparently contradictory aspects.]

TS: The poem's speaker is a "mischief"-maker, one who asserts the notion that the wall is an unnatural obstruction, a viewpoint likely shared at first by the reader.

[Here, the writer will define one aspect of this paradox: walls serve as barriers to human relationship.]

TS: The actions of both characters in the poem, the speaker and his "neighbor," demonstrate that, though the wall is man-made, it is in fact the natural, indeed instinctive, requirement of forming community.

[Here, the writer will define the other aspect of walls' paradoxical nature: they allow human beings to live in a well-ordered, amicable community.]

Definition Arguments not based on a literary work

TH: True friends respond selflessly, considering the needs of other human beings more paramount than their own.

[Here the writer defines friendship as selfless concern for the needs of others.]

TS: Authentic friends sacrifice their own time to help respond to someone else's need.

[Here, the writer elaborates with examples showing how one or more friends have acted selflessly with their time.]

TS: Genuine friends offer the moral guidance needed to navigate successfully the difficulties of life.

[Here, the writer explores one or more specific examples of a friend providing such

guidance.]

Thesis: Effective decision-making requires the ability to think logically, to seek wise counsel, and to recognize the limits of one's knowledge.

TS: Reacting rationally to situations that arise, rather than reacting emotionally, is more likely to result in beneficial decisions.

TS: Consulting others who have experienced similar situations—so long as time allows it—can lead to more advantageous conclusions.

Classification

When making an argument by classification, writers recognize that several examples—or pieces of evidence—within a text have like characteristics and, therefore, these examples belong to a distinct category. Like items in one category, then, are grouped into a body paragraph whose topic sentence identifies the unifying category. Like items in another category are grouped into a separate body paragraph whose topic sentence identifies that unifying category.

Classification Arguments from a literary work

Thesis: The government in the novel 1984 employs several methods for controlling its citizenry.

[The writer will explore and name in the topic sentence each of the "methods."]

Topic Sentence: Totalitarian governments often manipulate public information, both the details of history and the facts of the present.

[The method identified here deals with information control and all the examples from the novel elaborated in this paragraph will demonstrate such manipulation.]

Topic Sentence: Totalitarian governments impose physical restrictions upon its citizens.

[The writer will explore the government's imposition of physical restrictions in this paragraph, elaborating on examples from the text that illustrate this form of control.]

TH: Harry Potter demonstrates that the hero must overcome a variety of personal obstacles regardless of the physical powers of evil.

[In the following topic sentences, the writer will classify the types of personal challenges Potter confronts.]

TS: One of Harry Potter's challenges involves controlling his fear when confronting dangerous situations.

[One type of personal obstacle is classified: controlling fear when in danger.]

TS: Harry's own psychology must contend with memories of a painful past, which frequently prevents him from taking immediate action.

[The writer classifies another type of challenge: painful memories that haunt Potter. While both topic sentences above deal with obstacles of an emotional nature, subsequent paragraphs might classify other kinds of challenges, such as the mental challenge of using logic and reason to defeat evil.]

Classification Arguments not from a literary work

TH: Deception, or the deliberate concealment of the truth, can be justified when it protects the general well being of an individual or of society as a whole.

TS: When difficult situations arise involving one's child, deception shields innocence from the terror and cruelty of the outside world.

TS: During times of war, the government conceals certain details to protect its troops in battle.

TH: Friends fulfill a variety of needs, those which improve the body, the mind, and the soul.

TS: Friends on athletic teams urge their teammates to achieve physically that which others believe cannot be done.

TS: Friends, particularly those more gifted academically, help to teach us intellectual skills.

Comparison: Similarity or Difference or Degree

When making an argument by comparison, writers place two items side by side (characters, images, symbols, situations, setting, etc.). This side-by-side placement may yield any of three possibilities: that the two items are similar, that the two items reveal differences, or that the two items indicate a distinction of degree.

Similarity

This comparison argument that focuses on similarity identifies the common features of two distinct items under discussion; in other words, the writer believes the two items placed next to each other are analogous. When crafting literary arguments, writers often explore this analogy, which serves as a lengthy comparison, involving the resemblances discovered detail by detail between two items normally seen as distinctly different.

Similarity Arguments from a literary work

Thesis: The imagery Coleridge creates in "Kubla Khan" illustrates principles in his philosophy concerning how poetry is written.

Topic Sentence: Coleridge uses archetypal images in "Kubla Khan" to portray the fertility of the imagination, an idea also expounded upon in Coleridge's critical writings.

> *[The writer identifies the initial step in the writing process, the presence of a mind filled with ideas.]*

Topic Sentence: The visual imagery in "Kubla Khan" demonstrates another principle of poetic composition articulated in Coleridge's philosophy: the selection and elaboration of an idea.

> *[The writer focuses on one aspect of the writing process—selecting and elaborating upon an idea.]*

TH: The characterization in Mary Shelley's novel *Frankenstein* mirrors several qualities found in the characters created by John Milton in his epic poem Paradise Lost.

> *[The writer will define in each topic sentence a single quality that both*

Frankenstein and one of Milton's characters share.]

TS: Victor Frankenstein, like Satan, challenges God's omnipotent role as master of creation.

TS: Shelley borrows from Milton's Satan as she molds the character of the monster.

Similarity Arguments not from a literary work

TH: Musicians such as The Rolling Stones illustrate the salient characteristics normally associated with archeologists.

TS: As archeologists excavate the soil in search of revelatory artifacts, The Rolling Stones have spent years unearthing blues and country music composed long before anyone in the group could play an instrument.

TS: The instruments The Rolling Stones use to reveal musical relics have much in common with the tools the archeologist painstakingly employs.

TH: Fruits and vegetables both contain ingredients that help prevent cancer.

TS: Several green vegetables contain important antioxidants.

TS: A diet rich in berries can provide antioxidant protection against cancer.

Difference

The comparison argument that explores differences examines the contrasts between two items within the same class or grouping—between two athletes, two friends, two birthday gifts, two literary heroes, two sonnets.

Difference Arguments from a literary work

Thesis: Biddy and Estella in Dickens' *Great Expectations* influence Pip's maturation in contrasting ways.

Topic Sentence: Biddy models for Pip the virtue of humble selflessness.

Topic Sentence: Estella reinforces the idea that the value of individuals is based upon their social and economic class.

TH: Harry Potter and Hermione Granger reflect distinct sets of wizardry skills.

TS: Hermione possesses the ability to learn from situations in the past.

TS: Potter relies on his internal instincts when responding to danger.

Difference Arguments not from a literary work

TH: While small colleges and major universities provide a core educational foundation, small colleges emphasize excellence in teaching while universities stress the significance of research.

TS: Larger universities have gradually transformed their educational mission to emphasize the research its faculty conducts.

TS: The small college campus encourages its faculty to excel at classroom instruction.

Degree

Sometimes writers examine two items in juxtaposition, not to demonstrate they are completely different but that they differ by degree. One, for example, may be better than the other or worse than the other, one more effective than another, one more beneficial for the greater good than another, etc.

Degree Arguments from a literary work

Thesis: Although both are leaders, Odysseus more accurately exemplifies the ideal Greek hero than Agamemnon, the commander-in-chief of the armies.

> *[The writer will select for each topic sentence one quality of the ideal Greek hero to unify each paragraph.]*

Topic Sentence: The Greek hero must demonstrate prowess not only on the battlefield but also in the arena of language.

> *[The initial part of this paragraph will focus on Odysseus then shift to Agamemnon, whose use of language is less effective.]*

Topic Sentence: The ideal Greek hero ought maintain control over his emotions when in a position of leadership.

[Here, Agamemnon's confrontation with Achilles will be compared to Odysseus' with the suitors.]

TH: Hermione Granger demonstrates more potential as a young wizard than does Ron Weasely during their first year at Hogwarts.

[Each topic sentence will explore a singular trait where Hermione is more successful than Ron.]

TS: Hermione, unlike Ron, understands the importance of studying a variety of spells and potions.

[This paragraph might first explore Hermione's study habits, then contrast them with those of Ron.]

TS: Hermione's ability to think quickly in dangerous situations surpasses Ron's ability to react to threats.

[This paragraph develops the difference in degree further by examining both characters' contrasting responses in the midst of danger.]

Degree Arguments not from a literary work

Thesis: Fiddlers and violinists make music using the same instrument but the music they make reveals differing levels of artistry in the talents they possess.

TS: The type of music performed by violinists requires a longer period of time to master prior to performance than does that performed by fiddlers.

TS: While violinists must often integrate their instrument into the entirety of an orchestra, fiddlers work within a much smaller grouping of musicians.

Relationship: Contraries and Cause-Effect

When writers construct arguments by relationship, they argue the presence of a clear connection or correlation between the items—situations, events, characters, settings, etc.—under consideration. The two types of arguments by relationship emphasized herein are the contrary relationship and the cause-effect relationship.

Contrary Relationship

When writers argue a contrary relationship, they identify polar opposites of items within a category. Just as in the category of temperatures, where hot is the opposite of cold, and in the category of landscapes, where the desert is the opposite of the rain forest, when a writer constructs an argument based on a contrary relationship, he examines two ideas, two characters, two choices, two values that are incompatible, contradictory, or hostile to one another.

Contrary Arguments from a literary work

Thesis: In the play *Twelve Angry Men*, Juror Three and Juror Four spotlight the clash between the ethical and unethical conduct of jurors in the justice system.

[The thesis statement focuses on two opposing types of jurors—the ideal juror, who views matters logically, and the distinctly undesirable juror, whose response is largely an emotional one.]

Topic Sentence: Juror Three recognizes that the ethical approach to jury duty requires the ability to rely on reason rather than emotion when evaluating evidence.

[This paragraph will walk the reader through a series of examples, arranged chronologically, that highlight the use of reason by this juror.]

Topic Sentence: Juror Four responds to the details of the case with emotional responses, frequently demonstrating a series of fallacies in reasoning.

Contrary vs. Contrast

Students often confuse contrary and contrast. Contrast involves differences within a specific category, such as villains—Dick and Perry, the two villains of *In Cold Blood*, differ in their methods of deception. This is a Difference argument (see p. 152). Contrary involves inversions or opposites—Charles Dickens' Biddy as the ideal nurturing feminine and Estella as the femme fatale.

TH: In *A Tale of Two Cities*, Madame Defarge and Lucy Manette epitomize the struggle between the anarchic impulse and the desire for order.

TS: Madame Defarge seeks further destruction within her community.

TS: Lucy heals those within her community who are wounded.

Contrary Arguments not from a literary work

TH: John Locke and Karl Marx are philosophers who represent two contrary political visions regarding the role of government.

TS: Locke and Marx differ regarding the role government plays in the lives of the governed.

TS: Both philosophers hold distinctly incompatible views on the nature of the individual and private property.

Cause-Effect Relationship

The scientific world makes a clear distinction between correlation and causation, but when studying creative works, such absolute certainty is not possible and instead, the student often asserts enough evidence to indicate a pattern to reasonably suggest a non-scientific causation.

When writers construct arguments by cause-effect relationship, they argue the presence of a clear correlation between two or more events under consideration, a connection so essential as to suggest that one event would have been unlikely to occur without the prior or simultaneous existence of the other event.

To fashion an appropriate argument based upon a cause-effect relationship, the skillful writer observes patterns emerging in the literature being read, the history being studied, the issues of the day being debated. The reader of any literary work, for example, discerns the repetition of similar or contrasting situations that establish such a pattern. Perhaps a certain type of outcome is preceded by a pattern of similar events on more than one occasion. Perhaps every time a character acts in X manner or makes X choices, Y results.

Writers then reflect upon these multiple examples in a specific work—examples of effects or causes—and, after due consideration, associate a specific idea with the pattern of examples. Conceivably, all the examples connected to a specific cause can, for instance, be associated with the desire for power; and the examples connected to effect might be associated with the idea of chaos. Once writers have completed identifying the nature of the cause and the effect, they are ready to write a thesis statement that might read like this: The untrammeled desire for power ultimately leads to chaos within the community.

One error that young writers sometimes make is to isolate one example of a cause-effect relationship in the text and use that single incident for their thesis. For example, in Homer's *Iliad,* Agamemnon refuses to return Chryses' daughter, a refusal that leads the god Apollo to inflict a plague upon the Greek armies.

Here, we clearly see causality, but this example reflects one of several similar instances in the epic where a similar type of causality takes place. So a thesis that states, "If a leader refuses to return the daughter of Apollo's priest, Apollo will destroy his army," merely calls attention to one example of a cause-effect relationship without articulating exactly what the universal cause-effect relationship is. In other words, the thesis is merely built out of L1 instead of L2.

The writer needs to locate other similar examples in the poem that follow this same pattern. For instance, later on in this opening book of Homer's epic, Agamemnon refuses to allow Achilles to keep his prize, Briseis, which causes Achilles to withdraw from war, leaving the Greeks vulnerable to the Trojans.

At this point, as the writer begins to locate additional examples, he will need to assert an associative category [**unrestrained emotion**] for both the causes of several similar examples and the effects [**chaos**]. He will then be prepared to craft a thesis statement anchored in L2. In this case, a writer examining the leadership of Agamemnon in the Iliad might formulate this thesis: *A leader whose decisions are anchored in* **self-centered** *emotion* **imperils the existence** *of the community he leads.*

For the purposes of the English coach's playbook, cause-effect arguments can be constructed by the writer in two primary ways.

1. A cause producing one or more effects.

The writer can first begin with the cause, formulating a thesis that contends Event A is (was or will be) the cause of Event B. Of course, in many cases, more than one effect can be attributed to a single cause.

A student may be constructing a paper that examines an historical event such as the Great Depression. His research on the subject may lead him to argue that the Great Depression caused the rise of dictatorship in Europe: countries focused resources and attention on providing for the basic needs of its citizens (food and employment), and scant attention being paid to military defense in democratic countries made national borders increasingly vulnerable to attack by enemy nations.

A student may decide to write a paper after reading a literary work such as Leo Tolstoy's *Anna Karenina*. Her study of the novel leads her to argue that uncontrolled passions inevitably lead to tragedy. She explicates her thesis by examining the title character's descent once she becomes thoroughly enamored of Count Vronsky.

A third example of a cause producing an effect, or effects, can be observed when a student constructs an essay in support of a specific position concerning a topical issue of the day. Let us say, for example, that Congress is considering legislation that would grant amnesty to any immigrants who have arrived in this country illegally. Passage of that legislation, according to this writer's thesis, would be the cause producing a variety of negative effects, each effect being elaborated in the essay's body paragraph. As with any contemporary issue, another writer's thesis might contend that passage of such legislation would be the cause leading to a number of positive effects.

2. An effect resulting from one or more causes

A second method of constructing the cause-effect argument is for the writer to begin with the effect, and argue back from the effect to its cause. Using this approach, the writer develops a thesis proposing that Event D happens because of the prior existence of Event C. Of course, more than one cause (which might be labeled Event C2 and Event C3) can be ascribed to a single effect.

If a writer, for example, is working on an essay that examines what precipitated the French Revolution in 1789 [Event D], her research may lead her to argue a number of causes. Such causal factors [Events C1, C2, and C3] might involve the following: the philosophical ideas concerning political freedom and equality that had saturated much of the populace; the high taxation to support an aristocracy that was no longer respected by the citizenry being taxed; and the French troops' prior involvement in supporting the American colonists in their revolution against the British, such involvement a decade earlier serving as a model for revolution.

Were a writer to analyze a work of literature such as Shakespeare's *King Lear*, he might argue that King Lear's tragic fall was caused by his disproportionate pride, manifest in his two ambitious daughters and their husbands and his faithlessness to friends.

In the following examples, some thesis statements will focus on exploring the causes of a particular effect and other thesis statements will focus on exploring the effects generated by a cause.

As in previous examples of thesis statements followed by topic sentences, that there are two topic sentences listed does not preclude other topic sentences. The fact is every thesis statement in this section is likely to necessitate more than two body paragraphs to prove and, therefore, more than two topic sentences. These examples merely serve as a guide for how such thesis statements and their topic sentences might be constructed.

Cause-Effect Arguments from a literary work

Thesis: Thomas Hardy argues in his poem "Convergence of the Twain" that human pride resulted in the destruction of the Titanic, a ship emblematic of man's arrogance.

> *[Cause produces effect: This paper argues that Hardy's poem demonstrates a singular cause producing a decisive effect.]*

Topic Sentence: The initial section of the poem explores images of wealth and beauty now decayed, the effect of human pride.

Topic Sentence: The second half of the poem introduces the primary symbol of human pride, the Titanic, inevitably destined for tragedy.

TH: Shakespeare's *Macbeth* serves as a study in the effects of unbridled political ambition.

[Cause produces effects: The writer of this essay posits a singular cause for a number of effects observed in Shakespeare's play.]

TS: When *Macbeth's* closest confidant, his wife, nurtures his ambition, the restraints that shield his moral compass gradually loosen.

TS: Once he becomes king, Macbeth abdicates all moral principles as he seeks to maintain his ill-gotten power.

TH: King Lear's tragic fall is precipitated by an unrestrained vanity that adversely affects his judgment.

[Effect resulting from a cause: The writer of this paper indicates that each topic sentence will elaborate evidence of such vanity clouding his ability to make wise decisions.]

TS: Lear's insistence that each of his daughters must declare how much she loves him makes him unable to distinguish genuine familial love from the feigned.

TS: Because his arrogance brooks no dissent, Lear banishes his most perceptive adviser.

Cause-Effect Arguments not from a literary work

TH: Aspects of our culture have led to an increase in overweight Americans.

[Single effect resulting from causes: Here the writer focuses on the single effect of obesity and will explore in each paragraph one of a number of causes.]

TS: The proliferation of fast food has enticed people with its speed of preparation but not with its nutritional value.

TS: Limited time given to physical activity, starting at a young age, has produced a generation of sedentary Americans.

TH: Americans who smoke face a variety of medical and social problems.

[Cause produces effects: Here the writer introduces a single cause—smoking—and proceeds to explore a variety of effects, one effect per paragraph.]

TS: Americans who smoke increase their risk for stroke and heart attack.

TS: Smoking decreases the immune system's ability to combat illness.

Using the Topics to Develop Thesis Ideas for *Twelve Angry Men* (Sample Google Form Responses)

Definition	Classification	Comparison - similarity	Comparison- difference	Comparison- degree	Contrary Relationships	Causal Relationships
Juror 8 is an ideal juror	Jurors fall into types, driven by personal bias, focused on ethical responsibility, malleable to reason	Juror 5 & Juror 6 allow themselves to be open to persuasion	Juror 9 and Juror 1 contrast in their ability to accept how reason brings about clarity	Juror 3's bias driven by more intimate conflict proves more lethal than Juror 10's generalized bias	Juror 9 and Juror 3 reflect the tension between emotion and reason	Insistence on reason's power to break down emotion produces genuine justice
Jury process requires reflection, reassessment			Juror 10 and Juror 3 use contrasting emotional appeals and fallacies	Juror 9 demonstrates more shrewdly his ability to employ attention to detail than Juror 4	At conflict initiated at the play's open is a battle between the ideal and unideal roles of a juror	Juror 9 demonstrates that the consistent application of appeals ot logic bring about justice
Unideal juror examines through emotion rather than reason						

The chart above assembles the responses from the class Google Form, in which the teacher asks students to use the Topics to develop ideas for thesis statements about the Jurors in *Twelve Angry Men*.

Practicing Four Syntactical Patterns

Core Plays Involved

L1, L2, L3 Plays   **L2-L1-L2 Play**   **TOPIC STRING Play**

Learning Objectives

- Students will develop and control their interpretive voice as they increase the quantity and quality of associations (L2), placing L2 both before the quoted evidence (in the topic string) and after it (to the right).

- Students will understand how the assertiveness of their written voice correlates with the quantity, quality, and the placement of their own interpretive words.

WHY IT WORKS

Placing L2 in different parts of the sentence and recognizing how location and omission affects the presence of an interpretive voice triggers the **metacognitive** parts of the brain. These exercises force students to be aware of their use of the L1, L2, topic string plays. This conscious awareness reinforces their understanding of the plays and moves them into longer term memory so that these movements become internalized.[141]

---

[141] Marzano, Pickering, & Pollock, 2001; Marshall & Bredy, 2016.

Procedure

- First, the teacher selects a brief passage from the text the class is reading, up to one page in length. This passage may be, for instance, the description of a character or setting, or a pivotal moment of action within a chapter.

- The class reads this passage together.

- Afterwards, students, working individually or with a partner, have a few minutes to select a quotation (L1) from the passage that they will use during the writing practice to follow. Students write this quotation out on a white board or sheet of paper.

- Below this quotation, students then have ten to fifteen minutes to write out four sentences.

- Each of these sentences will incorporate all or part of the quotation. The differences between the four sentences lie in where the student places his or her associations (L2). Each sentence will follow one of the patterns on the next page.

- Students may work in any order they find helpful, from the sentence with the strongest pattern to the weakest, or from the weakest to the strongest.

- The teacher provides feedback regarding the correct placement of L2 and L1.

The Four Patterns for Literary Analysis

1. **Strongest voice: L2 – L1 – L2 [L2 before and after]**

2. **Strong voice: L2 – L1   [L2 before]**

3. **Weaker voice: L1 – L2 [L2 after]**

4. **Weakest: L1 only [No L2 appears in the sentence]**

Below are examples of sentences that follow each of these patterns, using quoted L1 from *The Great Gatsby*.

Bold = [L2] associations / [L1] evidence

1. **Strongest**: Even the **faint hope of success** remains **elusive**, for "the dust-covered wreck of a Ford" **cowers from sight**, merely "crouched in a dim corner," emphasizing the **ruined and spoiled ambitions** of Wilson.

2. **Strong voice**: **Bleakly unsuccessful**, "the dust-covered wreck of a Ford," **remains barren**, for it is merely "crouched in a dim corner."

3. **Weaker voice**: Inside Wilson's auto shop sits "the dust-covered wreck of a Ford," where it is "crouched in a dim corner," showing Wilson's **failure**.

4. **Weakest voice**: Inside Wilson's auto shop is his "dust-covered wreck of a Ford" and all it does is stay "crouched in a dim corner."

To help students visualize the four patterns, we display these examples on the board each time we do this activity.

Sample Student Sentences on Countee Cullen's poem "Simon the Cyrenian Speaks"

Strongest: L2-L1-L2	Strong: L2-L1	Weak: L1-L2	Weakest: L1-L1
Blatantly denying Christ, Simon cries out, "I will not bear his cross upon my back," revealing his resistance or unease towards Christ's calling.	Blatantly denying Christ, Simon cries out, "I will not bear his cross upon my back".	Simon says, "I will not bear his cross upon my back," revealing his resistance towards Christ's calling.	Simon says, "I will not bear his cross upon my back," and he's mad "because my skin is black."
Simon, intrigued by Christ's offering of himself, recognizes Christ is "dying for a dream," his suffering embodying the virtue of sacrificial love.	Simon, intrigued by Christ's sacrifice, sees he was "dying for a dream."	Christ is "dying for a dream" and Simon is intrigued by Christ's sacrifice.	Simon observes that Christ is "dying for a dream."
Simon perceives Christ's servile and gentle nature, as "he was meek," personifying Christ's humility.	Simon perceives Christ's servile and gentle nature as "he was meek."	Simon perceives Christ as "meek," personifying his humility.	Simon perceives Christ as "meek."

Get Creative with Organizing Evidence

Core Plays Involved

Learning Objectives

- Students will apply the Organization Play when creating multiple paragraphs from evidence and when arranging the evidence (L1) within a single paragraph.

- Student will arrive at their organization choices inductively by first examining the textual evidence (L1), then observing how the evidence can be grouped by time, place, idea, or a combination of the three methods.

Procedure

- The teacher reviews the "Organization Play" (see p. 96).

- The teacher selects a number of quotations from a section of the novel (~10 short quotations) to create a list of evidence (L1).

- The teacher requires students to select a specific number of quotations from the list.

- In pairs or triads, students must decide two possible ways to organize the evidence into **multiple paragraphs**. Students have ___ minutes to write their two organizational methods on the board.

- As an alternative, the teacher may assign a specific method—time, place, or idea–that students must employ to organize the provided list.

- **Continuation option**: After having grouped the pieces of evidence into multiple paragraphs, the students can then select **one** of these paragraphs and decide how they wish to organize the pieces of evidence inside it, using the same strategies of time, place, or idea.

WHY IT WORKS

The brain loves to predict, to examine details and draw conclusions, the basic **inductive** process of arriving at some claim, some decision. And as the brain sifts through data, its impulse is to see **patterns,** to locate how evidence might be grouped together in similarity. What equally helps the brain, particularly with this activity, is that students can be taught general patterns to use when organizing L1. Knowing the strategy to assemble by time, place, or idea [and any combination of the three] makes the brain work even more efficiently. The more we **repetitively** practice organization exercises, the more rapidly the skill becomes part of a stronger long-term memory circuit, reminding us of the wonder of **neuroplasticity.**[142]

---

142   McTighe & Willis, 2019.

Sample - *The Adventures of Huckleberry Finn,* Chapter 5

- How would you organize?
    - Time by chronology?
    - Place by scene-space?
    - Idea by [L2]?
    - Time <u>and</u> Place
    - Time <u>and</u> Idea
    - Place <u>and</u> Idea
    - Time, Place <u>and</u> Idea (all three methods at once)
- As a group, come up with **two different ways** to organize at least 8 pieces of evidence from the list below into **multiple paragraphs** about Pap, Huck's father. Write your two combinations (on the whiteboard, sheet of paper, Google Doc).

Evidence to Organize

1. "the new judge said he was going to make a man of him"
2. "took him to his own house"
3. "dressed him up clean and nice"
4. "had him to breakfast and dinner and supper with the family"
5. "he talked to him [Pap] about temperance"
6. "the old man cried"
7. "now he was agoing to turn over a new leaf"
8. "so he [the judge] cried and his wife she cried again"
9. "There's a hand that was the hand of a hog; but it ain't so no more"
10. "the judge said it was the holiest time on record"
11. "they tucked the old man into a beautiful room"
12. "in the night sometime he got powerful thirsty"
13. "traded his new coat for a jug of forty-rod"
14. "And when they come to look at that spare room, they had to take soundings before they could navigate it."
15. "The judge he felt kind of sore. He reckoned a body could reform the ole man with a shot-gun, maybe, but he didn't know no other way."

Using the Organization Play to create multiple body paragraphs with Huck Finn, Chapter 5

*One possible combination: Paragraphs organized by **Time**.*

- Paragraph 1 = Quotes 2-4. Topic Sentence: First, Pap demonstrates the potential for change.

- Paragraph 2 = Quotes 6-7, 9. TS: Then, the community's response increases the possibility of transformation.

- Paragraph 3 = Quotes 12-13. TS: Lastly, change remains a consistent human struggle, requiring control of emotion.

*Organized by **Idea** (in this case, character.)*

- Paragraph 1 = Quotes 5-7, 9, 12-13. TS: Pap practices manipulation and deception.

- Paragraph 2 = Quotes 1, 2, 5, 10, 15. TS: The judge reflects a tension between the purity of hope and the reality of naivety.

*Organized by **Time and Idea***

- Paragraph 1 = Quotes 2-5, 9-10. TS: First, Pap demonstrates the virtue of humility and self-awareness.

- Paragraph 2 = Quotes 12-15. TS: However, Pap's emotion later defeats reason.

Using the Organization Play to organize a single body paragraph

- Paragraph = Quotes 1, 2, 5, 10, 15. TS: The judge's hopefulness shifts into a stark awareness of evil's grip on man.

- Organize chunks by *Idea-Time*

    - Chunk 1 = Judge virtuously offers… Quotes 1, 2.
    - Chunk 2 = Believing in the power to change… Quotes 5, 10.
    - Chunk 3 = The result, however, exposes evil's grip…Quote 15.

Sentence Imitation

Many students enter our classrooms with a limited knowledge of the sentence. Consequently, they rely on the few syntactic possibilities they are familiar with, even if they are grammatically incorrect. One student's writing may be rife with sentence fragments. Another's sentences may begin with the same subordinating conjunction "when." Another may write sentences with content incorrectly placed in independent clauses. These are the patterns that have "stuck."

Sentence imitation develops "an awareness of the variety of sentence structure of which the English language is capable."[143] As K. Anders Ericsson might put it, this exercise expands students' "mental representations" of what a sentence can be.[144]

Additionally, the visual effect of breaking the sentence into different parts develops students' ability to see the sentence's various elements.

Core Plays Involved

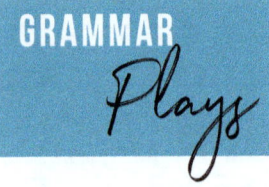

- absolute phrase [the "AP"]
- present participle phrase [the "PrPP"]
- past participle phrase [the "PaPP"]
- gerund phrase [the "GP"]
- infinitive phrase [the "IP"]

---

143 Corbett, 1971.
144 Ericsson & Pool, 2016.

- adverb subordinate clause [the "AdvSC"]
- noun subordinate clause [the "NSC"]
- adjective subordinate clause [the "AdjSC"]

Learning Objectives

- Students will master sentence syntax as they deepen their knowledge of parts of speech, sentence components, and sentence types.
- Students will internalize sentence patterns that they would not necessarily produce on their own.

WHY IT WORKS

Weekly sentence imitation relies on the power of both **retrieval** and **repetition.** With each sentence imitation activity, the teacher repeats a similar montage of questions about the sentence—sentence type, phrases, clauses, subject-verb, parallel structure. The goal is not to achieve 100% retrieval of grammatical knowledge. However, because of the regularity of the activity, more students will proceed to respond accurately each week.

During this questioning period, students are asked to recall details about a learning task from memory, without the aid of notes or discussion. Routine retrieval activities like this help the brain activate the neural networks where learned information is stored in memory. The more the brain retrieves this information, the more it then uses this information to perform a cognitive task (like writing a sentence with particular structures), the stronger and more efficient the brain becomes at doing so, a key feature of neuroplasticity.[145]

---

[145] McTighe & Willis 2019.

Procedure

The teacher selects a model sentence for the class to imitate.

- The model can be chosen from the current literary work, or one created by the teacher.

- If quoted from the literary work currently being studied, the sentence could open the class's discussion of the text.

- The model might contain a new sentence structure for students to discover and practice.

- It could be a new combination of familiar structures, a new pattern for students' brains to move through.

- In selecting a sentence, the teacher should consider the class' pre-existing skills and choose a pattern that will stretch students' understanding of syntax.

- To help students visualize the sentence's different components, the teacher may present it as a series of bullet points, as with this sentence from *The Great Gatsby*:

  - In my younger and more vulnerable years,
  - my father
  - gave me
  - some advice
  - that I've been turning over in my mind ever since.

The teacher initiates discussion of the sentence

- Before imitating the sentence, the teacher asks students a variety of questions about the sentence's structure. The goal is for the teacher to discover how much students know about the sentence by observing its components.

  - "How many clauses are in the sentence?"
  - "What is the subject and verb?"
  - "Can you find the participle phrase?"
  - "What's the sentence type?"

- Whether through discussion between the class and the teacher, or several quick rounds of student-generated responses (at the whiteboard, online, on scratch paper), the teacher uses this part of the activity to reinforce student knowledge of grammar and syntax through quick repetition and feedback.

Students begin to write.

- Students imitate the model sentence by replicating its structure using different words. For example, given the sentence

    His voice courtly,
    his face calm,
    his body singing of ease,
    I will trust him completely.
    [Charles Bowden, "The Teachings of Don Fernando"]

    A student may write:

    The atmosphere tense,
    the fans expectant,
    every player longing for victory,
    they will play the game ferociously.

- Students may create their imitations in their writing journals, on the whiteboard, or online in a Google Form. It may be helpful, particularly when practicing new sentence structures, to talk about different imitation possibilities so that students do not simply *copy* elements of the model. "Okay, besides the word "because," what are some other subordinating conjunctions that you could use? Since…although…when…"

> **Variation: Incorporate physical movement when recognizing sentence types**
>
> Place cards/posters around the room, each card one of the four sentence types. After reading the model sentence, students must get up and stand near one of these signs. The teacher may then question students about their choices: "So, you think this sentence is complex? How many clauses are in a complex sentence? Where is the dependent clause?"

- Finally, the teacher provides feedback on student sentences, highlighting quality examples and pointing out mistakes.

- As students practice imitation, the precision of feedback is important. Many novice imitators will mimic the larger parts of the sentence (independent clause, adjective clause, participle phrase) but pay less attention to smaller elements within these structures. The more intense the feedback –"Nice adjective clause. But do you see that yours does not contain a direct object?" – the more students are pushed to pay greater attention to a sentence's parts.

Sentence Combination

Core Plays Involved

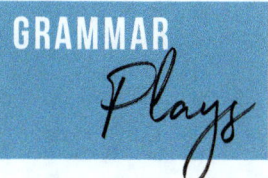

- absolute phrase [the "AP"]
- present participle phrase [the "PrPP"]
- past participle phrase [the "PaPP"]
- gerund phrase [the "GP"]
- infinitive phrase [the "IP"]
- adverb subordinate clause [the "AdvSC"]
- noun subordinate clause [the "NSC"]
- adjective subordinate clause [the "AdjSC"]

Learning Objectives

- Students will understand the many possible sentence patterns.
- Students will successfully create and correctly punctuate individual grammar structures within sentences.
- Students will demonstrate awareness of syntactical choices by moving from simplistic patterns towards more sophisticated combinations.

WHY IT WORKS

Sentence combining helps students see clearly how knowledge of grammar is useful—that it is **relevant.** The exercises show students how to use their knowledge of an absolute phrase, for instance, in their own writing, to make their sentences more efficient and to respond appropriately to teacher **feedback**—"To add more L2 to the right of your L1, use an absolute phrase." When students quickly see the applications for understanding grammar, the teacher opens a doorway to purpose and "the chances of its being learned, remembered, and internalized increases."[146] Sentence combining also has a **metacognitive** function; it helps students begin to think more consciously about what to do with their sentences, where combining might need to occur, how combining can eliminate wordiness, and correct problems with coordination and subordination.

Procedure

- To make the combination, students will turn one of the sentences into the specified grammar structure, and join it with the other sentence.

- The teacher should at times specify further requirements for the combination: "place the adverb clause after the independent clause," "place the present participial phrase before the noun it modifies," and so on.

- The combination exercise may be completed at the board, on a miniature board or desk (w/ dry erase marker), digitally using a Google Form.

---

146   O'Keefe & Linnenbrink-Garcia, 2014.

Sample Combination Exercises[147]

Sentence Combining with Present Participial Phrases

Directions:

- Combine the following sentences by turning one of them into a present participial phrase.
- Make two combinations per pair, *one before* the noun it modifies and *one after* it.
- Underline, italicize, or otherwise highlight each present participial phrase.
- Use commas where necessary.

e.g. Miami's citizens have already experienced two hurricanes this year.

They are very well prepared for any future catastrophe.

The writer has FOUR OPTIONS for combining these two sentences. Note comma locations.

Miami's citizens, *having already experienced two hurricanes this year*, are very well prepared for any future catastrophe.

Having already experienced two hurricanes this year, Miami's citizens are very well prepared for any future catastrophe.

Miami's citizens, *being very well prepared for any future catastrophe*, have already experienced two hurricanes this year.

Being very well prepared for any future catastrophe, Miami's citizens have already experienced two hurricanes this year.

1. Sergeant Simpson reprimands the private very severely. He forcefully removes one of his stripes.
2. Tamika traveled to the airport in a yellow van. She arrived twenty minutes early.
3. The coach has called two straight running plays with no success. He then decides to signal for a long pass.
4. The philosopher spoke to the English II classes at Garland High. She urged the students to study metaphysics before they graduate.

---

147 See chapter five of *Crafting Expository Argument*, 5th ed. (Degen, 2012) for the complete set of combination exercises that we use.

5. My cat refused to eat any food in his tray. He seemed to be on a hunger strike until we allowed him to lick off the dinner plates.

6. Hiroshima, Japan, had been destroyed by an atomic bomb in 1945. It was rebuilt over a period of fifteen years.

7. The robin eats at the bird feeder each morning. The bird is occasionally joined by a pair of sparrows.

8. The oak was struck by lightning. It split in half and fell to the ground.

9. The Secretary of State flies into Kashmir this weekend. She attempts to work out a peaceful settlement in the region.

10. Michael Stipe promotes the sale of his autobiography. Each weekend he visits bookstores and signs autographs.

Sentence Combining with Past Participial Phrases

Directions:

- Combine the following sentences by turning one of them into a past participial phrase.
- Make two combinations per pair, one before the noun it modifies and one after it.
- Underline, italicize, or otherwise highlight each past participial phrase.
- Use commas where necessary.

e.g. The coach of the basketball team was concerned about Randolph's inability to make free throws. He decided to bench him for the second half.

In this example, the writer has two options for combining these sentences.

The coach of the basketball team, *concerned about Randolph's inability to make free throws*, decided to bench him for the second half.

Concerned about Randolph's inability to make free throws, the coach of the basketball team decided to bench him for the second half.

Hint: When looking at a pair of sentences, YOU MUST FIRST FIND A VERB PHRASE CONTAINING A PAST PARTICIPLE. The verb phrase with a past participle is the one that contains a helping verb. TO FORM THE PAST PARTICIPIAL PHRASE, JETTISON THE HELPING VERB AND RETAIN THE PAST PARTICIPLE. In the above case, of the two sentences involving the coach and Randolph, only the first sentence has a past participle in the verb—*was concerned*, with *was* being the helping verb and *concerned* the past participle form of the verb. IF BOTH SENTENCES IN THE

PAIR HAVE PAST PARTICIPLES, THEN YOU WILL LIKELY HAVE FOUR OPTIONS FOR COMBINING the sentences because you may select either past participle to begin the past participial phrase.

1. Columbus was exhausted by a series of storms on his fourth voyage. He stayed in his cabin for the duration of the journey.
2. Magellan was enraged by the actions of two mutinous captains on his journey. He executed them posthaste.
3. The caterpillar is denied an opportunity to live. It is swatted onto the floor a few feet in front of me.
4. The free safety for the football team was injured in the play. He writhes helplessly on the ground.
5. Shannon's softball team was defeated in the state championship game. It was awarded the Hollander Trophy for Highest Team Batting Average.
6. Primal Scream's "Exterminator" was played online four times in one hour on 3WK Underground Radio. It drove my little sister out of my bedroom.
7. He was surprised at the violence contained in the news report. He quickly turned the channel to MTV.
8. Odysseus was instructed by Athena to disguise himself in his own house. He dined with the suitors and restrained his outrage at their supercilious behavior.
9. Her finished poems had been placed in a secret drawer by Emily. They were found twenty years after she died.
10. Grendel was easily defeated by Beowulf. The monster fought and yelled but fled to the swamps to bleed to death.

Sentence Combining with Absolute Phrases

Directions: Combine the following sentences by creating an absolute phrase out of one sentence in the pair and joining that phrase to the other. Underline, italicize, or otherwise highlight the absolute phrase.

- Removing the "be" verb from the sentence creates an absolute phrase.

Original

Julia listened in stunned silence. Her smile was vanishing from her face.

Revision

Julia listened in stunned silence, *her smile vanishing from her face.*

Original
The furnace was broken. We huddled under blankets and waited for dawn.

Revision
The furnace broken, we huddled under blankets and waited for dawn.

- Turning an active voice verb into a participle creates an absolute phrase.

Original
She looks up and smiles at her uncle. Long strands of silky hair fall limply on her face.

Revision
She looks up, *long strands of silky hair falling limply on her face*, and smiles at her uncle.

1. She cheerfully punches the keys T-H-E E-N-D and looks up with a proud crescent stretching across her lips. Her eyes gleam brightly as she reads over the masterpiece.
2. My mother keeps bellowing names, and soon her friends and relatives converge on the house. Her voice draws life from the dream's dark corners. [from Bernard Cooper's Maps to Anywhere]
3. John waited in the classroom. His fingers tapped on the desk nervously.
4. The community was restored. Prospero decides to throw away his magic staff and leave his recent past behind him.
5. The bank robbers fled the scene within minutes. The security guard saw part of the license plate numbers.
6. Mrs. Jones stared at the class. She had two research papers in her hand. She gritted her teeth.
7. John knelt on the fifty-yard line. He looked up at the tied score. He realized the team only had ten seconds.
8. Her heart races as she rushes away from the foreboding footsteps. The freezing wind chills her to the bone.
9. Mark's bedroom was a disaster. He had dirty underwear draped on the waste paper basket. He had soiled socks under the bed.
10. Three rugby players walked into the locker room together. One was soaked in sweat.

Grammar Dice

Core Plays Involved

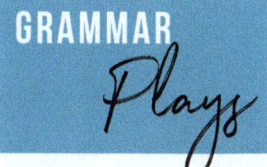

- absolute phrase [the "AP"]
- present participle phrase [the "PrPP"]
- past participle phrase [the "PaPP"]
- gerund phrase [the "GP"]
- infinitive phrase [the "IP"]
- adverb subordinate clause [the "AdvSC"]
- noun subordinate clause [the "NSC"]
- adjective subordinate clause [the "AdjSC"]

Learning Objectives

- Students will produce in their writing a variety of sentence patterns with speed and accuracy.
- Students will notably increase their personal knowledge and awareness of syntax.
- Students will imitate the patterns of established writers in the context of this competitive game.

WHY IT WORKS

Grammar Dice sets up an environment much like the athletic **scrimmage,** wherein student-writers execute a variety of plays within a competitive environment. This provides a fun opportunity to test the degree to which the plays have been internalized.

Like the athletic field, grammar dice can impose demands on their players' minds that mirror the demands of high stakes timed writing (the game), forcing the students (players) to adapt in ways that will improve their performance. During the game, the most successful players must retrieve knowledge quickly, a process which serves to further help the brain activate the neural networks where a learning task is stored. The more the brain **retrieves** the remembered grammar "plays," the stronger and more efficient it becomes at executing them, a key feature of **neuroplasticity.**[148]

Procedure

- This game is fast-paced, and involves all students writing sentences, whether on their device (laptop, iPad), on paper, or on a miniature whiteboard.

- Each round, the teacher rolls a die or dice, depending upon how many grammatical categories are included. For example, a teacher may focus only on six grammar plays: 1-PrPP; 2-PaPP; 3-AdvSC; 4-NSC; 5-AdjSC; 6-AP. If additional categories are needed, an additional die is used.

- After each roll, students race to complete a sentence containing the required structure. The first __(teacher chooses the number) students with correct sentences (all accurately punctuated) earn a point.

- When using a Google Form for this game, the teacher may open

---

[148] McTighe & Willis, 2019.

the "Responses" spreadsheet on the large screen to see sentences as students complete them. The teacher may also keep score by typing a "W" (for "win") next to the sentences that are correct.

- The teacher may declare a winner at the end of the period, or keep track of students' points over the course of the semester. After several rounds, seed students based on their point totals, and play a bracket tournament!

The requirements for each roll depend on the dice categories determined by the teacher. They can be easy:

1 = action verb
2 = prepositional phrase
3 = compound sentence
4 = proper noun
5 = adverb
6 = adjective

More difficult:

1 = past participial phrase
2 = adverb subordinate clause
3 = adjective subordinate clause
4 = gerund phrase
5 = infinitive phrase
6 = absolute phrase

Or devilishly challenging!

1 = parallel phrases inside correlative conjunctions

You may do your homework **either** *at the kitchen table* **or** *at your desk.*

2 = parallel clauses inside correlative conjunctions

Either *Victor Frankenstein will create a bride for his creature,* **or** *the creature will seek to make his life a misery.*

3 = parallel phrases or clauses with coordinating conjunctions

Running track **and** *playing baseball* **and** *competing in debate* makes for a very busy semester.

Winston tries to rebel against the Party, **but** *the torture of O'Brien ultimately breaks his spirit,* **and** *in the end Winston claims to love Big Brother.*

4 = parallel phrases/clauses flanking the independent clause

Her heart broken by suffering, **Miss Havisham teaches Estella to break other's hearts,** *the young girl practicing the old woman's cruelty on the innocent Pip.* (parallel absolute phrases)

When it is 9:00 a.m., **the students in the classroom will look to the teacher** *as the school bell starts ringing.*

6 = parallel gerund phrases

Odysseus employs many devious tricks: *constructing the Trojan Horse,* *blinding the Cyclops,* and *infiltrating into his own palace unbeknownst to the suitors.*

7 = parallel present participial phrases

Escaping from Pap's cabin and *faking his own death,* Huck acts with resourceful cleverness.

8 = parallel past participial phrases

Tormented by his own guilt, manipulated further by Roger Chillingworth, Dimmesdale exemplifies the suffering of all sinners.

9 = parallel adjective subordinate clauses

John Grady Cole, *who loves the life of the cowboy* and *who cannot accept his mother's decision to sell the ranch,* boldly runs away to Mexico.

10 = compound sentence with a semicolon and conjunctive adverb

Don John attempts to destroy Claudio and Hero's love; **however,** *the two overcome his machinations with the help of the community.*

11 = parallel adverb subordinate clauses

Odysseus is the greatest hero **not only** *because he survives so many encounters with incredible monsters* **but also** *because he learns to master his own emotions.*

12 = parallel absolute phrases

> Macbeth cannot believe what he has done, *his hands shaking, the blood on them filling his mind with horror.*

Variations

- **Add vocabulary to Grammar Dice:** Each round, select a vocabulary word from the class list and talk about how the word is typically used. Students' sentences must not only contain the correct sentence structure, but correctly use the word. For example, round one may roll the die for a sentence with an absolute phrase + the vocab word "gregarious." And a student may then submit the following sentence: "Mark's **gregarious** nature made him many friends, *the boy always wanting to bond with others in conversation.*"

- **Use Grammar Dice to continue your discussion of a literary text:**

  - This variation incorporates the Reading and Writing plays into the game.

  - To play it, the teacher must first select a few small passages from the book the class is reading, such as is listed on pp. 121-122. In each round of Grammar Dice, the class will write a sentence about one of these passages.

  - In this variation, students' sentences must not only contain a particular sentence structure, but also execute a specific Reading or Writing Play. For example, the teacher may require that students use the **L2-L1-L2 Play** (see Chapter 3, p. 82). In this instance, students must quote or paraphrase L1 from a given passage and place their L2 around it. Alternatively, the teacher may ask students to practice the **Topic String Play** (see p. 100). In this instance, students must place L2 at the beginning of the sentences they produce.

  - At the beginning of each round, the teacher selects one of these passages and the class reads it together.

  - Then, before the teacher rolls the die, students—working on their own, with a partner, or in a group—have a specified amount of time (five minutes, for example) to discuss the passage and begin writing.

- The teacher provides this additional time to account for the complexity of the task: it allows students to select L1 and make L2 before they have to begin thinking about creating a particular sentence structure.

- When time's up, the teacher rolls the die, and students add the required sentence structure to their sentence before they submit it. For example, before the die is rolled, a student might write the following sentence:

    > "Telemachus' mentor directs him to think of his own **responsibility** when she asks him, 'And what part do you play yourself?'

- If the roll indicates "Adjective subordinate clause," the student then has to modify his sentence to contain this structure:

    > "Telemachus' mentor, *who knows the young hero must rise to* **accept responsibility** *for his own fate*, asks him, 'And what part do you play yourself?'

- This variation enables the teacher to continue discussion of the story—to see how students are understanding a particular passage or scene—even when reviewing important sentence patterns. This form of the game will be less fast-paced than one that focuses solely on imitating a particular sentence structure.

See examples of student work.

Sample—Grammar Dice with *The Scarlet Letter*

The spreadsheet below displays sentences produced during a round of Grammar Dice in which students wrote about *The Scarlet Letter*. The "W" column indicates those students who earned "a win" (a point) for their sentence. In this round of the game, students were required to use the **L2-L1-L2 Play** to create sentences that place their associations before and after a piece of evidence. One student did not earn a win because his sentence did not incorporate textual evidence, while another student did not get a win because his sentence included no commentary to the right of the quotation.

Last Name	W	Sentence
Chostner	W	A **theological testament to the lack of redemption** present in Puritan communities, "she [was] a living sermon against sin, until the ignominious letter be engraved upon her tombstone," the **permanent** mark suggesting that God's **forgiveness** is **overshadowed** by **death's dominion**.
Brady	W	Connoting an action of **immorality**, Hester's "sin-born infant" **contrasts** the ideas of the **new life** of the infant with the **iniquity** of Hester's actions, connoting a sense of **irony** between the two.
Archie	W	Following her **shameful** appearance in front of the crowd at her trial, Hester's child born due to her *illicit* **adultery** is deemed a "token of infamy," contrasting the purity and innocence of a typical newborn child.
Johnson		Hester **loses grace** from the town, an **abandonment** of her **redemption** due to her nature of **sin**. [The sentence contains no L1.]
Archie, Crooms	W	Due to Hester's **earthly shame and willingness to repent**, she may become "more saint-like," growing into a new sense of **purity** and **innocence** "because of the result of her martyrdom," an action that causes her to appear **better in the eyes of God** and at the time of her final **punishment**.
Brady	W	Sealed in her fate of **punishment** her sin was "the roots she struck into the soil," **a shunned action** of **vice** that exemplifies the **immense sinful** action she has committed.
Watkins		The A on her bosom, a symbol of **adultery** shown through the "scarlet letter flaming on her breast," [This is a fragment, with no L2 to the right.]
Manne and Vo	W	Hester Prynne's **torture** from her **shame** had "purg[ed] her soul," **an expulsion of the devil** from her body.
Archie -- Crooms	W	**Attracted** to her lover living in **secrecy**, **bound** to her home **by her adultery**, the **permanent** scar of Hester's **sin** lingers with her like "a force of doom," preventing her from obtaining true **earthly purity** and causing her to live in **shame**.

Human Sentences

Core Plays Involved

GRAMMAR Plays

- absolute phrase [the "AP"]
- present participle phrase [the "PrPP"]
- past participle phrase [the "PaPP"]
- gerund phrase [the "GP"]
- infinitive phrase [the "IP"]
- adverb subordinate clause [the "AdvSC"]
- noun subordinate clause [the "NSC"]
- adjective subordinate clause [the "AdjSC"]

Learning Objectives

- Students will apply core grammatical knowledge to the building of sentences.
- Students will further reinforce their knowledge of phrases and clauses (and thus, their grammatical long-term memory) through physical movement and social engagement.

Procedure

- Human Sentences is a team game in which students race to create sentences by placing cards (each one representing a particular part of speech) in a specific sequence.

WHY IT WORKS

Human sentences aptly demonstrates what recent research underscores about physical **movement** and cognition. Once thought only to control our physical movements, the cerebellum actually directs messages to the cognitive areas of the brain. In fact, the majority of neural circuits in the cerebellum, triggered by even low intensity movement, branch outward[149] towards regions of the brain that deal with memory and learning functions.[150] In other words, the cerebellum is intimately linked to the learning and cognitive modalities of the brain.[151] During physical movement—in this case, the arrangement of the parts of speech cards—several **neurotransmitters** are released, most importantly BDNF, a protein or "Miracle-Gro for the brain,"[152] which strengthens the circuitry of memory networks and enhances overall learning.

To play this game, the teacher needs to create a few sets of cards, one for each team.

- Each set will contain **parts of speech cards** and **punctuation cards**. These cards can be made out of cardboard, corrugated plastic, poster board, laminated sheets of paper, or another material. In our classroom sets, a "card" is an 8" x 6" rectangle of corrugated plastic.

- Students will be placing these cards in sequence, either on a table, on the sill of the whiteboard, or another surface available in the classroom. As one alternative, the teacher might make cards out of paper, and give students magnets to hang the sheets in a specific order on the whiteboard.

---

149   Middleton & Strick, 1994.
150   Chen, Zhu, Yan, & Yin, 2016.
151   Jensen, 2005.
152   Ratey, 2008.

- A complete set of cards will contain the following:
    - 4 noun cards
    - 3 pronoun cards
    - 2 linking verb cards
    - 2 action verb
    - 2 adjective cards
    - 2 adverb cards
    - 2 preposition cards
    - 1 coordinating conjunction cards
    - 2 subordinating conjunction cards
    - 2 relative pronoun cards
    - 2 correlative conjunction cards
    - 2 present participle cards
    - 2 past participle cards
    - 4 comma cards
    - 2 semicolon cards
    - 1 period card
    - Note: We have not included articles in this list. In our classrooms, students write the required articles above the nouns in their arranged sequence of cards. If the teacher wants to add articles to the deck, 6-8 article cards (with the words *a*, *an*, *the* written on them) will suffice.

- To make the **parts of speech** cards, write 3-5 examples of the part of speech on each card.
    - A noun card in the deck might have the words *microscope, beauty, shoes, Albert Einstein*, and *airplane* written on it. Another noun card in this same deck might have different nouns: *Sherlock Holmes, dog, math, beach*, and *music*.
    - A linking verb card would have written on it 3-5 examples of this part of speech: *am, would be, seems, looks, was*.

- So too would the correlative conjunction card: *both...and, neither...nor, not only...but also.*

- A present or past participle card should have 3-5 examples of each: *laughing..., investigating..., ruling..., imagining...* (present), *confused..., eaten..., promoted..., criticized...* (past).

• Part of the fun of Human Sentences is that the sentences created by arranging the cards are usually whacky and nonsensical, reading like "mad libs." For this reason, the teacher will want to use a wide variety of nouns, verbs, adjectives, and other parts of speech to make each set (For instance, do not put the same 3-5 nouns on every noun card in the deck). The greater the variety of words, the more sentence possibilities students have to play with, making the act of arranging the cards more enjoyable.

• To make the **punctuation cards**, simply write the punctuation mark on each card (for example, all 4 comma cards should have only a large comma written on it).

Once the teacher has made the required sets of cards, the class is ready to play the game.

• Place students in teams, and give each team a set of cards (for variations of this activity, see p. 193).

• Develop a list of dice categories—the sentence structures that correspond to each number of the die (see additional examples on p. 183-185). In each round of Human Sentences, the class will roll the die to find out which sentence structure they must incorporate into their sentences. For instance, the class might play the game with these dice categories:

- 1 = compound sentence
- 2 = sentence with a present participle phrase (PrPP)
- 3 = sentence with a past participle phrase (PaPP)
- 4 = sentence with an adjective subordinate clause (AdjSC)
- 5 = sentence with an adverb subordinate clause (AdvSC)
- 6 = sentence with an absolute phrase (AP)

- In each round, after the die is rolled, teams must arrange some of the cards in their set to form a sentence that contains the required structure.
    - For example, if the teacher rolls a 2, then each team has to create a sentence containing the present participle phrase structure.
    - A team might do this by arranging the following sequence of cards: a present participle card, a noun card, a comma card, a pronoun card, a verb card, a noun card, and the period card. Doing so would form a sentence like this one: *Eating bumblebees, we chant computers.*
    - Another team might do this by starting with a noun card, then an action verb card, then a comma card, followed by a present participle card, another noun card, and a period card. This sequence would look like this: *Math leaps, investigating footballs.*
- Once one team completes its sentence alignment at the board, all play stops. All students sit down, while one representative from this team reads their completed card sequence, selecting one word off of each card to form a sentence.
- The other teams can vote on whether this sentence is correct or incorrect.
- At this point in the game, the teacher awards points to all teams, to the finishing team for their card sequence, and to the other teams for their votes. The teacher should create a **point system** that makes sense for their students, with one example being the following:
    - +2 for a correctly aligned sentence by the finishing team
    - +1 for a correct vote on whether or not this sentence contains the required structure
    - -1 for an incorrect vote
- Play continues for as many rounds as the teacher decides.

Variations

- In one variation of Human Sentences, the teacher divides the class into an even number of teams.

- During a round of the game, half of the teams arrange sentences using the physical sets of cards, while the other teams **enter sentences into a Google Form.** This variation is useful if the teacher does not want to make (and keep organized) several sets of cards.

- The teams with physical cards play the game as previously outlined.

- Teams typing in the Google Form enter as many sentences as they can before a team with cards completes their sequence. These teams are not assembling nonsensical word sequences; they do not have a word bank or deck of cards they are required to sift through. They can write about any topic. The teacher may require them to write about the text the class is reading.

- Once a team with the cards has finished arranging their sequence of physical cards, all play stops. Teams with cards may not continue to move them, and teams entering sentences into the Google Form may not continue to type.

- All students sit back down. One representative from the finishing team reads the arranged sentence, and the other teams vote on whether or not the sentence contains the required structure.

- The teacher awards points to the team who completed a sentence using the cards, to the teams who voted correctly on that sentence, and then scores the sentences submitted digitally to the Form.

    - +2 for a correctly arranged sequence of cards
    - +1 for a correct vote on the arranged sequence
    - -1 for an incorrect vote
    - +1 for a correct sentence submitted digitally to the Google Form
    - -1 for an incorrect sentence
    - **Optional**: Award a +5 "speed bonus" to the team with the fastest time completing a sequence of physical cards.

Labeling

Core Plays Involved

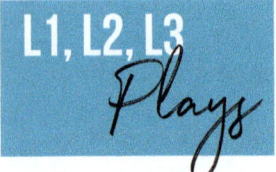 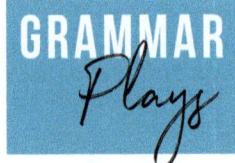 

Learning Objectives

- Students will pay attention to their use of core "Plays" by identifying them in their own written work.

- Students will begin to use the "Plays" strategically, when and where they might be most effective, as they reinforce knowledge of them in long-term memory.

Procedure

- The teacher develops a labeling system for essential elements of the playbook. During in-class writing activities, on essay assignments, or in the revision process, students follow the labeling requirements the teacher sets.

- The labeling system we use in our classes is below:
    - **L2 (associations) and L3 (relationships) labeled in bold**
    - Topic strings underlined
    - L1 (evidence) in blue
    - *Label in italics three words from our class' vocabulary list.*
    - [Sentence structures bracketed] Ex. [Walking down the street--PrPP], I saw Ivy.

WHY IT WORKS

Metacognition broadly refers to students' abilities to consciously reflect on a learning task and its components. In many ways, when we ask students to label "Plays" in their essays, we force them to replay the initial lessons for each writing strategy. The act of labeling calls their attention to their own execution of these writing strategies; the goal is that this conscious focus refines their skills and pushes them to practice the "Plays" further. And the triggering of a specific metacognitive neural network in the brain strengthens the **long term memory** network that binds all the writing plays.[153]

---

153   Vacarro, 2018.

Sample of a labeled body paragraph

Shelley critiques the **abdication** of a **moral framework, [warning** of the **dangers** of the **intoxication** of knowledge—PrPP]. First, in Volume 1 of *Frankenstein*, Shelley highlights the **dangers** of using **knowledge** as an **end in itself** when Frankenstein states "I ardently hope the gratification of your wishes may not be a serpent to sting you as mine has been," Frankenstein's **warning** to Walton paralleling Shelley's **warning** to the reader about the **addictive** nature of obtaining **new knowledge**—AP] (23). Shelley's biblical allusion to Satan's **distortion** of **morals** in the garden and the "serpent to sting you" contributes to her pathos appeal that **excoriates** Satan's **elevation** of **emotion** and **desire** above **reason** (23). Second, Shelley repeats her **warning** to the reader about the **dangers** of **abandoning** a **logical framework** when Frankenstein remarks "of what a strange nature is knowledge! It clings to the mind when it has once seized it, like a lichen on the rock," the **chronic diction** of "clings" contributing to her argument about the **intoxication** of **knowledge** by revealing its **chronic nature** (113). Shelley reveals the **deceptive nature** of the **unbridled pursuit** of **knowledge** in her description of **knowledge** as a "strange nature," **surprising diction** that subverts expectation and informs that **knowledge** is not always what it seems (113).

Memory Work

"Thus I got into my bones the essential structure of the ordinary British sentence—which is a noble thing."

– Winston Churchill

Susan Wise Bauer argues that memorization "builds into children's minds an ability to use complex English syntax." The student "who memorizes… will internalize" the "rhythmic, beautiful patterns" of the English language. These patterns then become "part of the student's 'language store,' those wells that we all use every day in writing and speaking." Without memorization, the student's "language store," Bauer says, will be limited: memorization stocks "the language store with a whole new set of language patterns."[154]

Core Plays Involved

Learning Objectives

- Students will internalize complex syntactic patterns as part of a student's default writing style.
- Students will employ patterns of analysis (L2) blended with evidence (L1).
- Students will reinforce syntax that contains an assertive interpretive voice.

---

154   Bauer, 2003.

WHY IT WORKS

Memorizing "distinctive" models engages students in complex and **challenging tasks,** igniting more cerebellar activity, more neurons firing and fusing into emerging networks. Establishing parameters to evaluate appropriate intellectual challenge, the Russian psychologist Lev Vygotsky argues for placing students in the zone of proximal development. ZPD is "the distance between the actual developmental level ... and the level of potential development ... under adult guidance, or in collaboration with more capable peers."[155] To assist in the memorizing component, the brain also responds to the **movement** of handwriting, which triggers[156] neural activity and learning, activity not seen when working on a computer.[157] Hence, requiring students to handwrite their notecards increases the success of committing the ideal sentences to memory, increases oxygen flow to the brain, and triggers neurons to fire off connecting signals, strengthening **memory networks.**[158]

Procedure

- Students memorize 1-6 model sentences created by the teacher, which could come from a sample paragraph, or could involve a thesis and topic sentences only.

- They imitate the sentence(s) using assigned content from current reading material. For example, if they are currently revising an essay for *The Scarlet Letter*, their sentences should use L1 from their draft. If they're not yet drafting, they might select L1 connected to their essay topic.

---

155 Vygotsky, 1978.
156 Plebanek D. and James K, 2022.
157 Li, J. X., and James, K. H. 2016; Smoker, T. J., Murphy, C. E., and Rockwell, A. K. 2009.
158 Vinci-Booher SA, James KH. 2017; Midling AS. 2020; Ose Askvik E, van der Weel FR and van der Meer ALH, 2020.

- Below is a topic sentence discussing Dickens' *A Tale of Two Cities*. Students memorize this sentence.

    The unnecessary execution of the guiltless seamstress reflects the Revolution's chaotic and destructive nature, its departure from preserving righteous virtues.

- In addition to having students memorize this model sentence, the teacher may have them imitate its syntax in their own writing. The sentence above contains the following components:

    *The unnecessary execution **(subject)** of the guiltless seamstress **(prepositional phrase)** reflects **(verb)** the Revolution's chaotic and destructive nature **(direct object)**, its departure from preserving righteous virtues **(absolute phrase)**.*

- The student writing about the *Lord of the Flies* would imitate the memory sentence with content from his own emerging paper draft. In this particular case, students imitate the syntax of the memory sentences, using these sentence patterns to give form to their own thoughts.

    *Jack's brutal actions **(subject)** towards other boys **(prepositional phrase)** suggest **(verb)** his malevolent and narcissistic character **(direct object)**, a threat to preserving the tribe's order **(absolute phrase)**.*

Initial exercises of rote memory must move toward an application of the memorized syntax to a student's own sentences. When students apply the syntax of a memorized sentence to their own sentence[s] with content from their specific essay assignment, they shift a short-term memory exercise into a long term memory. Their continued use of a formerly memorized syntactic pattern has a greater chance of becoming part of their internalized style.

Sample Memory Assignment: *Great Expectations*

Directions

- Memorize the first three sentences of the sample provided below.
- Write out all six sentences on index cards, one sentence per card. For each sentence, create your own imitation of the sentence. The content of your sentences should be your paper topic.
- On the announced "quiz" day, you will write out from memory the first three sentences of the paragraph.

Memory Sample

- Note: In the sentences below, evidence is labeled in blue, **associations are bolded**, and topic strings are underlined.

Topic Sentence: Throughout Volume 1, Dickens develops Joe's **yin** characteristics, those **traditionally associated with the feminine, causing us to rethink our stereotype of the father.**

<u>Initially,</u> Joe Gargery's semblance to a **physically imposing** "muscular blacksmith, [with a] broad chest" connotes **stereotypical masculine** imagery, but Joe later **contradicts** this imagery (6).

<u>As a mother</u> **protects her offspring from danger,** Joe, too, assumes this task at the dinner table on Christmas Eve.

<u>Hearing Pip being</u> **verbally battered by the family,** Joe extends his "restoring touch" unto Pip, "aiding and comforting [him]…by giving [Pip] gravy," a **benevolent deed that demonstrates not just his concern for Pip, but his willingness to help and care for him** (23; ch. 4).

<u>In fact,</u> Joe, instead of seeing Pip **suffer**, would also "wish to take [the Tickler] on himself," showing his **legitimate concern for Pip's well-being** (43; ch. 7).

<u>Apart from his concern</u> for Pip, Joe also desires the **unification of the household,** his concern for the ***oikos,*** an important **yin** characteristic.

Isolating Plays in Sentence Creation

Core Plays Involved

Learning Objectives

- Students will execute specified playbook skills.

Procedure

- The teacher selects, from the current unit, a quotation, passage, or page for the exercise. See, for example, pp. 121-122.

- Place students in partners or groups of three.

- The class reads the selected quotation, passage, or page aloud.

- Students have five minutes to select evidence (L1) from the literary text and develop associations (L2), the interpretive words they will use in their sentences.

- Students then have fifteen minutes to create three sentences, following the L2-L1-L2 pattern (See p. 82). In each sentence, they will attempt to successfully execute a specific play: Modified L1, L3, and To the Right.

- Students should use the model provided on the next page, which includes a quotation from *Othello* followed by three sample sentences. In each sentence, the writer uses the same piece of evidence, but focuses on a different play.

WHY IT WORKS

Sentence work converges expert performance, athletics, and brain research. **Breaking down complex movements** (like composing an expository argument) **into shorter sequences** allows the brain to efficiently develop skills and incorporate them into long-term memory.[159] Since researchers have found that we can take in only three to seven chunks of information before we overload and begin to miss new incoming data, sentence work proves the ideal instructional choice, especially for our weakest students.[160] Working with the single sentence also allows the teacher to provide **feedback** to students at the very moment of the movement, allowing students to immediately correct[161] their performance of a specific play. The timeliness of feedback increases the likelihood that the skill becomes part of a permanent long-term memory.[162]

---

159   Thalmann, Souza, & Oberauer, 2018; Jenson and McConchie, 2020.
160   Linden et al., 2003; Jensen, 2005.
161   Kopp, B., & Wolff, M., 2000.
162   Black & William 1998; McTighe and Willis, 2019.

Sample of isolating specific plays in blended sentences

Text chosen by the teacher

Roderigo: It is silliness to live when to live is torment; and then have we a prescription to die when death is our physician. (*Othello* Act 1, Scene 3)

Modified L1: Identify the type of L1 (diction, detail, imagery) used by the author to create meaning

> **Envy** has so **blinded** Roderigo, he believes that "death" is the only "physician" for his **pain**; this contradictory image of **death as a healer,** an **unideal archetype,** reveals the utter **confusion** that **evil** cultivates in its **victims.**

L3: Identify a relationship created by the piece of evidence

> Shakespeare **juxtaposes** Roderigo's **despondency** with his **irrational thinking**, depicting him as a **man ruled by his emotions,** his **obsession** with Desdemona causing him to believe it is "silliness to live" without her.

To the Right: Identify precise L2 after the quotation

> **Unable to fulfill his desire** for her, Roderigo proclaims that "to live is torment," life itself appearing to be **an agonizing affliction** in the absence of Desdemona's love.

Peer-Editing / Critic's Walk

Core Plays Involved

Learning Objectives

- Students will learn to use the Writing Plays to peer edit effectively, as teachers provide them specific feedback about peer sentences, paragraphs, thesis statements.

- Students will learn successful peer editing through training in limited specified tasks, which focus on evaluating a single play, such as the L2 Play or the Topic String play.

WHY IT WORKS

This peer editing activity sets up the **scrimmage**—a class period for the teacher to observe the degree to which students have internalized the writing plays, can retrieve the strategies efficiently, can respond to immediate teacher feedback, and can recover from moments of failure without the assistance of the teacher. Finally, the **metacognitive** aspect of the activity reinforces each "Play," embedding it into long-term memory in a way that mere direct instruction cannot. As teachers use peer editing activities, they provide opportunities for students to practice their skills, with swift feedback regarding flaws as well as the apt application of each play, thus increasing students' metacognitive skills.[163] These students demonstrate higher academic performance than those students who lack metacognitive awareness.[164]

---

163 Stanton JD, Sebesta AJ, Dunlosky J., 2021.

164 Clements 2016; Lin et al. 2007; McCutchen 2006; Saddler & Graham 2007; Harris, S. 2010; Karlen 2017; Graham & Harrison 2000; Wang, et.al 1990.

Procedure

Designing your peer-editing form: the "Critic's Ticket"

- Before class, teachers need to create a peer-editing form "Critic's Ticket" (a physical slip of paper, or a Google Form) that students will use to record their editing comments for their partners. **See sample tickets below**.

- Each student fills out **one ticket during each round of the activity**, looking at a different partner's work each time.

- The teacher has several options when it comes to creating the form used in this activity. The design of the ticket depends on the type of peer-editing movement you wish students to perform. You may find a few samples on the next page.

Sample Critic's Tickets

Peer-editing a thesis statement and its topic sentences

Students complete a peer-editing form that contains simple yes or no questions.

Writer's Name: _____

Editor's Name: _____

- The writer's thesis statement contains logical associations (L2) for the writer's topic:

    ☐ Yes   ☐ No   ☐ I'm not sure / I have a comment: _____

- The writer's topic sentences contain logical association (L2) for the topic.

    ☐ Yes   ☐ No   ☐ I'm not sure / I have a comment: _____

- The L2 in the writer's topic sentences link logically to the L2 in the thesis statement:

    ☐ Yes   ☐ No   ☐ I'm not sure / I have a comment: _____

Peer-editing another student's writing for a single play

Students score each other's sentences for a specific play that the teacher identifies at the beginning of the peer-editing round. The class discusses what is required to properly perform the play before peer-editing begins, looking at samples on the class' Mastery Handout (see pp. 272-283).

Writer's Name: _____

Editor's Name: _____

- Score the writer's sentence(s) for the specified play:
    - Insufficient
    - Progressing
    - Mastery
    - Distinctive

Suggesting revisions to another student's writing

Students propose their own ideas to improve their classmate's sentences.

Writer's Name: _____

Editor's Name: _____

- Write out the evidence (L1) that appears in the writer's sentence.

- Write out the associations (L2) that appear in the writer's sentence.

- Cross out the L2 that are not viable, too vague, or redundant.

- Look at the L1 in your partner's sentence. Pick a word or short phrase from this L1 and create more L2 for this small piece of the evidence–associations that do not already appear in your partner's sentence.

- Write out these new associations here: _____

Digital peer editing rounds

- At the beginning of the activity, students must provide their peers with access to their writing, either by

    - submitting part of the essay to a Google Form, or

    - pasting a link to their work on a Google Doc shared with the teacher and the class.

- Once students have completed this step, the teacher designates the partners for the first round of peer editing.

- Students move across the classroom to their partner's workstation.

- Once students arrive at their partners' stations, they have ____ minutes to fill out a critic's ticket for their partners.

- If the ticket is a Google Form, pull up the responses spreadsheet on the digital board or teacher device to see which students are engaged and efficient.

- The teacher tells students to rotate to the right, moving to the next student's workstation.

- At their new stations, students repeat the above process, filling out a new ticket.

Concluding the activity

- Ensure that students have access to the results of the peer-editing exercise: post the Google Form responses where students can see them.

- At the end of the peer-editing rounds, have students return to their seats and examine the feedback they were given.

- At this point, open the responses spreadsheet on the digital board for all to see.

- Conclude the peer-editing activity by giving the editors feedback and by clarifying particular students' performances—resolving differences of opinion.

- For example, Tim and Stacy gave Joan feedback on her thesis statement during the rounds, but their feedback is contradictory. Joan does not know which of her peers is right, and is confused about how to revise her sentence. You might say, "It looks like there was some disagreement about the quality of Joan's thesis statement. Let's move over to her space on the board and take a closer look at it as a class."

- Once there, pick another student to read the sentence aloud. "Okay, Tim rated this thesis as 'Mastery,' but Stacy said it is 'Distinctive.' Based on the sentence on the board, what do the rest of you think?"

- You can even incorporate further movement into the discussion: "Move over to this side of the room if you think it's Mastery, and go over there if you agree with Stacy that it's Distinctive..."

Writing Conference Memo

Writing conferences between the teacher and student can occur inside or outside the classroom. The conference occurs after student have completed a writing assignment and have received teacher feedback regarding how well they have demonstrated mastery of the writing plays.

When student come to the conference, they show evidence of revised sections of the essay where mastery of the plays was not achieved. The focus of the conference is to review the attempts at revision and to clarify possible misunderstandings of each play. During the conference, the teacher may direct students to examples of mastery that they should imitate.

The purpose of this memo activity is to prompt students to recall the conference in their minds, and by doing so, reinforce the understanding of their deficiencies and the understanding of how improve to their performance of the writing plays. Students' written reflections also serve as feedback for the teacher, verifying the degree to which the plays have been internalized correctly.

Core Plays Involved

The memo activity involves any plays that the student discussed with the teacher during a writing conference.

Learning Objectives

- Students will strengthen their knowledge of the plays by recalling feedback they receive from the teacher.
- Students will develop the necessary understanding that their own learning is their responsibility and no one else's.

Procedure

- Create a physical memo for students to fill out by hand, or create a Google Form.

WHY IT WORKS

One of the challenges English teachers face is simply getting their students to listen to feedback they receive.

While many students either ignore teacher feedback or lack the organization and initiative to respond to it effectively, the Writing Conference Memo requires them to recall the strategies the teacher has reminded them of during the conference and verbalize the next steps they need to make. This **retrieval** exercise increases the likelihood that our feedback about the reading and writing plays becomes part of their permanent long-term memory.[165] It also develops their **metacognitive abilities**, training their brains to pay attention to aspects of their own performance.[166] This ability to think about thinking is one that ultimately enables higher academic achievement.

- The teacher decides what questions to ask on the memo. Ideally, these questions require students to recall (i.e., what neuroscientists call "retrieval") the specific feedback given by the teacher during the writing conference. See the sample memo provided on the next page.

- In our classrooms, students fill out a memo after each conference with the teacher. The teacher posts a QR code on the teacher's desk or classroom wall, through which students access the memo form.

- To ensure students thoughtfully complete the memo, the teacher may assign it for a grade, assessing either the quality of the student's responses or simply their completion of the memo.

---

165 McTighe & Willis, 2019.
166 Vacarro, 2018; Sekeres et al., 2016.

Sample Student Writing Conference Memo

Directions

Referencing the reading and writing plays, answer the following questions. The goal of this assignment is to reflect on your experiences in writing conferences: how you have participated in them, how the teacher has attempted to guide your performance, how you have responded to this feedback with specific actions.

Name: _____

Date of Conference: _____

Essay Assignment: *Beowulf* Essay

1) **At the beginning of the writing conference, did you provide revisions for the teacher to review?**
    I tried to revise my thesis and topic sentences before the conference.

2) **Did you follow all labeling instructions prior to the conference?**[167]
    I forgot to underline my topic strings, and had to switch conference times so that I could take care of that.

3) **According to the teacher's comments during the writing conference, which plays [thesis statement, topic string, etc.] need to be addressed in your essay?**
    The plays in my *Beowulf* essay that needed to be addressed were the **L2** and **To the Right** plays. My first paragraph had a long quotation with no explanation for the reader on how the quotation proved my topic sentence. I had no L2 to the right of this quotation, I simply stated it, then started my next sentence with "Second…" and moved on to a new paragraph chunk.

---

[167] See the "Labeling" activity on page 194.

4) **Specifically, what revisions will you make to address these plays?**

I will rewrite several sentences of the paragraph chunk where I talk about how Beowulf faces Grendel. I will focus on the To the Right play when I'm doing this, trying to put stronger L2 after the L1 I use.

5) **What strategies did you learn that you can apply to your next essay, or which plays will you be especially aware of when drafting your next essay?**

This is my second conference about this essay. In the first conference, we talked about how you can make stronger L2 by doing factoring. In today's conference I showed the teacher how I already tried this with the L2 "brave" and "great." He liked two L2 I had come up with: "facing death" and "a trial no other warrior had succeeded." I will try to create more specific L2 for the other chunks in my essay before I meet with him again.

Sample Conference Memo - Google Form Responses

Using a Google Form for the Writing Conference Memo allows the teacher to keep track of previous conferences with students. The table below is a sample of student responses for the form we have used.

Name:	Did you provide revisions for the teacher to review?	Did you follow all labeling instructions prior to your meeting?	Which plays were addressed during your revision conference?	What do you need to work on prior to your next revision conference? What are at least two plays that need to be addressed?
Greg	no revisions completed; I only typed up and labeled the original	Yes	Thesis Statement	Revising thoughts
Max	thesis, topic sentences	Yes	Thesis Statement, Topic Sentences	I have the right ideas for thesis and topic sentences, they just need some touch up and a few words changed and rearranged.
Jake	topic sentences, blended sentence	Yes	Thesis Statement, Topic Sentences, L1 (Quantity and Quality), L2 (Quantity and Quality), L2-L1 Pairings	Revisit the passage and change structure of paper to include diction about theological concepts (forgiveness) and the bigger meaning of passage.
Ale	no revisions completed; I only typed up and labeled the original	Yes	Thesis Statement, Topic Sentences, L1 (Quantity and Quality), Conclusion	Summarizing the passage in the thesis, and improving the L1 quality.

05

PUTTING THE PLAYS TOGETHER

— SCRIMMAGE AND
REFLECTION ACTIVITIES —

The Scrimmage

In this chapter, the English teacher will find activities that combine the playbook's core plays and place students in situations that more closely resemble "the game" of English, the timed performance involving close-reading, writing, and/or verbal explication of the literary text.

The coaching concepts of scrimmage and silence, introduced in Chapter 1 of this book, inform the design of these activities (see pp. 36-38).

Through scrimmage, coaches evaluate players' abilities before an actual game, judging the degree to which they have internalized the key movements of the sport. In relative silence, they observe their athletes' performance to identify weaknesses that future training sessions must address. They tend to speak only at brief moments to provide quick feedback, reminders, or encouragement before allowing their athletes to keep playing.

Similarly, the activities in this chapter allow the English teacher to observe the degree to which students have internalized the reading and writing plays and are able to do them on their own.

In the English classroom, activities like the *Discussion Quiz, Literary News Conference, Tournament of Scholars,* and *Quotation Game* assess students' readiness for upcoming essay assignments, and allow us to provide feedback to help them improve. These activities require students to

- explain how textual evidence, when repeated, juxtaposed, or contrasted, contributes to character, theme, setting, tone, etc.;
- articulate original interpretations supported with logical textual evidence;
- verbalize a new way to view the text—a character, a theme, or setting, for example;
- posit intelligent connections (contrasts or similarities) with other characters in the text or with other works of literature and contemporary life;
- generate thoughtful questions about the literary text.

With any of these activities, the teacher can specifically decide if some of the core plays need particular attention, and modify the activity (by changing the rules or adding additional requirements) to focus students on a particular play.

Students Reflecting on Performance

In addition to these larger, scrimmage-like activities, this chapter includes a reflection exercise that engages students in evaluating their own writing performance, identifying specific challenges and areas for improvement.

We have designed the *Revision Chart* activity (p. 260) to respond to what neuroscience and psychology research tell us about "metacognitive activity" in the brain, which occurs when the performer consciously thinks about his or her own performance and thought process. Both fields have demonstrated that awareness of one's own performance, and the ability to evaluate it, enable higher achievement. This activity engages students in practicing this metacognitive awareness, asking them to

- define the plays (how to perform them, what they demand, why they are useful, when they are applicable),
- perceive the decisions they make when trying to execute them,
- articulate the reasons behind their mistakes,
- verbalize changes they need to make to achieve a greater level of performance.

Furthermore, the *Revision Chart* involves *retrieval*: by having students recall information about reading and writing plays, it strengthens memory networks related to them.

> **Note:** To engage students in this reflection activity, students will need to look back over their previous written work. The teacher must ensure that students keep previous writing assignments in an organized fashion. If students complete essays on paper, the teacher may keep a filing cabinet or crate in the classroom/office with graded student work. For students' digital work, the teacher can require students to create a shared folder online (Google Drive, Microsoft OneDrive, etc.) and store all work here.

Types of Questions to Consider When Reading

For the *Discussion Quiz*, the *Literary News Conference*, *Tournament of Scholars*, and *Quotation Game,* the teacher requires students or teams to develop questions for discussion.

WHY IT WORKS

Having students develop questions for discussion is one way teachers can practice **inductive instruction,** which fosters their intellectual growth more effectively than deductive methods through which they passively receive information from their teachers.

Moving inductively places greater intellectual demand on students, which stimulates their brains to *adapt* to meet the challenge (see chapter 1, "The SAID Principle – Specific Adaptation to Imposed Demands, for more on this idea). More cerebellar activity ignites, more neurons start firing and fusing to form memory networks when students are challenged to sift through the many events and characters in the literary text, recognize patterns, draw conclusions, and form their own questions – while the teacher refrains from supplying answers.[168]

Questions about Character

These questions inquire into the motivations or personal traits of individual characters in a story. They require us to draw conclusions or make inferences about a character because of what he or she says or does. Do not ask general or broad questions, such as "Who is this character?" or "What does this character do in chapter one?"

- What are the most important details that we learn in chapter 1 about

---

[168] McTighe & Willis, 2019; Richard et al., 2013; Wiggins & McTighe, 2012.

Piggy, and what do these details suggest about him as a character?

- What drives Odysseus' decision-making during the Cyclops episode?
- What does Daisy Buchanan reveal to the reader about her own moral character through what she says to other characters?
- What motivates Holden to insist that others are "phonies?"

Questions Concerning the Author's Purpose or Technique

These questions inquire into *why* the author does something. They challenge students to acknowledge that the literary text is a work of art, and that the author crafted the story with specific purposes in mind, using specific techniques to communicate these to the reader.

- The author emphasizes a specific detail involving a character: Why does Dickens repeatedly draw attention to Madame Defarge's knitting in *A Tale of Two Cities*?
- The author places an image in a specific location in a story: Why is a rose bush growing outside the prison in *The Scarlet Letter*?
- The author uses a specific simile or metaphor or other literary device in a key moment in a story: What does Romeo's comparison of Juliet to the sun tell us about Romeo?

Questions That Require Making Perceptive Connections within the Text

These questions concentrate on how one part of the story is connected to another, how one character is like or unlike another, or how one sequence of events is like another.

- In Homer's *Odyssey*, how does the bard's song about Hephaestus, Aphrodite, and Ares relate to Odysseus' return to his own palace?
- How does Macbeth's descent into evil mirror his wife's?
- How does the party scene in Chapter 6 of *The Great Gatsby* anticipate the scene in Chapter 7, where Gatsby confronts Tom?
- Compare and contrast Pip's care for Magwitch at his death with Joe's care for Pip during his convalescence?

Questions That Require Making Perceptive Connections among Stories

These questions demonstrate students' abilities to perceive how characters, situations, and themes in one story compare and/or contrast with characters, situations, and themes from other stories.

- Which qualities of leadership are revealed by Ralph (*Lord of the Flies*) and the 8th Juror (*Twelve Angry Men*)?

- Sydney Carton, like Macbeth, loses his life by the end of the story. How do these characters' deaths differ, and what larger moral lessons can we draw from them?

Questions about the Narrator as Narrator

These questions consider the narrator's effect on the meaning of the literary work. Beyond considering the type of narrator (first-person, second-person, third-person limited or omniscient), students should consider the particular effect the narrator's voice has on the reader's understanding of events, or the role the narrator plays in establishing the main associative ideas in the text.

- Imagine Twain telling *The Adventures of Huckleberry Finn* from a third-person omniscient narrator. How would the story be different? What if it was told from Tom's first-person perspective rather than Huck's?

- In *The Great Gatsby*, how might the reader understand Gatsby differently if Nick were not telling the story from his own perspective?

- Is the first-person narrator in "The Cask of Amontillado" by Edgar Allan Poe a reliable one? If so, how do you know? If not, why should he be seen as unreliable?

Questions That Apply the Novel to Life in General

Throughout the novel, students may find situations that apply to people or events today. Again, general questions will not be appropriate. Their question(s) should refer to specific situations in the story.

- Which characteristics of the adolescent male can the reader perceive in Huck during his interactions with Miss Watson and the Widow

Douglas at the beginning of the novel?

- Does Telemachus' journey mirror the journey of high school students in today's world? Why or why not?

- Does the relationship between Claudio and Hero mirror the adolescent's experience of romantic love today? If so, how? If not, in what ways are they different?

- Do the portrayals of the costs of unrestrained ambition that we see in *Frankenstein* and *Macbeth* ring true in today's world? Can you think of any present-day examples of people who resemble Victor Frankenstein or Macbeth?

Questions from Critical Research

Students may read a short comment or passage from a critical essay and ask a group to react—agree or disagree, providing textual evidence for the position. The critical research may be a handout or document that the class has already discussed, or a resource that students have found on their own. Remind students that they must cite the source and author.

- In *The Terrain of Comedy*, Louise Cowan claims that comic stories depict worlds that are "growing, healing." In William Faulkner's *The Reivers*, how does the community grow; which characters are healed?

- In *Bumper Sticker Ethics*, Steve Wilkins writes that the moral system of Egotism is grounded in "the pursuit of immediate desires and impulses," making choices based on what is in our interest now. Which characters from *Macbeth* exemplify this ethical system? How do you know?

The Discussion Quiz

Core Plays Involved

Learning Objectives

- Students will apply the core plays in a more complex situation, often considering the literary text as a whole rather than examining a single or small number of passages.

- Students will develop their abilities to create "glue" by responding to their peers' answers in a clear, logical way.

- Students will prepare for future writing assessment (timed essay) by discussing the literary text the class has finished reading.

WHY IT WORKS

Complex and **challenging tasks** like the Discussion Quiz (or "DQ") ignite cerebellar activity in our students' brains: more neurons start firing and fusing into emerging networks. Less challenging tasks and learning objectives, which require little cognitive effort, result in static brain activity. For instance, simply asking students to recall a fact from their reading or restate an idea that the teacher told them about the novel does not stimulate their brains to develop in the direction of improved performance in reading. The Discussion Quiz, by contrast, asks students to locate evidence that supports an answer to a discussion question, identify a relationship between one scene in the novel and another, respond to another student's answer with their own associations, and other challenging movements.

Additionally, the Discussion Quiz helps students understand why mastering the core reading plays (L1, L2, L3) matters. Research demonstrates that establishing this behavioral relevance increases "the chances of [a desired behavior] being learned, remembered, and internalized."

Procedure

The Discussion Quiz works best at the culmination of a unit or before an upcoming writing assessment. For instance, a teacher might hold a discussion quiz over the entirety of *Things Fall Apart*, or over Part I of *Crime and Punishment*. Holding the discussion at this point helps students to identify the most important evidence (L1), associations (L2), and relationships (L3) that occurred in the story. Their discussion helps to generate, clarify, and refine possibilities for the upcoming essay.

This activity can last for as long as the teacher deems useful; typically, one to two class periods is a sufficient amount of time.

Before the day of the Discussion Quiz, the teacher lays the groundwork for the activity by providing the questions and giving students time to prepare.

- **Questions.** Prepare several discussion questions in advance, and make them available to students. Usually these are directly related to essay topics; as students answer them, they are really talking about ways to approach the essay (See pp. 228-229 for examples).

  The teacher may show students the questions a week or two before the Discussion Quiz to give them time to prepare responses.

- **"Prep" work.** Many high school students believe that they can simply "wing it" in a live discussion. Clearly, requiring some advance preparation and defining the process redounds to most students' benefit. Students who complete prep work have something to refer to and rely on (See p. 230 for an example student chart).

  Most importantly, they will need to have L1 and L2 prepared in order to answer the questions and provide textual support.

  For this reason, it is helpful to assign an **Evidence-Association Chart** (see p. 132) for homework, or to develop one in class in the days leading up to the discussion quiz.

  For example, the teacher might assign every student 1-2 questions from the list, and require them to build an EAC chart containing some or all of the following:

    - L1, L2, and L3
    - L2-L1-L2 sentences

- thesis statements
- topic sentences

The demands of the prep work assignment must be realistic and achievable for the class. The goal should be to challenge them at their current stage of development.

How to run the activity

- On the day of the Discussion Quiz, the teacher arranges the desks in a circle.[169]

- The teacher appoints a student moderator to lead discussion for the day.

- The moderator calls upon another student to read the first question aloud.

- This student then has two options: 1) answer the question, or 2) say, "I'm not sure how to answer this; can someone help me?"

- After a student answers the question, other students can add additional comments. Students have two options: 1) Agree with all or part of a previous student's commentary and add further elaboration based on details from the literary text; 2) Disagree with all or part of a previous student's commentary and explain reasons based on evidence from the text.

> **Appoint a moderator**
>
> Ideally, the Discussion Quiz is student-led. To facilitate this, it is helpful to appoint a student to be the one who calls on others to speak.
>
> The teacher can then focus on student performance, and decide when to intervene and with brief feedback: directing the class' attention to a neglected element of the discussion question, a passage in the text that none have referenced, or a student's insightful observation that warrants recognition.

---

169 This is our preferred way of holding a large group discussion. If setting up the desks in a circle is not practical for your classroom space, this is not required. Have students sit in the usual desk formation and call on them as they raise their hands. Or, if you like, designate a physical object that the speaking student must hold (i.e., a foam ball, a fake microphone…a conch shell?) and then hand or toss to the next student who wishes to speak.

- If there is a lull in the conversation, the teacher, or student moderator, can say, "Does anyone have any further comments on this question?"
- If the class is ready to move on, the student moderator asks for a volunteer to read the next question. This volunteer can then offer an answer to the question, or ask for other students to help.
- The discussion continues by repeating the above steps: after a question is read, students take turns responding.

Directions for students

Below are some guidelines to provide students, particularly for the first time the class holds a Discussion Quiz.

- When it is your turn to speak:
    - Speak loudly and clearly.
    - Look at other students. Do not look down at your desk or at the teacher.
    - Be polite. Do not ridicule other students or make rude, inappropriate comments.
    - Stay on the topic/question the class is discussing.
    - Do not repeat the same idea (L2) as another student.
    - Speak to individuals by name when responding to their questions or ideas.
    - Use spoken transitions. (See examples of transitions below).
- When it is your turn to listen:
    - Be polite. Look at the student who is speaking and give him or her your attention.
    - Open your book to the page the speaker is referencing.
    - Have a pen or pencil ready to write down L1 and L2 that are mentioned during discussion.
- You can only earn credit for what you actually say during discussion.

Helpful Transitions for Students

Many students have not internalized the moves that effective speakers use to connect their ideas to others during a live discussion. Giving students a list of possible transitions enables them to practice creating logical glue (see p. 103).

"I agree with…"

"Agreeing with John's idea, I want to add…"

"I see your point, Mary…"

"I think it is better to…"

"I would like to ask Jane this question:…"

"I disagree with Mary's idea that…for this reason…"

"Building on Dan's idea, I would like to add this point…"

"In addition to what Bob said…"

"Adding to what Michael said…"

"Carrying what Jim and Alice said a step further, I would like to say…"

"Summing up, the majority seems to think…"

"Most of you seem to think…but what I understand is…"

Sample – *Beowulf* discussion quiz

Prepare responses to **at least two of the questions below** by creating an Evidence-Association Chart in your writing journal. Your chart must contain **at least six pairings of evidence from the text with your own associations**. You must also draft a thesis statement in response to each question you choose.

When developing your EAC chart, be sure to record the page numbers and line numbers clearly. During discussion, you will need to reference these so that others can find these L1 in the text.

Questions

1. Literary critic John Halverson writes, "So there are a number of suggestions in the representation of Heorot and Hrothgar of God and his creation...the idea of creating or making, which is seen as a God-like act. As God brought form out of chaos, light out of darkness, so the king brings order to his world and maintains it."

   How does the poet employ diction, detail, and imagery to emphasize this God-like quality of the king as a creator and bringer of order?

2. Literary critic George Clark writes, "In Heorot, Grendel's mother's flight suggested her vulnerability to the weapons of the Danes—the narrator measured her strength and found it inferior—but in the depths of the mere, Grendel's mother becomes the archetypal enemy and assumes the powers of the place itself, chaos, the antiworld."

   What is the *Beowulf* poet trying to convey about evil through this shift Clark describes?

   How does this shift underscore the poet's Biblical, Christian perspective?

3. What are the various functions of feasting in the Anglo-Saxon tradition? Which moments in the text reveal these different functions?

4. What are the functions of the various tales sung by the "scop" [bard] during the feasts? How do these stories from the past relate to the events going on in the present moment of the story?

5. In what forms does evil appear in Beowulf? Discuss both its external and internal forms.

* **Note:** The class need not have read literary criticism on the novel, play, or poem for the teacher to select a relevant quotation from an academic source. In this scenario, the academic source should be accessible to students, perhaps with some brief clarification by the teacher when the discussion questions are unveiled.

Here is an example of an EAC that a student might prepare before discussion (See "Prep" Work on p. 224).

Sample - Student Prep Work for *Beowulf* Discussion Quiz			Question 1
L1	L2	L3	L2-L1-L2 Sentence
Hrothgar builds "a great mead-hall meant to be a wonder to the world forever"	creation, architect, awe, sign of power, majesty, glory, eternal		A majestic creation, Heorot is "meant to be a wonder to the world forever," words that imply its glory will be eternal. This diction compares what the king creates to something only God can accomplish, a perfect "wonder."
"there he would dispense his God-given gifts to young and old"	generosity, absolute, blessing. Hrothgar recognizes source of wealth and power is God.	juxtaposition (1,2): the mead-hall's majesty juxt. w/ the blessings it offers the people	
Thesis Statement (Question 1): The *Beowulf* poet's initial description of Hrothgar's construction of Heorot establish a parallel between the majestic, benevolent king who rules the Danes and the Creator God who rules the heavens.			

Tips for Managing Discussion

While some students may already know how to participate in a verbal discussion, the goal of Discussion Quiz is for all students to learn how to do so. The teacher's role is to facilitate a setting in which productive discussion actually occurs. Below we have included suggestions for how to address situations that may arise during discussion.

- If no students raise their hands or volunteer to talk, the teacher can direct them to their prep work.

    "Raise your hand if you prepared for question 1. Okay, let's take turns sharing our answers to this question."

- If students are not listening and responding to each other's ideas, but taking turns monologuing (simply reading from their prep work charts), the teacher can require the class to keep talking about a particular page in the text before moving to a different one.

    "Jennifer, where in the book can we find the quotation you just mentioned? Everyone, turn there."

    "I want us to stay here for a few minutes. I want you to practice listening and responding to each other's ideas, not just reading off your own."

    "Remember, in a discussion you can make additional L2 for the L1 Jennifer is talking about, or you can introduce another L1 that appears on that same page. You may see something you did not already have in your prep work chart."

- If one or a group of students are monopolizing the discussion, the teacher can implement a limit.

    "We need to add a rule. From now on, students who have already spoken three times have to wait until we finish discussing this question. Before we read the next question, I'll allow final comments from students who still have something to add."

- If a more introverted student is struggling to speak up, it is easiest and least disruptive to intervene when the class has finished their discussion of one question and is about to transition to a new one:

    "Before we go further, I wanted to be sure we could hear from Ryan, Lisa, and Cesar. Did any of you prepare for this question?"

- If a student says, "Someone already said what I was going to say," here are some helpful ways the teacher can engage him or her:

    "What did you have written down (or typed) in your chart?"
    "Do you have any L1 in your chart that we haven't mentioned?"
    "Read to me the thesis statement you prepared in advance."

    Sometimes, a student is unprepared and needs to experience the consequences for it.

    However, some students will struggle with the Discussion Quiz because they have not internalized the movements involved in discussion. The teacher can use questioning to lead these students through that process.

Rubric

For *The Discussion Quiz, Literary News Conference, Tournament of Scholars*, and the *Quotation Game*, the teacher steps back and largely adopts the role of an observer and data collector. While students are engaged in playing the game, the teacher notes strengths and weaknesses, moments of insight and consistent issues. The teacher scoring rubric for these activities looks like this:

Student Name	# of responses	L1 Play Cites the text in responses	L1 Play Expands on the language of the text (diction, detail, imagery)	L2 Play Asserts associations	L3 Play Identifies relationships between associations (repetition, contrast, juxtaposition, shift)	Comments
Joe						
Estella						
Hester						
Ralph						

In the "Comments" section, the teacher can write down notable observations that students make during discussion, as well as recurrent issues (students not referencing L1, L1 and L2 not matching, L2 being too vague, etc.).

This scoresheet assists the teacher in tracking individual student performance, tallying points for team games (*Tournament of Scholars, Quotation Game*), and giving specific feedback at appropriate intervals during the activity (at the end of a round in the *Tournament of Scholars,* for example).

The Literary News Conference

Core Plays Involved

Learning Objectives

- Students will enrich their understanding of the literary work through role-playing, which allows consideration of the characters and events in the work from a different perspective.

- Students will strengthen their neural circuits related to the L1, L2, and L3 plays, and those related to creating word and logic glue in discussion.

Procedure

The News Conference activity occurs near the end of a unit, after the class has finished reading the literary work. The activity is particularly entertaining with a class of more extroverted students who embrace its role-playing aspects, but is designed to be effective even with more introverted students.

In this activity, the class is divided into two groups:

- student performers role-playing a character from the literary work, and
- student reporters interviewing them.

Directions for All Students

- Every student reporter is assigned a character or characters to interview; student performers are assigned a character to role-play.

- Locate as many passages concerning these character(s) as possible.

- Create an **Evidence-Association Chart** (see p. 132) for your character(s). At a minimum, you should have at least five L1-L2 pairings for each character.

- Follow any directions below that apply to you, depending on your role in the activity.

- Turn in all written preparation at the end of the period.[170]

Directions for Performers Role-Playing "Characters"

- Familiarize yourself with the list of questions provided by the teacher (see p. 238). How would you respond to them?

- Choose at least four of these questions and write down a response. Each of your responses must include at least one piece of evidence from the text that supports your answer.

Directions for Reporters

- Prepare at least four questions per character assigned to you.

- Half of these may be versions of the sample questions provided (see p. 238).

- Half of your questions must be ones you have developed on your own (see p. 239).

Make It Fun

Come up with your reporter/publication name. It can be silly, but must be appropriate (e.g., Jim Hrothguy, reporter for *The Daily Wulf*; Cassandra, reporter for *Bad News* magazine).

---

[170] The teacher assigns this written preparation for a homework or classwork grade; the goal is to make sure that students prepare for the activity in advance. If necessary, devote class time to preparing for the News Conference.

- Do *not* simply ask the character to summarize what happened in a particular scene: ask the character to explain what this moment in the text reveals about his or her personal traits, motives, beliefs, perspective, etc..
- After each question, write down how you anticipate the character might answer based on your understanding of him or her.

WHY IT WORKS

The Literary News Conference employs **inductive-predictive instruction** to enhance students' enjoyment of literature and motivate them to engage with it more attentively. The characters on the page are far more interesting and complex than our students first assume, and this fact becomes more evident to them in the role-playing performance, during which they must consider specific details and move inductively towards reasonable conclusions.

This activity also takes advantage of what we know about specific **neurotransmitters** in the brain (namely, dopamine, acetylcholine, and norepinephrine) that affect how students learn. Dopamine enhances focus, motivation, and memory (as one online blog puts it, "Dopamine = engagement + retention");[171] acetylcholine supports memory function;[172] and norepinephrine increases focus, supports memory, and enhances neuroplasticity, the characteristic of the brain that enables it to change, adapt, and become more efficient at specific tasks. The news conference stimulates the release of these chemicals as students interact with one another socially in a context involving play (dopamine), as they experience novelty and surprise in performance (acetylcholine), and as they ask and answer questions spontaneously under pressure (acetylcholine, norepinephrine). Harnessing these neurochemical factors enhances students' motivation to engage with a subject matter that some might otherwise find boring.

---

171   Rollins, accessed 10 August 2023.
172   Huang et al., 2022.

Holding the News Conference

Here are the steps for running this activity in class.

- Arrange seating for student performers at the front of the class; student reporters can sit at desks or tables or chairs facing them. Alternatively, performers sit in a small circle at the center of class, and reporters sit in a larger circle around them.
- A teacher calls on a student reporter to ask the first question.
- The reporter addresses his/her question to one of the performers.
- The performer has a few options:
    - Offer an answer to the reporter's question
    - Ask for clarification or context
    - Decline to answer the question*

    *Note: During the conference, a performer is allowed to decline up to two questions before losing points for doing so.
- After the performer offers an answer, the reporter has two options:
    - Ask a follow-up question (Scan the QR code at right to see a handout of the types of follow-up questions reporters may ask).
    - Thank the character for his/her response, and allow another reporter to ask a follow-up question
- Once any follow-up questions have been answered, the teacher calls on another reporter (or asks for volunteers) to ask the next question. Alternatively, the teacher can ask the student role-playing a character to call on a reporter who has a question for him or her.
    - Note: The teacher may decide to maintain the class' attention on a single character for a certain amount of time ("Who else has a question for Tom Buchanan?") or allow reporters to question characters at will, alternating between Tom, George, Jordan, Gatsby, Daisy, Nick, etc.
- The News Conference continues for as many rounds as the teacher decides.

Throughout the news conference, the teacher takes notes on student performance of the L1, L2, and L3 plays by filling out a scoresheet like the one found on p. 232. Although some students are asking questions and others are answering them, all students perform these same plays:

- L1 - referencing the text, and its language (diction, detail, imagery), directly

- L2 - asserting associations about the characters in the text

- L3 - identifying relationships between different associative ideas

The teacher grades student performance using the rubric on p. 241.

Access additional resources for the
Literary News Conference here.

Sample Questions Provided by the Teacher

Here is a list of questions that performers may study to prepare for the news conference. Reporters may select half of their questions directly from this list:

- Basing your answer on your actions in the story, what would you say motivates you in life; what desires lie behind the decisions you make?

- What do you regard as having been your principal strengths and weaknesses? Why?

- Who was most intimately involved in your fate? What was the nature of that involvement? What would you wish to say to the person now?

- What is an admirable or courageous action or decision for which you should be commended? Why?

- Were you ever a victim? When did you allow yourself to be taken advantage of? Explain how, why this happened.

- What was the nature of your power over others? How did you affect them?

- What moments of your life do you recall as having been most painful and distressing?

- How did you change because of your life's experiences?

- What does your story reveal about what it means to be a man (or woman)?

- What do your actions in the story reveal about the nature of love?

- Basing your answer on the decisions you make throughout the story, would you say that human beings are inherently good or bad? Or do your actions suggest that the reality is more complex?

- While you may not have explicitly voiced your religious beliefs in the story, what do your words or actions imply that your religiousbeliefs may be?

Sample Questions Created by Reporters

In addition to asking questions from the list provided them, reporters must also generate questions that refer to specific events in the story. Reporters should not ask characters to summarize what happened. They should prompt the character to explain what a particular moment in the story reveals about his or her personality, motives, beliefs, perspective, etc..

Below are several examples of such questions.

- "Hello Mr. Gargery, my name is Mick Jaggers, writing for *Pip's Post*. Given his unpleasant attitude and personality, can you explain why you hired Orlick in the first place? What does this action say about you as a person?"

- "Mr. Carraway, question from *American Archetypes* magazine: Who would you blame most for Gatsby's death, and why?"

- "Hello, Hero. I'm reporting for *Ado*, online blog for all things Shakespearean. Why do you forgive Claudio for what he did to you? Is it because of the way he repents, or does it have more to do with who you are as a woman?"

Preparing to Answer Questions Beforehand

All students (reporters and characters) write down anticipated answers to questions.

For student performers, doing so obviously prepares them to answer questions that will be asked during the news conference.

For student reporters, anticipating a character's answers to questions both demonstrates their thinking to the teacher and prepares them to ask follow-up questions. For instance, if the reporter's anticipated answer contains references to the text that the character does not mention, then the reporter may ask the character whether these details further support or contradict the character's stated answer.

Sample EAC & Prepared Answer to a Question

Character: Sydney Carton, Charles Dickens' *A Tale of Two Cities*

L1	L2
"I care for no man on earth, and no man on earth cares for me."	Bitter, alienated from the world (the reason why Carton drinks)
"Do you particularly like a man who resembles you?" he muttered, at his own image; "why should you particularly like a man who resembles you? There is nothing in you to like; you know that."	Embittered, ashamed of himself, feels contempt for himself
"Mr. Carton, who so long sat looking at the ceiling of the court, changed neither his place nor his attitude, even in this excitement. While his learned friend, Mr. Stryver, massing his papers before him, whispered with those who sat near, and from time to time glanced anxiously at the jury; while all the spectators moved more or less, and grouped themselves anew; while even my Lord himself arose from his seat, and slowly paced up and down his platform, not unattended by a suspicion in the minds of the audience that his state was feverish; this one man sat leaning back, with his torn gown half off him, his untidy wig put on just as it happened to light on his head after its removal, his hands in his pockets, and his eyes on the ceiling as they had been all day."	Carton feigns apathy for Darnay's circumstances

Q: Who was most intimately involved in your fate? How?

A: Charles Darnay is maybe the *most* intimately involved in my fate, because at the end of the novel, I trade places with him, giving him a future, a life, a world where he can live free from the terrors of the Revolution and be with Lucy. It's not just that we look alike – our resemblance gave me the opportunity to lay down my life for someone else. This shift in my character at the end of the novel marks a transformation, a redemption for me. Without Darnay, I (Carton) would have remained in my bitter, alienated state.

Rubric

	Reporter	Performer
A	• Frequently incorporates textual evidence when speaking. • Develops questions that reflect a sophisticated understanding of the text. • Makes frequent contributions to discussion. • Challenges the character to confront details with follow-up questions.	• Demonstrates a sophisticated understanding of the character being role-played. • Makes insightful comments in response to reporters' questions, both incorporating textual references and making reasonable inferences about the character's attitude, beliefs, etc..
B	• Demonstrates understanding of the plot, its main associative ideas, and the reasons why the characters act the way they do. • Makes consistent references to the text when speaking. • Asks characters some questions about their personal traits, motives, or perspective, but other questions may be merely plot-driven. • Attempts some follow-up questions that require the character to elaborate upon an answer or that reference additional details in the text.	• Performer demonstrates a solid understanding of the plot and its basic themes and reasons why characters act the way they do. • Could improve responses with additional associations (L2) and/or reference to the text (L1). • Makes reasonable responses to reporters' follow-up questions.
C	• Asks only basic plot questions or questions provided by the teacher. • Demonstrates occasional misunderstanding of the plot or the main associative ideas. • Participates infrequently.	• Answers occasionally without specific reference to the text. • At times is unable to respond to questions or follow-up questions.
D/F	• Not prepared to ask questions. • Does not reference the text directly, no quotations used. • Participates minimally, or does not participate.	• Is unable to answer several questions. • Does not reference the text directly, no quotations used. • Answers in a vague or illogical manner.

The Tournament of Scholars

Core Plays

Learning Objectives

- Students will identify important L1, logically pair L1 with L2, develop sophisticated L2, identify L3, and create modified L1 language.

- Students will practice verbal communication skills within small groups: presentation, organization, compromise, etc..

Procedure

In *The Tournament of Scholars*, teams (about three to four students per team) compete to determine which team can analyze and discuss the literary text most effectively. Taking place over several rounds (and approximately two to three class periods), the tournament allows the teacher to cover several key passages from the reading in an engaging atmosphere where students have an incentive to practice the core plays.

Before the tournament begins

- Organize the students into an even number of teams (usually four or six teams).

- At the beginning of the game, each team of students chooses its own passage (approximately 1 page of the text).

- The teacher can allow teams to find this passage on their own, perhaps designating a specific topic.

- Or the teacher provides them with a list of options, like the following list of passages from *The Odyssey* of Homer:

WHY IT WORKS

In the Tournament of Scholars, the training environment for students increases in complexity to simulate an actual reading and writing performance as closely as possible (see chapter 1, **"Look Like the Game"** and **"Scrimmage"**). Students receive a passage, read, annotate, develop thesis statements, draft paragraphs, orally present, and in discussion, delve deeper into the language of the passage to gain unclaimed points from other teams. The top performers in English internalize these behaviors and are able to do them on their own when tasked with writing an essay.

In addition to training for the game, this activity's structure permits the teacher to step back and observe, and intervene at the end of each round with actionable, timely, clear, and specific **feedback**. By providing feedback, then having students practice the plays again in another round of the game, the teacher creates a situation in which students can attempt to improve their performance and quickly receive additional guidance. The competitive nature of the activity, finally, incentivizes students' motivation to pay attention to and improve their performance. In other words, the tournament encourages **deliberate practice.**

We have seen this discussion game augment students' enjoyment and interest in English; one student, Matthew, explained that until he played the Tournament of Scholars, he had found reading boring. "I was pretty much just guessing on my Of Mice and Men and Odyssey quizzes. But the tournament showed me it could be interesting and fun to analyze things. Being on a team and going for the win made me read more carefully."

Passage #1: Odysseus deceives the Cyclops and blinds him (Book 9)

Passage #2: Odysseus' men encounter the Laistrygonians (Book 10)

Passage #3: Odysseus speaks with Agamemnon in the Underworld (Book 11)

Passage #4: Odysseus' companions decide to eat Helios' cattle (Book 12)

When selecting passages, the teacher can have teams submit their choices to a Google Form, or call them out. The teacher needs to make sure that no two teams have selected the same passage.

- After teams select a passage, teams work together to write an expository paragraph about their chosen passage. Each team gets to read its written analysis during that team's "rebuttal" round of the tournament. If desired, the teacher can require students to write their expository paragraph inside of the Paragraph Chart (see p. 140).

> **Variation**
>
> *Students develop a discussion question.* The teacher may decide to require groups to develop a **discussion question** about their chosen passage, too (see page 217-220 for types of questions that might be created).

Passage selection and paragraphing takes place on the day *before* the tournament rounds begin. During this class period, teams complete as much of a paragraph as they can.

- The game begins the next day, after this time of preparation.
- During the game, two teams at a time face off: in round 1, Team A vs. Team B; in round 2, Team C vs. Team D, and so on.

Sample Student Paragraph for Tournament of Scholars

Team: Nathan, Luke, and Kyle

Passage/Lines We Selected: *Odyssey* Book 9, lines 475-542

Our Question: What does the Cyclops episode reveal about Odysseus as a character?

Our Exposition:

In this passage, Odysseus' taunting of Polyphemus reveals his central **character flaw** as a hero, **his pride.** First, Homer suggests that Odysseus' taunting of Polyphemus was caused by the "great heart within" Odysseus and his injured pride (9.476). His heart is **torn over the loss** of his crewmates in the Cyclops' cave, and his **hubris** gets the better of him as he only continues to **endanger** his still living companions. Later, his **prideful taunts result in his downfall** when the Cyclops curses him: "Hear me, Poseidon who circle the earth, dark-haired. If truly I am your son, and you acknowledge yourself as my father, grant that Odysseus, sacker of cities, son of Laertes, who makes his home in Ithaca, may never reach that home" (9.528-536), making his homecoming much more **difficult.** Even though Odysseus believes he is **defending his honor,** this was **not worth the consequences,** because now, due to the curse, Odysseus will not return to Ithaca with any of his companions, nor will he return **peacefully,** for he will find "troubles in his household."[173]

---

173 In this sample, students' L1 is labeled in blue, L2 is bolded, and the topic strings inside the paragraph are underlined. We require students to label these plays in their writing; for more details, see "Labeling" on pp. 194-196.

How to Play a Round of the Tournament of Scholars

A tournament round follows these steps:

- To begin the first round, Team A will call out the passage they have chosen. The teacher may require students to develop a discussion question:

"We chose the passage on page __, where Odysseus' men encounter the Laistrygonians. Our question is: What does this passage reveal about the nature of evil?"

- Team B has **eight minutes** to read Team A's passage, discuss it amongst themselves, and deliver a verbal presentation about it to the class. It is up to Team B to decide how much time to devote to each of these tasks.

> **Tip: "Mind your time, Team B…"**
>
> If the class has never played a tournament before, teams may not understand that eight minutes is all the time they have for reading, annotating, and presenting.
>
> "Remember, when that timer goes off, your talking time is over. You have six minutes left. When do you want to start talking? At four minutes? At two minutes?"

- As Team B prepares to respond, all teams should be reading and annotating the passage, familiarizing themselves with the details in the text and making associations. Even Team A should use this time to add additional sentences to its rebuttal paragraph.

- When Team B signals that they are ready to talk, the teacher calls for quiet in the classroom. All other teams must be quiet and listen to Team B.

- Throughout the team's presentation, the teacher notes students' use of the L1, L2, and L3 plays (Use a form of the chart on p. 230) Teams that simply summarize the passage receive no points.

In the example below, all instances of L2 and L3 play are bolded; the L1 play (textual references) is highlighted in blue.

One student from Team B begins, "*In this passage where Odysseus meets the Laistrygonians, we noticed that Homer **repeats** the theme of **evil being deceptive**, **disguising its true intentions** from Odysseus' men. Like the suitors earlier in the book, like the Cyclops, the giants attempt to trap their victims. For example, when Odysseus' men arrive, the daughter of the Laistrygonian king is the first one they see, a girl drawing water, who welcomes them back to the palace. She appears **innocent** and **harmless** and also follows the laws of **hospitality** that the men are familiar with…*"

The other members of Team B add their own observations, as the team leads the class through the passage.

A second student might add, for example, *"After Odysseus' men **fall into this trap**, and enter the palace with the Laistrygonian girl, the violent death of one companion, whom the king "snatch[es] up" and "t[ears]" limb from limb for dinner, emphasizes the **barbarity** of these giants. The **cruel destruction** of the man's body and the king's **cannibalistic** devouring of him highlight a monstrous danger the men had failed to avoid."*

A third student: *"This moment also reveals a significant shift. The appearance of being in a **hospitable**, **civilized** place was a **deception**. It reminded me of how at the beginning of the Cyclops episode, Odysseus and his men also think they are dealing with a creature who, like them, respects the gods…but their flawed judgment has **deadly consequences**."*

The teacher awards points to Team B for their response, depending on the completeness of their answer, their knowledge and citation of textual evidence, and their understanding of larger thematic patterns in the work.

The teacher may deal out as many points as he or she sees fit, but it is important that the score be linked to students' performance of the L1, L2, and L3 plays. The teacher might, for example, award one point every time the team links a piece of evidence (L1) with logical associations (L2), or identifies a relationship emerging between associations (L3).

- After Team B's response, the members of Team A will have **two minutes** to provide its rebuttal.

  Rebuttal is an opportunity for the team that originally chose the passage to make comments heretofore unaddressed by their opponents (Team B). Here, Team A uses their own previously-written response, as well as any other ideas they might have developed. They should not repeat any comments that Team B has already made about their passage.

  The teacher awards points to Team A for the quality of their analysis in rebuttal.

- After this rebuttal, the other teams outside the pair-off (Teams C, D, E...) may each have **one minute** to add information that neither team addressed. The teacher awards the outside ring of teams points.

  > **Tip**
  >
  > Vary the order in which outside teams answer, to avoid one team gaining an advantage from always going first.

- At the end of the round, the teacher steps in to provide feedback by

  - highlighting the important L1, L2, and L3 that different teams mentioned,

  - asking questions about areas of the passage that no team addressed, and

  - providing guidance on how to improve performance (such as the quality of one's L2-L1 pairings).

  The teacher might mention, for example, that Team B's presentation (on page 247) only directly quoted the text twice; other comments made by the team involved paraphrase or general connections to other scenes. This is a problem with the **L1 play**. "Can you increase the quantity of L1 when you speak? I want you to show us more of what's on the page."

Moving on to the next round(s)

- Once the outside teams have contributed, Team B now presents its question to Team A (repeat steps 1 through 5). After repeating the above steps, round 1 of the tournament is over. Round 2 (Teams C and D) can begin, following the above process.

- The class plays the game until all passages have been discussed.

Awards

The teacher may decide to award extra credit to the winning team, the top two teams, etc. An award might also be given to individual students who distinguished themselves in their performance. Here is an example of the "Winner's Pass" for tournament victors:

WINNER'S PASS

Entitles you to one of the following:

- Add 15% to a quiz or homework grade
- Cancel a quiz or homework grade
- Turn in an essay two days late w/o penalty

NAME: _____

REASON FOR AWARD: _____

DATE: _____

Hand in your completed pass (with reward circled) to the teacher. This pass is only valid during the semester it is awarded.

The Quotation Game

Core Plays

Learning Objectives

- Students will participate in activities designed to strengthen the essential reading plays: L1, L2, L3, modified L1, etc..
- Students will identify diction, imagery, detail, language, syntax, archetype, allusion, repetition, and other literary devices, and explain how these elements connect with developing themes in the literary work.
- Students will practice verbal communication and listening skills in discussion and small-group work.

Procedure

Setting it up: Gather a collection of important quotations (1-2 sentences in length) from the literary text.

- An apt quotation for the game does one or more of the following: reveals something important about a character, shows a character in an unexpected or otherwise unusual light, places our focus on a particular observation or description by the narrator.
- Quotations chosen should, for the most part, be relatively the same length and possess a similar degree of complexity or difficulty.

WHY IT WORKS

The Quotation Game is shaped by the concept of **chunking,** which refers to the action of breaking down complex tasks into manageable parts. This technique, essential for attaining expert performance, responds to the brain's ability to manage only a finite number of learning tasks at a time. Researchers have found that we can take in only three to seven chunks of information before we overload and begin to miss new incoming data.[174] Teachers need to avoid "too much content, too fast," because it "is unlikely to get processed correctly and saved accurately."[175] In other words, rather than seeking to cover everything in a given chapter, English teachers must focus on leading students to meaningfully interact with small selections from the text as they practice the plays.

In this game, students examine not an entire novel, an entire chapter, but a few key quotations (1-2 sentences each). By chunking the reading, paring down what students are asked to analyze, the game narrows the scope but raises the intensity. Students discover that even a single word might matter, suggesting an association that subtly changes the logical interpretation. Like the *Tournament of Scholars*, this activity uses competition to incentivize the reading plays; in the process, it establishes **clarity** and **behavioral relevance,** showing students "the why" behind effective close-reading strategies.

Preparing to play: After the list of quotations has been prepared, divide the class into teams (3-4 students per team).

- Each team selects a quotation from the list.
- Teams then have ten minutes to prepare their discussion of the quotation.
- After preparation time is over, the teacher decides which team will

---

174   Linden et al., 2003; Jensen, 2005.
175   Schacter, Guerin, & Jacques, 2011; Paas, & Ayres, 2014.

go first: ask for volunteers, call on a team at random, draw a slip of paper out of a jar, roll a die, or spin a wheel of team names.

Playing the game: Once the class has prepared to play, the game begins.

- The first team to play has **two minutes** to give a verbal presentation of their quotation. They must cover, as completely as possible, the following areas:

    - **L1:** Who is the speaker? What is occurring at this point? What are the most significant diction, detail, or imagery that may be observed in the quotation?
    - **L2:** What is significant about this passage? Does it reveal something about character? theme? conflict? Elaborate.
    - **L3:** Does it mark a repetition, contrast, shift? Elaborate.

    The team is not required to present the above elements separately; rather, they are elements that the teacher wants to hear students refer to at some point during the presentation.

    All members of the team must speak during their presentation. Teams will be penalized for not meeting this requirement.

    All other teams must listen carefully during the presentation (The teacher will deduct points from teams for talking and other disruptions).

- After one team presents, the remaining teams each have **one minute** to make additional comments about the passage. Teams will lose points if they merely repeat comments already made by another team.

- After each listening team has had an opportunity to respond extemporaneously, the teacher provides feedback on the class' comments about the quotation.

- Then, the next presenting team begins with its quotation.

- When all presenting teams have had their turns and the extemporaneous comments have taken place, the Quotation Game is over.

- The game can go on for as many rounds as the teacher decides (e.g., three times during the unit, once every few chapters, etc.).

Sample Quotation Game Round: *The Great Gatsby*

Here is a list of five quotations from the first chapter of *The Great Gatsby*:

1. "When I came back from the East last autumn I felt that I wanted the world to be in uniform and at a sort of moral attention forever; I wanted no more riotous excursions with privileged glimpses into the human heart."

2. "If personality is an unbroken series of successful gestures, then there was something gorgeous about [Gatsby], some heightened sensitivity to the promises of life, as if he were related to one of those intricate machines that register earthquakes ten thousand miles away."

3. "No—Gatsby turned out all right at the end; it is what preyed on Gatsby, what foul dust floated in the wake of his dreams that temporarily closed out my interest in the abortive sorrows and short-winded elations of men."

4. "The [house] on my right was a colossal affair by any standard—it was a factual imitation of some Hotel de Ville in Normandy, with a tower on one side, spanking new under a thin beard of raw ivy, and a marble swimming pool, and more than forty acres of lawn and garden. It was Gatsby's mansion."

5. "Her husband [Tom], among various physical accomplishments, had been one of the most powerful ends that ever played football at New Haven—a national figure in a way, one of those men who reach such an acute limited excellence at twenty-one that everything afterward savors of anti-climax."

The team that chose Quotation #3 volunteers to go first. They present to the class:

> **Student 1**: So, the speaker in our quotation is Nick, the narrator, and it comes from the beginning of the chapter where he first mentions Gatsby. In this quote, Nick reveals his personal feelings about Gatsby as a person he can approve of despite his flaws,

saying, "Gatsby turned out all right in the end." The words "all right in the end" tell us of a shift in Nick's thoughts on Gatsby, that it is only at the end of this story that Nick is able to make this favorable judgment.

Student 2: The second part of the quotation reveals that Nick's troubling view of New York comes from "what preyed on Gatsby," which he describes as a "foul dust" that "float[s] in the wake of [Gatsby's] dreams." This sinister image carries connotations of death. It conveys to the reader that Gatsby's hopes or ambitions are snuffed out or covered by something dark, evil, or corrupt.

Student 3: This "foul dust" is the cause of Nick's dreadful perspective, and because of what happens to Gatsby, he now views life bleakly, filled with "abortive sorrows" and "short-winded elations," depressing diction that cast the world as fundamentally tragic.

The teacher awards points to this team depending upon the quality of their presentation:

- Did the team clearly identify the speaker and the context of their quotation (L1)?

- Did the team draw the class' attention to specific diction, detail, and imagery within the quotation (L1)?

- Did the team clearly present the quotation's significance, stating logical, precise associations (L2)?

- Did they identify any relationships of repetition, contrast, juxtaposition, or shift within the passage (L3)?

After the team presents this quotation, other teams are allowed to add comments:

Student from Team B: "I would also like to point out that in the last part of the quotation, the writer uses the diction of "abortive" to suggest that men's sorrows are in vain. They do not have purpose or meaning. This suggests a world where suffering does not cause individuals or those around them to change for the better."

Student from Team C: "This passage also shows how Nick views Gatsby in a positive way, even after everything that happens in the book." **(Note: The teacher would take points away from this team – they merely repeated what the presenting team said.)**

Student from Team D: "They also did not mention how the quotation points to the tragic world because mens' joys are "Short-winded elations" and do not last."

Student from Team E: "Everything's already been said."

In each round of the game, the teacher varies the order in which other teams get to speak, in order to avoid giving one team a disadvantage for always speaking last. In the next round of this game, for instance, Team E might be the first group with the chance to make additional comments.

After all teams have had a chance to speak, the round is over. At this moment, the teacher gives students feedback on their participation in the round (See our suggestions on the next page).

After the teacher provides feedback, the game then moves on to another team's quotation, until all quotations have been discussed.

Giving Feedback During the Quotation Game

✓ **Highlight moments of ideal close-reading, and have students explain the process behind these moments:**

> "I heard several good associations during the round, particularly Mr. Asche's comment about Daisy Buchanan being an example of how in the world of tragedy, feminine figures tend to be victimized by masculine ones. Can anyone tell me which details in the passage most clearly suggest that Daisy is a victim?"

✓ **Use questioning to guide students to refine vague, imprecise, or illogical L2:**

> "Alicia's team claimed that it was tragic and depressing that "Tom was God knows where" when his daughter was born. While accurate, the L2 of "tragic" and "depressing" could be more specific. *Why* is it depressing that Tom abandoned his wife and daughter in this situation? What does it reveal about his attitude towards them?"

✓ **Direct the class' attention to neglected L1:**

> "I noticed that no teams made any comments about the fact that when Daisy finishes telling her story, Nick tells us that "in a moment she looked at [him] with an absolute smirk on her lovely face, as if she had asserted her membership in a rather distinguished secret society to which she and Tom belonged." This is something important that we should not have skipped over. Who can explain what this part of the quotation is saying?"

✘ **Do not just say that a student's answer is wrong.**

"That's not really a good interpretation."

✘ **Do not just tell students that they need to do better (without saying how).**

"I think we need to try to go a little deeper with the quotation in the next round."

✘ **Do not give students the answer.**

"Well, all teams mentioned that Daisy and Tom's marriage is tragic, but no one pointed out the irony in the passage. Do you see where it says that Daisy smirks at Nick after finishing her story? The irony here is that Daisy not only suffers in her marriage to Tom, but that she enjoys the pity others show her when they learn of his infidelity."

The Revision Chart

Core Plays

Learning Objectives

- Students will strengthen memory networks related to the core plays.
- Students will examine feedback more closely.
- Students will identify plays they have not yet mastered.
- Students will verbalize (define) and practice these plays in revision.
- Students will set goals for future improvement.

WHY IT WORKS

The *Revision Chart* is an activity that stimulates **"metacognitive activity"** in our students, as they become aware of their own knowledge and thought processes. Actively reflecting on a learning task to evaluate performance is the skill that enables top performers to achieve, but is one that many students in English class lack. The chart facilitates its practice, **chunking** (breaking down) the thought process behind looking at one's own writing and trying to improve it. Training this skill is vital, for students who possess it demonstrate higher achievement than students who lack metacognitive awareness.[176]

---

[176] Clements, 2016; Lin et al., 2007; McCutchen, 2006; Sadler & Graham, 2007; Harris, S. 2010; Karlen, 2017; Graham & Harrison, 2000; Wang, et.al 1990.

Procedure

To complete this activity with students, two things are required.

- First, students must be able to look through their past written work and quickly identify the plays that they have not mastered. To do so, they use the **scoring guide** that we give them with each graded essay. On this rubric, we evaluate their performance of each writing play. There are four levels of performance specified on the scoring guide: Insufficient, Progressing, Mastery, and Distinctive:

Four Levels of Performance (see the Scoring Guide on p. 272)

Distinctive (A, 90-100)	Strategic and sophisticated application of the play.
Mastery (B, 80-89)	Application of the play that is not merely a mechanical implementation but reasonable, consistent, and effectively linked to the overall argument.
Progressing (C, 70-79)	Merely mechanical demonstration of a play, occasional absence or ineffective use of the play in advancing the larger argument.
Insufficient (D/F, <70)	No demonstrated attempts to perform the play.

- Second, students must be able to see examples of performance at each of these levels, in order to guide their revision efforts. In our classrooms, we provide students with **mastery samples** for each writing play (see pp. 272-283). These samples are tailored to the course, just beyond students' current level of development. The samples provided to a junior AP Literature course would not, therefore, be the same ones given to a freshman English 1 class.

The Revision Chart activity requires students to identify the plays that they performed at a "Progressing" or "Insufficient" level in their past writing.

Using the provided mastery samples as a guide, students find sentences in their essays that exemplify these lower levels of performance, and attempt to revise them.

The teacher has a few options regarding the scope of this activity:

- **Students complete a revision chart for a single essay, focusing on their performance on this one assignment.** This option is best for students who are beginning to learn the plays: the teacher will want to narrow the scope of the activity to help students learn how to identify areas in their paper where they have not executed the plays correctly. Looking at a single essay facilitates setting goals for performance on an upcoming essay.

- **Students complete a revision chart that tracks their performance of the plays on *multiple* essay assignments.** This option is, naturally, easier to do at the end of the semester or school year. In this context, students can examine the trends across multiple assignments to gain a new perspective on their performance. "If you look back at your fall semester essays, what are the trends that you notice on your scoring guide sheets? For which plays do you typically receive a low score?" Doing the activity this way gives students the opportunity to think about how they have developed over the course of several units, and set goals for the future (the next semester, next school year).

The chart may be completed in class or assigned for homework.

Directions for students

- In column 1, identify the particular essay assignment(s) you are examining.

- In column 2, list the play(s) for which you received a score of "Progressing" or "Insufficient." These plays are the areas that most require your attention and effort to improve.

- In column 3, define each of these plays in your own words.[177]

- In column 4, copy a sentence from the original essay that exemplifies "progressing" or "insufficient" performance.

---

[177] Students who do not understand the writing plays will naturally provide imperfect definitions for them. For this reason, it is appropriate for the teacher to provide a key for students to check against their own definitions. See the "Mastery Samples" section of the Appendix.

- In column 5, revise this sentence, aiming for mastery.
- After you have completed one entry in the chart for every "progressing" and "insufficient" play, complete a brief reflection on your writing progress in the final box of the chart.
- When you have completed the chart, turn it in to the teacher with your original essay draft(s) attached.
- See a sample completed chart on the next page.

Sample Revision Chart

Essay Assignment	Play scored "Progressing" or "Insufficient"	Definition of the Play	Original	Revised
Infernal Comedy	Topic Sentence	The topic sentence must contain L2.	TS: The main character, Oliver, is wearing grey clothes, just like the other kids in the workhouse.	TS: The main character, Oliver, **suffers dehumanization** within the workhouse.
Infernal Comedy	Topic Strings	Put L2 at the beginning of my sentences – these L2 must link to the ones in the TS.	TS: In the film Oliver, the main character Oliver is wearing grey clothes, just like the other kids. <u>During the children's song, they sing</u> "Food, glorious food" …	TS: The main character, Oliver, suffers dehumanization within the workhouse. <u>The children's song reveals their</u> **desperate need** for "food, glorious food" …
Infernal Comedy	L2 to the right	Put L2 after the L1 that is very specific to it – I cannot use this L2 for any other evidence.	During the children's song, they sing "Food, glorious food" while the wealthy governors enjoy a feast.	The children's song reveals their desperate need for "Food, glorious food" while the wealthy governors enjoy a feast, **an ironic contrast between destitution and gluttony.**

Reflection: In a few sentences, comment on how your understanding of the plays is developing. What did you learn about the plays through this exercise? Which plays do you want to focus on improving on the next essay assignment?

I got Progressing for my **Topic Sentence** because I think I don't always realize when I'm putting L1 in this sentence. This chart helped show me the difference between a TS without L2 and one that has L2. On the next paper, I want to try to earn Mastery for this play.

Sometimes I'm rushing to get my thoughts out on paper and so I forget to put associations in my **topic strings.** On the next essay, I could list out associations that I want to use in my topic strings before I start writing the paragraph.

Variation: Using a Google Form for the Revision Chart

Should the teacher wish to modify the activity to create more opportunities for direct, immediate feedback, a Google Form is a helpful tool to accomplish this.

In this format, students submit individual chart entries through the Google Form. This allows the teacher to see all students' work at once, highlight ideal examples, and identify gaps in the class' understanding of the plays.

It also allows the teacher to walk the class through the columns of the chart step-by-step, if desired. With each submission to the Google Form, students slowly move from simply identifying a "progressing" play from their scored essay and defining it (first response) to finding an example sentence inside the essay (second response), then finally to revising this sentence (third response), with the teacher able to provide guidance at each step in the process.

For this variation to work, make sure to post the Google Form responses spreadsheet where students can access it. Sharing the spreadsheet allows them to copy and paste their work from a previous response back into the Google Form to complete additional steps.

Sample Google Form

Name:

Essay Assignment:

Play scored "Progressing" or "Insufficient":

Definition of the play:
[What is the play? How do you execute it?]

Original Sentence:
[A sentence from your paper that is an example of progressing/insufficient performance of the play]

Revised Sentence:
[A revised version of your original sentence above]

- First, the teacher creates a Form like the sample on the previous page.
- In the first round of the activity, students submit a response in which they identify one play that received a progressing or insufficient score, and they define this play in their own words.

"For your first response, I want you to tell me one of the plays that received a 'progressing' or 'insufficient' score, and then I want you to define this play in your own words. What do you have to do to execute this play? Note: You do not have to complete the sentence boxes in the form yet."

- After looking over student responses, the teacher provides feedback: Did students correctly define the plays they referenced? Do any definitions require further clarification?

"Okay, it looks like a lot of students struggled with the Topic String play. But reading some of these definitions, I think it would be helpful for us to talk about what 'mastery' performance looks like."

- The teacher then asks students to submit another response to the Form, in which they also provide an example sentence for one of their "progressing" or "insufficient" plays (This step is akin to completing the fourth column of the chart on page 262). After this round, the teacher stops the activity to further guide students: Are the sentences that students provided in fact good examples of progressing or insufficient performance?
- In the next round, students attempt to revise the original sentence for the particular play. Teacher feedback focuses on highlighting the sentences that have now achieved mastery of a given play, or guiding students to see the flaws in their revision attempts.

"I see that you tried to add L2 to the right of that quotation, Garrett. Can you tell me which words in the quotation gave you these L2?"

"Good, Adam: I'm now seeing L2 in that topic string that matches the L2 in your Topic Sentence."

PUTTING THE PLAYS TOGETHER

APPENDIX

KEEPING THE PLAYBOOK CLOSE—BOOKMARKS FOR STUDENTS

Students should have the playbook cues with them at all times. One way to do this is to print them off in "bookmark" form, so that all students can keep the plays close at hand inside the book they are reading. On the next few pages, we have reproduced "The Reading Plays" and "The Writing Plays" charts. Each appears in two columns so that it may be printed off and laminated to create a bookmark—the left column indicating the front of the bookmark and the right indicating the back.

First, for "The Reading Plays," we list the basic plays on the front of the bookmark—level one (L1), level two (L2), and level three (L3)— basic language that directs specific student action. The backside of the bookmark contains a list, which can be modified for your audience, of potential associative words. At the bottom of the back side is a writing sample that students can imitate; again, you may adapt this sample to the skill level of your students, selecting a sample that reaches just beyond development.

"The Writing Plays" chart includes the remaining cues/plays for writing. You may adapt this to your situation, but the basic formula remains – keep the cues simple and make sure the corresponding action is clear.

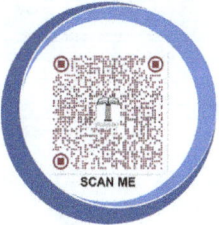

Scan the QR Code if you would like to print playbook bookmarks for your students.

The Reading Plays

Front of the bookmark | Back of the bookmark

The Reading Plays

Level One [L1]

Identify the **evidence** observed by you, the reader.

- Details: What's the setting? Who are the characters? What is the situation?
- Diction: What types of words are used or repeated?
- Imagery: How is the image created? What are its parts? What senses are provoked?

Level Two [L2]

Identify the conceptual **associations** [ideas, qualities, conditions] that emerge from the details, diction, and imagery of the literary work you are reading.

Examples of concepts that might be associated with pieces of evidence include, but are certainly not limited to, the following:

- Fear. Excitement. Joy. Love. Disdain.
- Violence. Chaos. Control. Order. Arrogance.
- Submission. Humility. Confidence. Authority. Wisdom.
- Confinement. Freedom. Tyranny. Benevolence. Refinement.
- Skepticism. Faith. Greed. Penury. Parsimony.

Level Three [L3]

Identify the **relationships** among the associations linked to details, diction, and imagery in the text.

- Repetition [similarity, recurrence, echo, parallelism]
- Contrast [difference, incongruity, opposition, tension]
- Juxtaposition [proximity, adjacency]
- Shift [change, turn, transformation].

Association Words

Unfriendliness
boorish, caustic, disparaging, derisive, scornful, insolent, insulting, impudent, belittling, contemptuous, scolding, spiteful, envious

Comedy
Facetious, ironic, satiric, amused, mocking, sarcastic, humorous, hilarious, uproarious.

Animation
energetic, vigorous, ardent, passionate, rapturous, ecstatic, feverish, inspired, exalted, hasty, brisk, hopeful, euphoric, exuberant.

Apathy
inert, sluggish, languid, dispassionate, colorless, indifferent, stoical, resigned, defeated, helpless, hopeless, monotonous, vacant, feeble, blasé

Pain
worried, uneasy, troubled, disappointed, vexed, annoyed, bored, disgusted, miserable, sorrowful

Pleasure
peaceful, satisfied, contented, happy, cheerful, jubilant, playful, elated, joyful

Self-control
calm, quiet, solemn, serene, simple, mild, gentle, temperate, imperturbable, nonchalant, cool, wary, cautious, confident, laconic, stern, remote.

Sample — Blending L1, L2, L3

In *The Great Gatsby*, the **bleak** details of Wilson's auto shop, both "unprosperous and bare," reflect the **hapless condition** of its proprietor, a financial **prosperity absent and barren**. Even the **faint hope of success**—"the dust-covered wreck of a Ford"—remains **elusive, for it almost cowers from sight**, merely "crouched in a dim corner," the **repetition** of "dust" and "dim" further emphasizing the **failed, ruined, and spoiled ambitions** of Wilson. In fact, these **spoiled aspirations shroud** Wilson, who wipes "his hands on a piece of waste," a gesture that underscores the **futility of his efforts**.

The Writing Plays

Front of the bookmark

The Writing Plays

Quantity of Associations (L2)

Highlight the number of associations you have in your sentence, paragraph, or paper. Can you add?

Do you remember that the **major parts of speech** can be associative? **Nouns** [tyrant]; **verbs** [guide, manipulate]; **adjectives** [supercilious, benevolent]; **adverbs** [furtively, graciously]. Do your sentences contain this variety?

Voice strengthens when the quantity of associations increases in sentences.

Quality of Associations (L2)

Examine the quality of your associative diction: do you say "mean" or "bad" when "malevolent" or "tyrannical" is more precise?

Voice strengthens when the quality and precision of your associative voice increases.

Lower quality: In fact, these **bad ideas take over** Wilson, who wipes "his hands on a piece of waste," a movement that says his efforts are not worth it and even the word "waste" shows sorrow.

Higher quality: In fact, these **spoiled aspirations shroud** Wilson, who wipes "his hands on a piece of waste," a gesture that both underscores the **futility of his efforts** and functions, through the selection of the word "waste," **metaphorically to suggest a life of despair.**

Syntax: L2-L1-L2

Do your associations appear at the beginning and ends of sentences?

Ex: Even the **faint hope of success**—"the dust-covered wreck of a Ford"—remains **elusive, for it almost cowers** from sight, merely "crouched in a dim corner," the **repetition** of "dust" and "dim" further emphasizing the **failed, ruined, and spoiled ambitions** of Wilson.

Back of the bookmark

Topic Strings

Does the diction to the left of the midpoint of each sentence contain associative diction linked to that in the topic sentence?

Do you vary the content of what's in your strings? 1) Exact repetition of words from the topic sentence, 2) synonyms, 3) pronoun references, 4) varied syntax?

Do you need to increase the quality and quantity of your associations inside the topic string?

Logic of L2-L1 Pairings

Inside the sentence, does the juxtaposition of your association and the evidence from the text make sense? Do you have L2 without evidence?

Ex. George lacks **monetary resources, a lower class man,** one "spiritless," "anemic," "damp." [L2 & L1 don't quite match] **vs.** George's **moribund** description as a man "spiritless," "anemic," and "damp," lacking **vitality** [L2 matches with L1]

Modified L1 Language

Ex. tyrannical **diction;** the **imagery** of entrapment; deceptive **details.** L2 + L1 word or L1 word + L2

To the Right

Examine L2 to the right of quoted material in your sentences; is the analysis so precise that you cannot move the comment to another piece of evidence in your paragraph?

Ex. Even the **faint hope of success**—"the dust-covered wreck of a Ford"—remains **elusive, for it almost cowers** from sight, merely "crouched in a dim corner," the **repetition** of "dust" and "dim" further emphasizing the **failed, ruined, and spoiled ambitions** of Wilson.

THE SCORING GUIDE & MASTERY HANDOUT

Below is the scoring guide that we attach to each student's essay. The scoring guide lists each play and allows the teacher to indicate the student's level of achievement—distinctive, mastery, progressing, insufficient.

The sample Mastery Handout lists examples for each play on the scoring guide. We've given you an example of what the entries for a thesis statement and topic strings might look like. What course teachers need to do is agree on the samples for each level of achievement. The samples for a distinctive thesis, for instance, will look different in English 1, Honors English 2, and AP Lit. Only the course teacher[s] can determine the appropriate samples for the intended audience.

SCORING GUIDE — THE PLAYS

Insufficient: [0-65] the student has not demonstrated knowledge of the plays

Progressing: **[70-79]** merely mechanical demonstration of the plays, occasional presence, ineffective, or absent in advancing the larger argument.

Mastery: **[80-89]** An application of the plays that is not merely a mechanical implementation but reasonable, consistent, and effectively linked to the overall argument.

Distinctive: **[90-100]** Strategic and sophisticated application of the plays.

— **See Mastery Samples handout and the Reading & Writing Plays Bookmarks for Examples of Mastery and Distinction.**

Thesis

— **insufficient / progressing / mastery / distinctive**

Topic Sentences

— **insufficient / progressing / mastery / distinctive**

Paragraphing

L1 — quantity & quality

— **insufficient / progressing / mastery / distinctive**

L2 — quantity & quality

— **insufficient / progressing / mastery / distinctive**

L2-L1 pairings

— **insufficient / progressing / mastery / distinctive**

Topic strings w/ L2

— **insufficient / progressing / mastery / distinctive**

To the Right

— **insufficient / progressing / mastery / distinctive**

Syntax: L2-L1-L2

— **insufficient / progressing / mastery / distinctive**

Word & Logic glue

— **insufficient / progressing / mastery / distinctive**

Organization of chunks: time, place, idea

— **insufficient / progressing / mastery / distinctive**

L3

— **insufficient / progressing / mastery / distinctive**

Modified L1

— **insufficient / progressing / mastery / distinctive**

MASTERY HANDOUT— SAMPLES

We provide students with mastery samples for each of the plays. These models help them visualize the target performance, recognizing the differences between mere mechanical execution of a given play and its effective application. Below are mastery samples for two writing plays, the Thesis Statement and Topic Sentence.

Thesis Statement

Distinctive: The apt, sophisticated diction of the thesis statement produces a precise, insightful claim.

> In "Sonnet 18," in a tone of **consummate assurance,** the speaker **exults** in the **power of verse to lend immortality** to beautiful youth, a **power that overcomes time's destructive force.**

Mastery: The L2 present in the thesis statement articulates an interpretive point of view, but the writer's claim requires revision for precision and clarity.

> In Shakespeare's Sonnet, "Sonnet 18," the speaker **tenderly** illustrates his beloved's **beauty as greater than a force of nature**.

Progressing: The quantity and quality of L2 in the thesis statement decrease; the thesis statement begins to drift towards summary of the literary text.

> In sonnet 18, the author expresses his **admiration** for his lover and how their **love does not fade.**

Insufficient: The thesis statement does not contain L2.

> In sonnet 18, Shakespeare says that the person's beauty is better than the beauty of summer.

Topic Sentences

Distinctive: Topic Sentences contains precise L2 that articulate an aspect of the thesis statement; clear coherence exists between thesis and topic sentences.

> Thesis: Macbeth, the commanding war hero, **follows ambition over reason**, a choice that actually **leads him toward demise rather than power**; Banquo, however, **depends more on reason** and acts as a **noble, but cautious skeptic**.

- Topic Sentence #1: Macbeth **asserts his power over others**, but his military might, **ironically, proves powerless** to withstand the witches' guile.
- Topic Sentence #2: Banquo, unlike Macbeth, **depends upon reason**, which he displays through his **repeated skepticism,** still **remaining cautious** after Macbeth becomes the thane of Cawdor.

Mastery: Topic sentences contain convincing L2 but require revision, either to make the interpretive point of view more precise or to strengthen coherence between thesis and topic sentences.

> Thesis: Macbeth, the commanding war hero, **follows ambition over reason**, a choice that actually **leads him toward demise rather than power**; Banquo, however, **depends more on reason** and acts as a **noble, but cautious skeptic**.
> - Topic Sentence #1: First, Macbeth **asserts his power over others**.
> - Topic Sentence #2: Banquo, unlike Macbeth, **depends upon reason**.

Progressing: L2 in topic sentences is too vague or general; the topic is too broad; the topic sentences contain evidence that should appear inside the paragraph; the link between topic sentence(s) and thesis statement is unclear.

> Thesis: Macbeth, the commanding war hero, **follows ambition over reason**, a choice that actually **leads him toward demise rather than power**; Banquo, however, **depends more on reason** and acts as a **noble, but cautious skeptic**.
> - Topic Sentence #1: First, Macbeth chooses to trust the witches in order to **gain power**, which is a **mistake**.
> - Topic Sentence #2: Banquo is a **noble hero** who makes choices totally different from Macbeth.

Insufficient: Topic sentence(s) absent; the student has not attempted to begin paragraph(s) with a claim containing L2.

> Thesis: Macbeth, the commanding war hero, **follows ambition over reason**, a choice that actually **leads him toward demise rather than power**; Banquo, however, **depends more on reason** and acts as a

noble, but cautious skeptic.

- Topic Sentence #1: First, Macbeth trusts the witches when he says, "This supernatural soliciting cannot be ill."
- Topic Sentence #2: (The second paragraph of the essay is missing.)

LI — Quantity & Quality

Distinctive: The writer incorporates several pieces of evidence from the text that support the topic sentence; the selection of evidence reveals an emerging sophistication in the writer's attention to detail.

Topic Sentence: George and Myrtle Wilson's marriage reflects the **darkness of the tragic abyss**, a relationship **trapped in sin**.

- Myrtle says that she "goes to see her sister in New York" whenever she leaves the garage to be with Tom.
- Myrtle tells her friends, "I married him because I thought he was a gentleman,... but he [isn't] fit to lick my shoe."
- Tom lies to Myrtle, saying that he and Daisy cannot be divorced because Daisy "is a Catholic."
- Myrtle is hit and killed by Gatsby's car, and mingles her "dark blood" with the "dust."
- George says, "You may fool me, but you can't fool God!"
- George kills Gatsby, then himself, the "shots" creating a "holocaust."
- George leaves life "a man deranged by grief."

Mastery: The writer incorporates reasonable examples from the text to support the topic sentence, though additional textual support would strengthen the argument.

Topic Sentence: George and Myrtle Wilson's marriage reflects the **darkness of the tragic abyss**, a relationship **trapped in sin**.

- Myrtle says, "I married him because I thought he was a gentleman,... but he [isn't] fit to lick my shoe."
- George says, "You may fool me, but you can't fool God!"
- George kills Gatsby, then himself, the "shots" creating a "holocaust."

Progressing: The writer needs to increase the quantity and quality of evidence so that the reader can see sufficient details from the text that support the topic sentence. Some evidence may not be linked to the topic sentence ideas. In some cases, the writer may have misunderstood the meaning of the text.

> Topic Sentence: George and Myrtle Wilson's marriage reflects the **darkness of the tragic abyss**, a relationship **trapped in sin**.
>
> - Myrtle says, "I married him because I thought he was a gentleman,... but he [isn't] fit to lick my shoe."
> - George is "spiritless" and "anemic," and he "wip[es] his hands on a piece of waste."
> - George kills Gatsby, then himself, the "shots" creating a "holocaust."

Insufficient: The writer uses minimal textual evidence to support claims; the evidence cited does not logically link with the writer's topic sentences, and indicates either a lack of reading or serious issues with comprehension.

> Topic Sentence: George and Myrtle Wilson's marriage reflects the **darkness of the tragic abyss**, a relationship **trapped in sin**.
>
> - George is "spiritless" and "anemic," and he "wip[es] his hands on a piece of waste."
> - George runs over Myrtle with the "death car."

L2 — Quantity & Quality

Distinctive: Sentences contain a high quantity of L2, with apt, sophisticated associations that link closely to the quoted L1.

> TS: Through numerous character descriptions, Homer utilizes armor to portray **the aristeia of a warrior**, **a core heroic value** that displays the **superior prowess** and **skill of the individual**. For instance, Homer, implying a sense of **royalty** and **supremacy**, describes Hector's armor as "the flashing bronze, the horsehair crest, the great ridge of the helmet nodding, bristling terror" (6.560-561). The **magnificence** of his gear, especially the shining metal and the imperial crest, emphasize Hector's **superiority** as an **heir to the throne worthy of such valuable material**. Not only does his armor imply his **royalty**, but it

also **strikes fear into his enemies** because it provides Hector with **seemingly insurmountable power and skill**.

TS: The speaker in the poem from Songs of Innocence responds to the **bleakness of child labor** by producing **hopeful images of heaven and redemption**. Opening with a **desolate image of a helpless child** whose "father sold [him]" (2), Blake's poem "The Chimney Sweeper" establishes the **malevolent** nature of life as a chimney sweeper, magnified in **bleakness** by the **failure of the father to protect and provide for his child**. This **abandoned** child, destined to the **squalid fate** of sleeping "in soot" (5), **suffers even in his time of rest**, sleep being no longer a source of **rejuvenation** but of further **defilement**.

Mastery: The quantity of L2 is consistent throughout the paragraph. The quality of L2 is acceptable, but needs revision to make the interpretive point of view more precise.

TS: Through numerous character descriptions, Homer utilizes armor to portray the **superior prowess** and **skill of the individual**. For instance, Homer, implying a sense of **royalty**, describes Hector's armor as "the flashing bronze, the horsehair crest, the great ridge of the helmet nodding, bristling terror" (6.560-561). The **magnificence** of his gear, especially the shining metal and the imperial crest, emphasize Hector's **excellence** and **worth** as a fighter. Not only does his armor imply his **royalty**, but it also **strikes fear into his enemies** because it provides Hector with **great power and skill**.

TS: The speaker in the poem from Songs of Innocence responds to the **bleakness of child labor** with **hope**. Opening with a **sorrowful image of a child** who is "sold" (2), Blake's poem establishes "The Chimney Sweeper" as a **dehumanized** youth from a **broken family**. This **abandoned** child, destined to **poverty** and sleeping "in soot" (5), finds **no relief** in the world.

Progressing: Sentences contain a low quantity of L2; occasional redundancy may exist. The quality of L2 is also low, with associations being too vague, general, or unclear. Some interpretive diction may be illogical or improperly used.

TS: Through numerous character descriptions, Homer utilizes armor to portray the **heroicness of the warrior**. For instance, Homer, implying a **great warrior,** describes Hector's armor as "the flashing bronze, the horsehair crest, the great ridge of the helmet nodding, bristling terror" (6.560-561), which shows how great of a fighter Hector is. Homer emphasizes Hector as a fighter whom **others are scared of**. Not only does his armor show how **frightening** he is, but he uses it to be **heroic in battle**.

TS: The speaker in the poem from Songs of Innocence responds to **depressing child labor** by saying that heaven waits for chimney sweepers when they die. Showing a **sad child** whose "father sold [him]" (2), Blake's poem "The Chimney Sweeper" establishes the boy's life as **tragic**. The child also lives in **disgusting poverty,** which further portrays his **sad** fate.

Insufficient: L2 occur rarely throughout the paragraph; the quality of associations is low, with the writer relying on diction that is colloquial and general.

TS: Through numerous character descriptions, Homer utilizes armor to portray the warrior. For instance, Hector's armor is "the flashing bronze, the horsehair crest, the great ridge of the helmet nodding, bristling terror" (6.560-561). Hector is a great fighter for Troy, and Homer is describing the **amazing** armor he wears.

TS: The speaker in the poem from Songs of Innocence shows the chimney sweepers waiting for heaven when they die. When the "father sold [him]" (2), "The Chimney Sweeper" was without a father. The child goes off into the darkness.

Topic Strings

Distinctive: Consistent, apt L2 in strings; precision of L2 increases; emerging ability to strategically introduce the evidence.

TS: As a minor character, Meyer Wolfsheim functions to establish the presence of **moral corruption in the tragic world**. In chapter nine, Wolfsheim reveals the **criminal influence behind Gatsby's prosperity** when he boasts of "rais[ing] him up out of nothing."

Mastery: Consistent placement of associations in topic strings that are related to the associations found in the topic sentence; however, some strings require revision to make the link more precise.

TS: As a minor character, Meyer Wolfsheim functions to establish the presence of **moral corruption in the tragic world**. In chapter nine, this **moral corruption** is suggested when Wolfsheim says that he "raised [Gatsby] up out of nothing."

Progressing: Inconsistent presence of associations in topic strings; when present, associations are too general, unrelated to the topic sentence or to the quoted evidence.

TS: As a minor character, Meyer Wolfsheim functions to establish the presence of **moral corruption in the tragic world**. In chapter nine, Wolfsheim **tragically** says that he "raised [Gatsby] up out of nothing," revealing how he **corrupted** Gatsby after the hero came back from the war.

Insufficient: The writer has not demonstrated an understanding that the topic string must contain associations linked with those found in the topic sentence.

TS: As a minor character, Meyer Wolfsheim functions to establish the presence of **moral corruption in the tragic world**. In chapter nine, Wolfsheim talks to Nick about how feels about Gatsby, and says that he "raised him up out of nothing," revealing how he **corrupted** Gatsby after the hero came back from the war.

To the Right

Distinctive: The L2 placed to the right of the quoted evidence achieves precision: these associations cannot be shifted to another piece of evidence.

In chapter nine, Meyer Wolfsheim proudly states that he "raised [Gatsby] up out of nothing," **arrogant** words that convey his **power** over the hero, a **power to elevate him out of poverty and anonymity.**

Antinous tells the assembly that Penelope "dangl[es] promises, drop[s] hints," the image of "dangling" illustrating a **puppeteer who easily**

manipulates the men's lust.

Mastery: The L2 placed to the right demonstrates an attempt to anchor the writer's idea in the quoted text, although some L2 may be even more precise.

> In chapter nine, Meyer Wolfsheim proudly states that he "raised [Gatsby] up out of nothing," **arrogant** about having **shaped Gatsby's destiny**. [Note: The same L2 could be used to comment on Wolfsheim's words "Start him! I made him."]

> Antinous tells the assembly that Penelope "dangl[es] promises, drop[s] hints," **taking advantage** of the suitors and **leading them on**.
> [Note: The same L2 could be placed to the right of "she [...] build[s] each man's hopes."]

Progressing: L2 is consistently present to the right, but tends to be too vague or general; it is not specifically anchored in the diction, imagery, or detail of the quoted text.

> In chapter nine, Meyer Wolfsheim proudly states that he "raised [Gatsby] up out of nothing," showing his **arrogance**.

> Antinous tells the assembly that Penelope "dangl[es] promises, drop[s] hints," diplaying his **anger** at Penelope's behavior.

Insufficient: L2 to the right is absent.

> In chapter nine, Meyer Wolfsheim proudly states that he "raised [Gatsby] up out of nothing." He then mentions that Gatsby "did some work" for one of his associates.

> Antinous tells the assembly that Penelope "dangl[es] promises, drop[s] hints" about marrying one of the suitors.

L2-L1-L2

Distinctive: The L2-L1-L2 pattern is predominant throughout the writer's paragraphs, with greater quality and precision of L2.

> In the opening passage of Chapter 2, Fitzgerald repeats a **deathly** image of "ashes," unveiling a setting whose **life is choked** by the

bleak substance, **ironically created by the hands of the American laborers** who inhabit it.

Mastery: The writer's syntax is predominantly L2-L1-L2 or L2-L1. The associations in the topic string or to the right of the quoted evidence requires some revision to clarify or strengthen the writer's analysis.

In the opening passage of Chapter 2, Fitzgerald repeats a **deathly** image of "ashes," a symbol of the **despair** that covers the lives of the people who live in the Valley.

Progressing: Inconsistent use of strong syntax. The writer tends towards the L1-L2 pattern, with occasional instances of L2-L1.

In the opening passage of Chapter 2, Fitzgerald uses the image of "ashes," which creates a **depressing** setting.

Insufficient: The writer's syntax rarely incorporates L2. If present, associations typically appear after quoted evidence, not before.

In the opening passage of Chapter 2, Fitzgerald repeatedly refers to the "ashes" in the Valley.

Word & Logic Glue

Distinctive: The writer consistently uses exact word repetitions, synonyms, and pronouns to create word glue between sentences in the paragraph. The use of transition words and phrases also creates logic glue, implying the logical relationships between sentences.

In the opening dialogue of A Christmas Carol, Dickens creates Scrooge's **shallow personality** by the **repetition of diction associated with money**. **Almost every comment Scrooge makes includes economic diction. For example,** when Scrooge's nephew first arrives to greet him a "Merry Christmas," **Scrooge disdainfully comments about his nephew's monetary status**: "You're poor enough" (13; ch.1), **a statement that shows how Scrooge evaluates individuals by their monetary value**. When his **nephew ignores this arrogant remark** and urges his uncle to enjoy the season, **Scrooge continues to see Christmas in terms of money**: "What's Christmas time to you but a time for paying bills without money; a time for finding yourself a year older, and not an hour richer" (14; ch.1).

Mastery: The writer mechanically employs transition words and word glue to create coherence between sentences.

> In the opening dialogue of *A Christmas Carol*, Dickens creates Scrooge's shallow personality by **the repetition of diction associated with money.** Scrooge **makes many comments with this kind of diction** in the opening chapter. **For example**, when Scrooge's nephew first arrives to greet him a "Merry Christmas," Scrooge says, "You're poor enough" (13; ch.1), **a statement that shows how Scrooge evaluates individuals by their monetary value. Scrooge <u>also</u> sees Christmas in terms of money** when he says, "What's Christmas time to you but a time for paying bills without money; a time for finding yourself a year older, and not an hour richer" (14; ch.1).

Progressing: The writer inconsistently uses transitional language; occasionally, a pair of sentences may not be connected by word or logic glue.

> In the opening dialogue of A Christmas Carol, Dickens creates Scrooge's shallow personality by the **repetition of diction associated with money**. When Scrooge's nephew wishes Scrooge "Merry Christmas," he says, "You're poor enough" (13; ch.1), **a statement that shows how Scrooge judges other people by how rich they are**. Scrooge sees **Christmas in terms of money** when he says, "What's Christmas time to you but a time for paying bills without money; a time for finding yourself a year older, and not an hour richer" (14; ch.1).

Insufficient: The writer does not demonstrate an understanding of word glue (the only glue may be, for instance, the name of the character being written about) and does not use transitional language to create implied logic glue.

> In the opening dialogue of A Christmas Carol, Dickens creates **Scrooge**'s shallow personality by the repetition of diction associated with money. Scrooge's nephew first arrives to greet him a "Merry Christmas," **Scrooge** says, "You're poor enough" (13; ch.1). **Scrooge** says, "What's Christmas time to you but a time for paying bills without money; a time for finding yourself a year older, and not an hour richer" (14; ch.1).

L3

Distinctive: The writer is able to employ the language of relationships (repetition, contrast, juxtaposition, and shift) to help the reader clearly see how part of the text's meaning is created.

> Homer **juxtaposes** Antinous' **unrepentant gluttony** with Odysseus' **moral act of restoring justice—virtue's** "stabbing arrow" **destroying evil** as it continues to **indulge** "drain the wine" of Odysseus' house.

Mastery: The writer employs the language of relationships (repetition, contrast, juxtaposition, and shift), but needs to clarify how this relationship creates meaning within the text.

> Homer **juxtaposes** Antinous' **gluttony**, symbolized by the golden cup he drinks from, with the "stabbing arrow," a sign that the villain is being **punished for his sins**.

Progressing: The writer employs the language of relationships (repetition, contrast, juxtaposition, and shift), but either does not specify the meaning created by the relationship, or uses associations that are too vague.

> Homer **juxtaposes** Antinous, the **chief villain of the suitors**, with Odysseus "stabbing arrow," which leads to his **brutal death**.

Insufficient: The writer does not employ the language of relationships to analyze the text.

> Homer portrays Antinous, the **chief villain of the suitors**, being killed by Odysseus "stabbing arrow," which leads to his **brutal death**.

Modified L1 Language

Distinctive: The writer comments precisely and insightfully on the diction, detail, or imagery employed by the literary author to create meaning.

> England finds itself in a decaying moral status, as it has become now "a fen / of stagnant waters,"(2-3) <u>**sordid imagery** that **metaphorically** conveys the nation's **vile descent** into **depravity.**</u>

Mastery: The writer logically identifies textual evidence as diction, detail, or imagery and uses reasonable L2 as modifiers; however, some associations may lack precision.

England finds itself in a decaying moral status, as it has become now "a fen / of stagnant waters,"(2-3) **filthy imagery that suggests the unideal landscape** of the country.

Progressing: The writer attempts to comment on the diction, detail, or imagery employed by the author to create meaning, but the L2 used as modifiers lack quality.

England finds itself with moral decay, transforming into "a fen / of stagnant waters," **gross diction to describe the forgotten place** (2-3).

Insufficient: The writer makes no attempt to identify the diction, detail, or imagery employed by the author to create meaning.

England finds itself with decay, transforming into "a fen / of stagnant waters," showing how gross it is becoming to live there.

PLAYBOOK QUIZ

Below is a sample "Playbook" quiz we administer to students every seven or fourteen days. The questions reflect the core knowledge and plays necessary to be successful throughout the year. On quiz day, we select five random questions from the list. Prior to the quiz, the answers are always posted for students to memorize.

Questions

1. What are the two types of clauses?
2. Which elements do all clauses contain?
3. What are the three types of dependent clauses?
4. Dependent clauses begin with what types of words [provide two examples of each type}?
5. What are the sentence types and their definitions?
6. Define a topic string.
7. Define L1, L2, L3.
8. A topic sentence must contain what?
9. Evidence can be organized how?
10. What phrase should go in the "Organization" column in the "Paragraph Chart"?
11. Identify at least two elements of logic glue.
12. Write an **absolute** phrase.
13. Write both a **present** participial and **past** participial phrase.
14. Write a sentence with a **noun clause**.
15. Write a sentence with an **adjective clause**.
16. Write a sentence with an **adverb clause**.
17. Explain the following sentence pattern: L2—L1—L2.

Answers

1. What are the two types of clauses? *independent & dependent*

2. Clauses contain what elements: *subject + verb*

3. What are the types of dependent clauses? *Noun, adjective, adverb*

4. Dependent clauses begin with what types of words [provide two examples of each type}? *Relative pronouns [who, that, which...]; subordinating conjunctions [if, when, because, although...]*

5. What are the sentence types and their definitions: *simple [1 independent clause], complex [one independent clause + dependent clause], compound [two independent clauses], compound-complex [two independent clauses + one dependent clause]*

6. Define a topic string. *The first 5-8 words at the beginning of a sentence*

7. Define L1, L2, L3. *L1 = evidence; L2 = associations; L3 = repetition, contrast, shift, juxtaposition*

8. A topic sentence must contain what? *L2*

9. Evidence can be organized how? *Time, place, idea*

10. What phrase should go in the "Organization" column in the "Paragraph Chart?" *The time, place or idea phrase that appears at the beginning of the sentence that starts a chunk: "At the cemetery..." or "Joe's humility emerges"*

11. Identify at least two elements of logic glue: *and; but-yet; or; that is; for example; therefore*

12. Write an absolute phrase. *His mind racing with grammatical knowledge.*

13. Write a present participial and past participial phrase. *Scribbling a participle phrase. Amazed by the musical genius of U2.*

14. Write a sentence with a noun clause. *John Grady decided <u>that he would run away to Mexico.</u>*

15. Write a sentence with an adjective clause. *Tom Sawyer, <u>who is less pragmatic than his friend Huck,</u> enjoys imagining himself on heroic adventures.*

16. Write a sentence with an adverb clause. *<u>Because she committed the sin of</u>*

adultery, Hester must wear the scarlet letter.

17. Explain the following sentence pattern: L2—L1—L2: *The most assertive interpretive sentence begins with associations, quotes the evidence to prove the associations, and adds additional associations anchored precisely in the quoted material.*

Feedback Memo

Learning Objectives

- Students will reflect on what they have and have not learned during the previous week or unit.
- Students will provide feedback for the teacher and the construction of future lessons.
- Students will identify for the teacher the plays that need reinforcement.

WHY IT WORKS

The feedback memo, given weekly or by unit, allows students to **retrieve** information about instruction from the week and to reflect on what they still don't understand. Retrieving information from prior lessons allows the brain to reinforce the content more deeply into long-term memory, and the deliberate act of evaluating the degree to which one understands course content triggers additional cognitive activity in the brain.

Procedure

- Create a Google Form with an area for students to submit a written response. As an alternative, students may complete a feedback memo on paper.
- This memo can be a Friday activity, or an activity done post-quiz, as students finish an assessment at their own pace.
- Students respond to questions like the following:
    1. What was most puzzling in class this week?
    2. What was most interesting?
    3. What was most difficult?
    4. What would help you the most?
    5. Any suggestions for activities/revisions?

What Did the Teacher Say?

Core Plays

- The teacher identifies the play(s) for students to retrieve.

Learning Objectives

- Students will strengthen their long-term memory circuits.
- Students will make predictions.
- Students will verbalize previous instruction.

WHY IT WORKS

Retrieval activities ask students to recall details about a learning task from memory, without the aid of notes or discussion. Routine retrieval activities help the brain activate the neural networks where a learning task is stored. The more the brain retrieves the remembered task, the stronger and more efficient the related neural circuits become, a key feature of neuroplasticity.[178]

Retrieval activities are considerably more effective than studying notes.[179] The teacher interrupts classroom activities to record student understanding—in a Google Form, on a sheet of paper, a list on the board, or a partner share. This data provides useful feedback for the teacher when deciding which areas of the playbook need strengthening.[180]

---

178 McTighe & Willis, 2019.
179 Jensen & McConchie, 2020.
180 Owens, 2017; Roediger & Butler, 2011.

Procedure

- Create a Google Form with an area for students to submit a response.
- The teacher may interrupt the lesson at any point to initiate the retrieval activity—"Okay, before we go on, I want you to tell me in your own words...What did I just say about _____?"
- This quick response allows you to see the range of understanding within the class about an assignment, about a writing skill, etc.
- The prompt to which students respond involves recall:
    - Tell me everything that you remember about _____.
    - How many pieces of evidence go in a paragraph?
    - What is a topic string?
    - What are the requirements for next week's timed write?
    - How do you make a Present Participial Phrase?
- It also gauges student understanding of content:
    - What did I just say?
    - In other words, what am I trying to tell you about the upcoming exercise?
    - What was the most important thing I just told you about the next essay assignment?
    - What can you tell me about the tragic hero?
    - What are some associations you remember from yesterday's poem, "A Noiseless, Patient Spider"?
- The retrieval request either precedes an activity or immediately follows it. It invites students to make predictions or evaluations about the task:
    - What do you think is most important to pay attention to when you're trying to do _____?
    - How is the exercise we're about to do going to help you?
    - Why did we just do that?
    - What was most difficult for you about the task we just completed?

GLOSSARY

Axons — The fibers that carry electrical messages from one neuron to the dendrites of another.

Amygdala — The part of the brain that filters emotion (fear, anxiety, frustration, despair); it can restrict learning by denying new information access to memory circuits.

BDNF — Brain derived neurotrophic factor: "protein produced inside nerve cells when they are active. It serves as Miracle Gro for the brain, fertilizing brain cells to keep them functioning and growing, as well as spurring the growth of new neurons." (Ratey 27)

Cerebellum — The part of the brain found near the brain stem that controls muscle movement; more recently, its activity has been found to stimulate other parts of the brain linked with cognitive functions.

Dendrite — Of a neuron, the fibers that receive electrical messages from the axons of other neurons.

Dopamine — A type of neurotransmitter that is released during movement or during moments when one receives a reward, such as praise, acknowledgment, positive feeling; helps develop memory.

Frontal lobe — The foremost part of the brain, responsible for higher cognitive functions; it organizes and arranges information, analyzes, sorts, plans, prioritizes.

Hippocampus — A region of the brain closely linked with memory and learning, transfering short-term memory into long-term memory.

Myelin — A substance that forms an insulating sheath around the axon of a nerve cell (neurons) in the brain and increases the speed at which signals may travel through it. The wrapping of myelin around the neuron, a process known as myelination, enables the brain to perform tasks more efficiently.

Neural networks — Groups of connected neurons communicating with each other through axons, dendrites, and synapses

Neurogenesis — The "process of stem cells dividing and developing into functional new brain cells, or neurons, in the brain." Research over the past several decades shows that even adults, through modalities such as physical exercise, can stimulate this process in their brains.

Neurons — The fundamental cells in the brain. They conduct electrical impulses, the messages that travel across our brains and direct our thought, feeling, and motion. Communication between neurons builds neural networks. Our memory is directly related to the formation of such networks, groups of neurons that fire together in response to stimuli.

Neuroplasticity — The ability of the brain to grow and change based upon its interaction with stimuli.

Neurotransmitters — Brain proteins that carry information between neurons; they animate and energize the connections between neurons, propelling messages throughout a network. They can block messages or modulate activity between cells. Examples of neurotransmitters include serotonin, which affects memory, mood, attention, sleep, arousal, and dopamine, which is primarily linked with motivation and reward.

Prefrontal cortex — Located at the back of the frontal lobe, the prefrontal cortex plays a central role in cognitive functions.

Synapse — The space between the axon of one neuron and the dendrite of another. Across this space, information passes from neuron to neuron by way of neurotransmitters.

Working memory — A term used to describe the part of short-term memory that the brain calls upon when completing cognitive tasks.

REFERENCES

Allen, D., & Tanner, K. (2003). Approaches to cell biology teaching: mapping the journey-concept maps as signposts of developing knowledge structures. Cell biology education, 2(3), 133–136. https://doi.org/10.1187/cbe.03-07-0033.

Askvik EO, van der Weel FR, van der Meer ALH. (2020) The importance of cursive handwriting over typewriting for learning in the classroom: A high-density EEG study of 12-year-old children and young adults. Front Psychol. 2020;11:1810.

Baeten, M., Kyndt, E., Struyven, K., Dochy, F. (2010). Using student-centered learning environments to stimulate deep approaches to learning: Factors encouraging or discouraging their effectiveness. *Educational Research Review*, 5(3), 243–260.

Bangert-Downs, R., Kulick, C., Kulick, J., & Morgan, M. (1991). The instructional effects of feedback in test-like events. *Review of Educational Research*, 61 (2), 213-238.

Baram, T. Z., Chen, Y, Dube, C. M., & Rice, C. J. (2008). Rapid loss of dendritic spines after stress involves derangement of spine dynamics by corticotropin-releasing hormone. Journal of Neuroscience, 28, 2903-2911.

Barber, N. (2014). *What Teachers Can Learn from Sports Coaches: A Playbook of Instructional Strategies*. Routledge.

Bauer, S. W. (2003). The well-educated mind a guide to classical education you never had. Norton.

Beyer, B (1997). *Improving student thinking: A comprehensive approach.* Boston: Allyn and Bacon.

Birnbaum, S., Gobeske, K. T., Auerbach, J., Taylor, J. R., & Arnsten, A. F. (1999). A role for norepinephrine in stress-induced cognitive deficits: alpha-1-adrenoceptor mediation in the prefrontal cortex. *Biological psychiatry*, 46(9), 1266-1274.

Black, P., & William, D. (1998), Inside the black box: Raising standards through classroom assessment. *Phi Delta Kappan*, 80(2), 1-13.

Black, JE., Isaacs, K.R., Anderson, B.J., Alcantara, A. A., & Greenough, W.T. (1990). Learning causes synaptogensis, while motor activity causes angiogenesi, in cerebellar cortex of adult rats. *Proceedings of the National Academy of Sciences*, 87, 5568-5572.

Bransford, J., Brown, A., & Cocking, R. (Ed.) (2000). How people learn: Brain, mind, experience, and school: Expanded edition. Washington, DC: National Academy Press.

Bromberg-Martin, E. S., Matsumoto, M., & Hikosaka, O. (2010). Dopamine in motivational control: rewarding, aversive, and alerting. *Neuron*, 68(5), 815-834.

Bruner, J. (1973). Beyond the information given: Studies in the psychology of knowing. New York: W.W. Norton.

Bryan, J. E., & Karshmer, E. (2013). Assessment in the one-shot session: Using pre-and post-tests to measure innovative instructional strategies among first-year students. *College & Research Libraries*, 74(6), 574-586.

Buch, E. R., Cohen, L. G., Bonstrup, M., Quentin, R., & Claudino, L. (2021, June 8). *Consolidation of human skill linked to waking hippocampo-neocortical replay*. Cell Reports. Retrieved June 8, 2022, from https://www.cell.com/cell-reports/fulltext/S2211-1247(21)00539-8.

Carter C., Grahn, J.. Optimizing Music Learning: Exploring How Blocked and Interleaved Practice Schedules Affect Advanced Performance. *Front Psychol. 2016 Aug 18*; 7:1251. doi: 10.3389/fpsyg.2016.01251. PMID: 27588014; PMCID: PMC4989027.

Clements, D. H., Sarama, J. & Germeroth, C. Learning executive function and early mathematics: directions of causal relations. *Early Child. Res. Q.* 36, 79–90 (2016).

Cleveland Clinic. (2022, March 14). Neurotransmitters: What they are, functions & types. Cleveland Clinic. Retrieved July 20, 2022, from https://my.clevelandclinic.org/health/articles/22513-neurotransmitters#:~:text=What%20are%20neurotransmitters%3F,muscle%20cell%20or%20a%20gland.

Corbett Barr. (n.d.). Retrieved August 1, 2022, from https://corbettbarr.com/

Corbett, Edward P. J. "The Theory and Practice of Imitation in Classical Rhetoric." College Composition and Communication, vol. 22 (1971), pp. 243-250.

Coyle, D. (2009). *The Talent Code: Greatness Isn't Born. It's Grown. Here's How.* New York, NY: Bantam Books. 18, 33-44.

Cozolino, L. (2010). The neuroscience of psychotherapy. New York, NY: Norton.

Cunha, C,. Brambilla, R, and Thomas, K.L. (2010). A simple role for BDNF in learning and memory? *Frontiers in Molecular Neuroscience*, (3), 1-14.

Cushion, C. (2010). Coach behaviour. In John Lyle, Chris Cushion (eds.), *Sports coaching: Professionalisation and practice,* (pp. 43-61), p. 47.

DeLong, Charles, personal communication, 5 October 2022.

Desmond, J., Gabrielli, J., Wagner, A., Ginier, B., & Glover, G. (1997). Lobular patterns of cerebellar activation in verbal working-memory and finger tapping tasks as revealed by functional MRI. *Journal of Neuroscience*, 17(24), 9675-9685.

Dewey J (1933). How We Think: A Restatement of the Relation of Reflective Thinking to the Educative Process, Boston: Heath.

Diamond, A. (2012). Activities and programs that improve children's executive functions. *Current directions in psychological science*, 21(5), 335-341.

Doherty, A., & Forés Miravalles, A. (2019, September). Physical activity and cognition: inseparable in the classroom. In *Frontiers in Education* (Vol. 4, p. 105). Frontiers.

Drost, D. K., & Todorovich, J. R. (2013). Enhancing cognitive understanding to improve fundamental movement skills. *Journal of Physical Education, Recreation & Dance*, 84(4), 54-59.

Dye, K. M., Stanton, J. D. (2017). Metacognition in upper-division biology students: Awareness does not always lead to control. *CBE—Life Sciences Education*, 16(2), ar31.

Eichenbaum, H. (2017). Memory: Organization and control. Annual Review of Psychology, 678, 19-45.

Elderton, W. (2008). Situation Training: Key to Training in a Game-based Approach. *ITF Coaching and Sport Science Review, 15 (44)*, 24-25.

Ericsson, K. A., Krampe, R., & Tesch-Romer, C. (1993). The Role of Deliberate Practice in the Acquisition of Expert Performance. *Psychological Review, 100, n. 3,* 363-406.

Ericsson, A. & Pool, R. (2016). *Peak: Secrets from the New Science of Expertise.* Boston, MA: Houghton Mifflin. 99, 238, 250-251.

Fazeli, D. & Hamidreza, T. & Saberi Kakhki, A. (2017). Random Versus Blocked Practice to Enhance Mental Representation in Golf Putting. *Perceptual and Motor Skills. 124.* 003151251770410. 10.1177/0031512517704106.

Fleur, D.S., Bredeweg, B. & van den Bos, W. Metacognition: ideas and insights from neuro- and educational sciences. *npj Sci. Learn.* 6, 13 (2021). https://doi.org/10.1038/s41539-021-00089-5.

Fogarty, R., Kerns, G. & Pete, B. (2018). *Unlocking Student Talent: The New Science of Developing Expertise.* New York, NY: Teachers College Press. 64-65; 77.

Germain, J. L. (2013) Guided discovery: a twentieth century model proves useful in the twenty-first century classroom. *United States Military Academy*, 20(12).

Girardeau, G., Benchenane, K., Wiener, S.I., Buzsaki, G., & Zugaro, M.B. (2009). Selective suppression of hippocampal ripples impairs spatial memory. Nature Neuroscience, 12(10), 1222-1223.

Gobet, F., Lane, P., Croker, S., Cheng, P., Jones, G., Oliver, I. & Pine, J. (2001). Chunking mechanisms in human learning. Trends in Cognitive Sciences, 5, 236- 243.

Harris, K. R., Santangelo, T., & Graham, S. (2010). Metacognition and strategies instruction in writing. In H. S. Waters & W. Schneider (Eds.), Metacognition, strategy use, and instruction (pp. 226-256). New York, NY: Guilford Press.

Harrison, W. (2015, October 1). *Soccer is a Thinking Man's Game.* Amplified Soccer. https://www.amplifiedsoccerathlete.com/coachguide/2015/10/1/soccer-is-a-thinking-mans-game).

Hattie, J. (1992). Measuring the effects of schooling. *Australian Journal of Education*, 36(1), 5-13.

Hattie, J. (2008). *Visible learning: A synthesis of over 800 meta-analyses relating to achievement.* New York: Routledge.

Hattie, J. (2013). *Visible learning for teachers: Maximizing impact on learning.* Thousand Oaks, CA: Corwin Press.

Hattie, J.A., & Timperley, H. (2007). The power of feedback. Review of Educational Research, 77, 81-112.

Haystead, M., & Marzano, R. (2009). *Meta-analytic synthesis of studies conducted at Marzano Research Laboratory on instructional strategies.* Englewood, CO: Marzano Research Laboratory.

Hiebert, N.M., Vo, A., Hampshire, A., Owen, A.M., Seergobin, K.N., & MacDonald, P.A. (2014). Striatum in stimulus response learning via feedback and in decision making. *Neuroimage*, 101, 448-457.

Hill, Chris, personal communication, 16 September 2022.

Hochanadel, A., & Finamore, D. (2015). Fixed and growth mindset in education and how grit helps students persist in the face of adversity. *Journal of International Education Research*, 11(1), 47-50.

Huang, Q., Liao, C, Ge, F. Ao, J Liu, T. (2022). Acetylcholine bidirectionally regulates learning and memory, *Journal of Neurorestoratology*, 10(2), 1-11.

Iigaya, K., Fonseca, M. S., Murakami, M., Mainen, Z. F., & Dayan, P. (2018). An effect of serotonergic stimulation on learning rates for rewards apparent after long intertrial intervals. *Nature communications*, 9(1), 1-10.

Ivry R. Cerebellar timing systems. *Int Rev Neurobiol*. 1997;41:555-573.

James, K.H. 2017. The importance of handwriting experience on the development of the literate brain. *Curr. Direct. Psychol. Sci.* 26, 502–508. doi: 10.1177/0963721417709821.

Jensen, E. (2005). *Teaching with the brain in mind, 2nd edition*. ASCD.

Jensen, E. (2013). What brain insights can boost your student's classroom success? jensonlearning.com. Retrieved from jensenlearning.com/news/brain-insights-boost-your-students-success/brain-based-learning.

Jensen, E., & McConchie, L. (2020). *Brain-Based Learning: Teaching the way students really learn*. Corwin Press.

Karlen, Y. (2017) The development of a new instrument to assess metacognitive strategy knowledge about academic writing and its relation to self regulated writing and writing performance. *Journal of Writing Research*, 9(1), 61-86.

Kilgard, M.P., & Merzenich, M.M. (1998). Cortical map reorganization enabled by nucleus basalis activity. *Science*, 279, 1714-1718.

Kontra, C., Lyons, D. J., Fischer, S. M., & Beilock, S. L. (2015). Physical experience enhances science learning. *Psychological science*, 26(6), 737-749.

Kopp, B., & Wolff, M. (2000, January). Brain mechanisms of selective learning: Event-related potentials provide evidence for error-driven learning in humans. *Biological Psychology*, 51(2-3), 223-246.

Kyska, L. (2012). "11 Steps Towards Deliberate Practice." 11 Steps Towards Deliberate Practice – Expert Enough. https://www.expertenough.com/deliberate-practice-steps/. Accessed July 20, 2020.

Lally, P., van Jaarsveld, C.H.M., Potts, H.W.W., & Wardle, J. (2010). How are habits formed: Modelling habit formation in the real world. *European Journal of Social Psychology*, 40(6), 998-1009.

Lemov, Doug. *Teach like a Champion 2.0*. John Wiley & Sons, 2014.

Lemov, D., Woolway, E., Yezzi, K. (2012). *Pracrtice Perfect: 42 Rules for Getting Better at Getting Better*. San Francisco, CA: Jossey-Bass Books. 49-50, 68, 183.

Light, R. (2001). *Making the most out of college: Students speak their minds. How should curriculum be reformatted?* Cambridge, MA: Harvard University Press.

Li, J. X., and James, K. H. 2016. Handwriting generates variable visual output to facilitate symbol learning. *J. Exp. Psychol. Gen.* 145, 298–313. doi: 10.1037/xge0000134.

Lin, S.-J. C., Monroe, B. W., & Troia, G. A. (2007). Development of writing knowledge in grades 2–8: A comparison of typically developing writers and their struggling peers. Reading & Writing Quarterly, 23(3), 207-230. doi:10.1080/10573560701277542.

Linden, D.E., Bittner, R.A., Muckli, L., Waltz, J.A., Kriegeskorte, N., Goebel, R., Singer, W., &

Munk, M.H. (2003, November). Cortical capacity constraints for visual working memory: Dissociation of FMRI load effects in a fronto-parietal network. Neuroimage, 20(3), 1518-1530.

Liston, C., McEwen, B. S., & Casey, B. J. (2009). Psychosocial stress reversibly disrupts prefrontal processing and attentional control. *Proceedings of the National Academy of Sciences, 106*(3), 912-917.

Love, D. (2017, August 7). *Advice from an NBA Shooting Coach: Random vs. Blocked Shooting Practice*. Basketball Immersion. https://www.basketballimmersion.com/random-vs-blocked-shooting-practice/

Luiten, J., Ames, W., & Ackerson, G. (1980). A meta-analysis of the effects of advanced organizers on learning and retention. American Educational Research Journal, 17(20, 211-218.

Marshall, P., & Bredy, T. (2016). Cognitive neuroepigenetics: The next evolution in our understanding of the molecular mechanisms underlying learning and memory? *NPJ Science of Learning* 1, 16014.

Marzano, R., Pickering, D., & Pollock, J. (2001). Classroom instruction that works: Research based strategies for increasing student achievement. Alexandria, VA: ASCD.

Matthews, R.C. (1977). Semantic judgments as encoding operations: The effects of attention to particular semantic categories on the usefulness of interim relations in recall. Journal of Experimental Psychology: Human Learning and Memory, 3(8), 160-173.

Mavilidi M, Okely AD, Chandler P, Cliff DP, Paas F. Effects of integrated physical exercises and gestures on preschool children's foreign language vocabulary learning. Educ Psychol Rev. (2015) 27:413–26.

Mavilidi MF, Okely AD, Chandler P, Paas F. Infusing physical activities into the classroom: effects on preschool children's geography learning. Mind Brain Educ. (2016) 10:256–63.

Mavilidi M-F, Okely A, Chandler P, Louise Domazet S, Paas F. Immediate and delayed effects of integrating physical activity into preschool children's learning of numeracy skills. J Exp Child Psychol. (2018) 166:502–19.

McCutchen, D. (2006). Cognitive factors in the development of children's writing. In C. A. MacArthur, S. Graham, & J. Fitzgerald (Eds.), Handbook of writing research (pp. 115-130). New York, NY: Guilford Press.

McDaniel, M., Waddell, P., & Einstein, G. (1988). A contextual account of the generation effect: A three factor theory. Journal of Memory and Language, 27, 521-536.

McDowall, A. (2008) Using feedback in coaching. In Jonathan Passmore (ed.), *Psychometrics in Coaching: Using Psychological and Psychometric Tools for Development* (pp.26-46). Kogan Page Limited.

McTighe, J., & O'Connor, K. (2005, November). Seven practices for effective learning. Educational Leadership, 63(3), 14.

McTighe, J., & Willis, J. (2019). *Upgrade your teaching: Understanding by design meets neuroscience*. ASCD.

Middleton, F., & Strick, P. (1994). Anatomical evidence for cerebellar and basal ganglia involvement in higher cognitive function. Science, 266, 458-461.

Midling AS. (2020) Norwegian SciTech News. Why writing by hand makes kids smarter.

Mueller, P. A., and Oppenheimer, D. M. 2014. The pen is mightier than the keyboard: advantages of longhand over laptop note taking. *Psychol. Sci.* 25, 1159–1168. doi: 10.1177/0956797614524581.

Nesbit, J. C., & Adesope, O. O. (2006). Learning with concept and knowledge maps: A meta-analysis. Review of educational research, 76(3), 413-448.

O'Donnell, J., Zeppenfeld, D., McConnell, E., Pena, S., & Nedergaard, M. (2012). Norepinephrine: a neuromodulator that boosts the function of multiple cell types to optimize CNS performance. *Neurochemical research*, 37(11), 2496-2512.

O'Keefe, P.A., & Linnenbrink-Garcia. L. (2014). The role of interest in optimizing performance and self-regulation. *Journal of Experimental Social Psychology*, 53, 70-78.

Ose Askvik E, van der Weel FR and van der Meer ALH (2020) The Importance of Cursive Handwriting Over Typewriting for Learning in the Classroom: A High-Density EEG Study of 12-Year-Old Children and Young Adults. *Front. Psychol.* 11:1810. doi: 10.3389/fpsyg.2020.01810.

Owens, M. T., & Tanner, K. D. (2017). Teaching as Brain Changing: Exploring Connections between Neuroscience and Innovative Teaching. *CBE life sciences education*, 16(2), fe2. https://doi.org/10.1187/cbe.17-01-0005.

Peters, S., Braams, B., Raijmakers, M., Cedric, P., Koolschijn, M. & rone, E. (2014). The neural coding of feedback learning across child and adolescent development. *Journal of Cognitive Neuroscience* 26(8), 1705-1720.

Petrigna L, Thomas E, Brusa J, Rizzo F, Scardina A, Galassi C, Lo Verde D, Caramazza G and Bellafiore M (2022) Does Learning Through Movement Improve Academic Performance in Primary Schoolchildren? A Systematic Review. Front. Pediatr. 10:841582.

Plebanek, D and James K (2022) Why Handwriting is Good for Your Brain. Front. Young Minds. 10:623953. doi: 10.3389/frym.2022.623953.

Robertson, E.M. (2019). Skill memory: Mind the ever-decreasing gap for offline processing. *Current Biology*, 29(8), R287-R289.

Potrac, P., Jones, R., Cushion, C. (2007). Understanding Power and the Coach's Role in Professional English Soccer: A Preliminary Investigation of Coach Behaviour. *Soccer & Society*. 8. 33-49. 10.1080/14660970600989509.

Puig, M., Rose, J., Schmidt, R., & Freund, N. (2014). Dopamine modulation of learning and memory in the prefrontal cortex: insights from studies in primates, rodents, and birds. *Frontiers in neural circuits*, 8, 93.

Raskin, Sarah (2017) (http://naplusa.org/blog/2017/05/08/the-teen-brain).

Ratey, John J. MD, Hagerman, Eric. (2008) *Spark: The Revolutionary New Science of Exercise and the Brain.* Little, Brown, Spark. 40-45.

Rhoads, M. C., Kirkland, R. A., Baker, C. A., Yeats, J. T., & Grevstad, N. (2021). Benefits of Movement-Integrated Learning Activities in Statistics and Research Methods Courses. *Teaching of Psychology*, 48(3), 197-203.

Richard, J.M., Castro, D.C., DiFeliceantonio, A.G., Robinson, M.J., &Berridge K.C. (2013). Mapping brain circuits of reward and motivation In the footsteps of Ann Kelley. *Neuroscience*

& *Biobehavioral Reviews*, 37(9), 1919-1931.

Rilling, J. K., Gutman, D. A., Zeh, T. R., Pagnoni, G., Berns, G. S., & Kilts, C. D. (2002). A neural basis for social cooperation. *Neuron*, *35*(2), 395-405.

Roediger, H. L., 3rd, & Butler, A. C. (2011). The critical role of retrieval practice in long-term retention. *Trends in cognitive sciences*, *15*(1), 20–27. https://doi.org/10.1016/j.tics.2010.09.003.

Rollins, A. *360Learning*. "The Link Between Dopamine and Learning Outcomes: What Does It Mean for Business?", https://360learning.com/blog/dopamine-and-learning/. Accessed 10 August 2023.

Saddler, B., & Graham, S. (2007). The relationship between writing knowledge and writing performance among more and less skilled writers. Reading & Writing Quarterly, 23(3), 231-247. doi:10.1080/10573560701277575.

Sanes, J., & Lichtman, J. (2001, November). Induction, assembly, maturation, and maintenance of a postsynaptic apparatus. *Nature Reviews Neuroscience*, 2(11), 791-805.

Schmidt, R. and Lee, T. (2020). *Motor Learning and Performance: From principles to application.* Human Kinetics.

Schneider, S., Beege, M., Nebel, S., & Rey, G. D. (2018). A Meta-analysis of how signaling affects learning with media. *Educational Research Review*, 23, 1-24.

Sekeres, M.J., Bonasia, K., St-Laurent, M., Pishdadian, S., Winocur, G., Grady, C., & Moscovitch, M. (2016). Recovering and preventing loss of detailed memory: Differential raters of forgetting for detail types in episodic memory. Learning & Memory, 23(2), 72-82.

Silver, H., Strong, R., & Perini, (2007). *The strategic teacher: Selecting the right research-based strategy for every lesson.* Alexandria, VA: ASCD.

Smith, M., & Cushion, C. J. (2006). An investigation of the in-game behaviours of professional, top-level youth soccer coaches. *Journal of Sports Sciences*, 24(4), 355–366. https://doi.org/10.1080/02640410500131944.

Smoker, T. J., Murphy, C. E., and Rockwell, A. K. 2009. "Comparing memory for handwriting versus typing," in *Proceedings of the Human Factors and Ergonomics Society Annual Meeting*, Vol. 53 (Los Angeles, CA: SAGE Publications), 1744–1747. doi: 10.1177/154193120905302218.

Smolen, P., Zhang, Y. & byrne, J.H. (2016). The right time to learn: Mechanisms and optimization of spaced learning. *Nature Reviews Neuroscience*, 17(2), 77-88.

Snow, Sam. (2015, January 9). *Improving Player Development with Guided Discovery*. Soccer Today. https://www.soccertoday.com/sam-snow-improving-player-development-guided-discovery/.

Spalding, K., Bergmann, O., ALkass, K., Bernard, S., Salehpour, M., Huttner, H., ... Frisen, J. (2013). Dynamics of hippocampal neurogenesis in adult humans. Cell, 1534(6), 1219-1227.

Stanton JD, Sebesta AJ, Dunlosky J. (2021) Fostering Metacognition to Support Student Learning and Performance. *CBE Life Sci Educ*, 20(2).

Sukel, Kayt. (2019, August 1). *Neurotransmitters*. Dana Foundation. Retrieved July 20, 2022 from https://dana.org/article/neurotransmitters/.

Tanner, K. D. (2012). Promoting student metacognition. *CBE—Life Sciences Education*, *11*(2), 113–120.

Terada, Y. (2022, April 21). *We drastically underestimate the importance of brain breaks*. Edutopia. Retrieved June 8, 2022, from https://www.edutopia.org/article/we-drastically-underestimate-importance-brain-breaks.

Thalmann, M., Souza, A.S., & Oberauer, K. (2019). How does chunking help working memory? Journal of Experimental Psychology: Learning, Memory, and Cognition, 45(1), 37-55.

Tharp, R.G. & Gallimore, R. (1976). What a coach can teach a teacher. *Psychology Today. 9*. 75-78.

Vaccaro, A. G., & Fleming, S. M. (2018). Thinking about thinking: A coordinate-based meta-analysis of neuroimaging studies of metacognitive judgements. *Brain and neuroscience advances, 2,1-14*.

Van den Heuvel, M., Stam, C., Kahn, R., Hulshoff Pol, H.E. (2009). Efficiency of functional brain networks and intellectual performance. *Journal of Neuroscience*, 29(23), 7619-7624.

Vinci-Booher SA, James KH. (2016) Neural substrates of sensorimotor processes: letter writing and letter perception. J Neurophysiol. 115(1):1-4. doi:10.1152/jn.01042.2014.

Vygotsky, L. S. (1978). *Mind in society*. Cambridge, MA: MIT Press.

Wang, M. C., Haertel, G. D., Walberg, H. J. (1990). What influences learning? A content analysis of review literature. *Journal of Educational Research*, 84(1), 30–43.

"What is the SAID Principle?" *National Federation of Professional Trainers*, 2013. https://www.nfpt.com/blog/what-said-says. Accessed 19 August 2023.

Wiggins, G., & McTighe, J. (2012). The Understanding by Design guide to advanced concepts in creating and reviewing units. Alexandria, VA: ASCD>.

Willis, Judy. (2016) "Using Brain Breaks to Restore Students' Focus.

Edutopia. Retrieved December 7, 2016, from https://www.edutopia.org/article/brain-breaks-restore-student-focus-judy-willis.

Willis, J. (2007). Cooperative learning is a brain turn-on. *Middle school journal*, 38(4), 4-13.

Willis, J. (2009). What you should know about your brain. *Educational Leadership*, 67(4), 1-3.

Wright, S., Horn, S., & Sanders, W. (1997). Teacher and classroom context effects on student achievement: Implications for teacher evaluation. *Journal of Personnel Evaluation in Education*, 11)1), 57-67.

Yan, W., Zhang, T., Jia, W., Sun, X., & Liu, X. (2011). Chronic stress impairs learning and hippocampal cell proliferation in senescence-accelerated prone mice. *Neuroscience Letters*, 490(2), 85-9.

Zull, J. (2002). *The art of the changing brain*. Sterling, VA: Stylus.

ACKNOWLEDGEMENTS

Thanks to Dan Maher for his brutal copy-editing, which landed us both in the ICU for several months (we thankfully survived).

We would like to thank Ari Magill, M.D. for his help in research. A neurologist based out of Arizona, Ari gathered numerous articles to complement our existing neuroscience references.

We would like to thank Charlie DeLong for his many visits to the English department commons to chat about athletics and the classroom, the impetus for this book. And his mother is no doubt pleased that he finally completed a decent essay.

To Chris Hill, Giuliano Sanchez, Jeremy Weeks, Brandon Hickman, and other coaches past and present at Jesuit College Preparatory School, for sharing their insights on our common craft.

Thanks to our colleagues in the Jesuit English department, who have continued to practice and share with us their different strategies to teach these plays.

And finally, thank you to our numerous faculty peers who proofread and provided helpful feedback for our activities: Jonathan Alexander, Leanne Applegate, Lynn Bolton, Will Ellis, Kenneth Gan, Brian Goll, Tiffany Holmes, Laura Hudec, Katie Johnston, Karen Lahey, Madeline Maggard, Shulamit Moed, Greg Nielson, Sheryl Row, Jonathan Segal, Billy Thompson, Ky Vu, Seth Waits, Don Woods, and Bob Wunderlick.

ABOUT THE AUTHORS

Ian Berry has been an English teacher at Jesuit College Preparatory School in Dallas for the past decade. He has studied literature at the University of Texas and the Sorbonne. He first practiced "the game" in English as a student in Degen's AP Literature course, and has been playing it ever since. When he is not thinking about the classroom, he enjoys long-distance running, page-turner detective stories, and French poetry.

Michael Degen has been practicing teaching at Jesuit College Preparatory School in Dallas for the past thirty years— sophomores, juniors, and seniors. He served as a College Board consultant for several decades and continues to provide workshop opportunities for teachers across the country.

OTHER TEXTS AVAILABLE FROM TELEMACHOS

Crafting Expository Argument: Practical Approaches to the Writing Process for Students and Teachers

Prospero's Magic: Active Learning Strategies for the Teaching of Literature

Understanding Written Grammar

Virginia Woolf: A Contribution to the Essay Form

INDEX

A

acetylcholine, 60, 235
The Adventures of Huckleberry Finn (Twain), 120, 168–69, 221
All the Pretty Horses (McCarthy), 74, 115
amygdala, 20
Analytical Voice chart, 64, 68
Anna Karenina (Tolstoy), 158
Aristotle's topics for invention, 144–61
    categories, 145
    cause-effect arguments, 156–60
    classification arguments, 149–50
    comparison arguments, 151–54
    contrary arguments, 155–56
    core plays involved, 144
    definition arguments, 147–49
    degree arguments, 153–54
    difference arguments, 152–53
    identify patterns, 144
    relationship arguments, 154–60
    similarity arguments, 151–52
Arnold, Matthew, 93
athletic coaching, 31–45
    English classroom, guided discovery in, 40–45
    English scrimmage, 37–38
    guided discovery, 38–40
    SAID principle and, 32–35
    scrimmage, 36–37
athletic paradigm, 47–48
axons, 29

B

Barber, Nathan, 43
basketball coaches, 32
Bauer, Susan Wise, 197
BDNF. *See* brain-derived neurotrophic factor
behavioral relevance, 50, 113
Beowulf discussion quiz, 228–30
    questions, 228–29
    student prep work for, 230
boardwork, 108–9

bookmarks, 267–69
    reading plays, 267, 268
    writing plays, 267, 269
brain
    absorbs stimuli, 49
    cerebellum, 16–17
    chemistry, movement and, 19–21
    movement of handwriting, 57
    natural memory function, 27
    neurotransmitters, 59–60
    pattern recognition, 58–59
    research on. See brain research
    retrieval activities, 59, 171
    teachers knowledge about, 48–50
brain break(s), 50–51, 114–15
brain-derived neurotrophic factor (BDNF), 19, 60, 189
brain research, 13, 16–21. *See* also neuroscience
    cerebellum, research on, 16–17
    dopamine, 20
    embodied cognition, 18
    endorphins, 20
    link between movement and learning, 16–18
    movement and brain chemistry, 19–21
    movement and memory, 18–19
    Preventive Medicine, 18
Bumper Sticker Ethics (Wilkins), 222

C

cause-effect relationship arguments, in Aristotle's topics, 156–60
    cause producing effect or effects, 156–57
    effect resulting from one or more causes, 157
    from literary work, 159–60
    not from literary work, 160
cerebellum, 16–17
    and movement, 57
    neurons in, 17
challenging texts. *See* difficult texts, engage

chunking, 23, 51–52
    quotation game and, 251
    revision chart, 258
clarity, 22, 52
class digital evidence chart, 137–38
classification arguments, in Aristotle's topics, 149–50
    from literary work, 149–50
    not from literary work, 150
coaches
    basketball, 32–33
    effective, 32
    right moments to speak for, 44
Coleridge, Samuel Taylor, 151
Colvin, Geoff, 22
comfort zone, 22
comparison arguments, in Aristotle's topics, 151–54
    degree arguments, 153–54
    difference arguments, 152–53
    similarity arguments, 151–52
composition
    crafting, 90–92
    sample, 83–86
conceptual associations, 67–70
    elaborate direct quotations with, 70
    from evidence, 77–78, 87–88
    selection of, 69–70
    for student-writer, 68
    well-crafted speeches and, 67
    writing about, 68–69
conference memo, writing, 210–14
    benefits of, 210
    core plays involved in, 210
    Google Form responses, 214
    learning objectives, 210
    sample, 212–13
contrary relationship arguments, in Aristotle's topics, 155–56
    from literary work, 155–56
    not from literary work, 156
contrast, 72–73
core plays
    involved evidence-association chart, 132
    L1 play, 66–67
    L2-L1-L2 play, 82
    L2 play, 67–70
    L3 play, 70–76
    logic glue, 103–4
    modified L1 play, 83–86
    organization, 96–100

thesis statement, 92–93
topic sentence, 94–95
topic string, 100–2
understanding, 65
word glue, 103
writer's analytical voice, 64–65
cortisol, 60
    negative emotional states and, 20
    stress-induced discharge, 20–21
Cowan, Louise, 222
Coyle, Daniel, 22, 29, 30
Crime and Punishment (Dostoevsky), 224
Cullen, Countee, 165

D

deductive classroom approach, 54
definition arguments, in Aristotle's topics, 146–48
    from literary work, 147–48
    not based on literary work, 148–49
degree arguments, in Aristotle's topics, 153–54
    from literary work, 153–54
    not from literary work, 154
deliberate practice, 8–10, 22–23
    automaticity and, 29
    develop creative players, 9
    identifying errors or weakness, 8
    principles of, 21–22
    in tournament of scholars, 243
DeLong, Charlie, 32
Dickens, Charles, 72–73, 85, 94, 125
    Great Expectations, 72, 74, 152, 200
    A Tale of Two Cities, 77–83, 156, 199, 220, 240
diction, 66
Diet Coke, 73, 74
difference arguments, in Aristotle's topics, 152–53
    from literary work, 152–53
    not from literary work, 153
difficult texts, engage
    core plays involved, 124
    deliberate practice in, 125
    The Great Gatsby, 131
    learning objectives, 124
    partial student responses, 130
    procedure, 125–28
    sample(s), 129–31
    Sonnet 29, 130
Dillard, Annie, 86–92

discussion quiz (DQ), 223–32
    activity, running of, 225–26
    appoint moderator for, 225
    Beowulf discussion quiz, 228–30
    as complex and challenging tasks, 223
    core plays involved, 223
    directions for students in, 226
    discussion questions, preparing, 224
    helpful transitions for students, 227
    learning objectives, 223
    managing discussion, tips for, 230–32
    prep work, 224–25
    procedure, 224–30
    rubric, 232
    sample, 228–29
dopamine, 19, 60, 235
    negative emotional states and, 20
    positive social interaction, response to, 57

E

EAC. *See* Evidence-Association Chart
endorphins, 20
English classroom, 15
    activities of, 217–18
    guided discovery in, 40–45
    scrimmage to, applying, 37–38
    secondary, 13, 22, 45
English coach
    engages students in daily practice, 27–28
    immediate feedback by, 31
    playbook for students, creates, 26–27
    profile of, 25–31
    struggle and failure, understands, 30–31
    training program, delineates, 25–26
    uses repetition, 28–30
English teachers, 31, 35
    concept of silence and, 44–45
    decisions in light of brain's response to stress, 21
    secondary, lessons for, 24–25
    use movement-based activities, 20–21
Ericsson, K. Anders, 22–25, 27, 170
    ideal coach, trait of, 31
    principles to classroom, 23
evidence
    conceptual associations from, 79, 87–88
    observing, 77–78, 87–88
    recognizing relationships among associations linked to, 89–90, 88–89

evidence-association chart (EAC), 228
    applications of, 136–39
    class digital evidence chart, 137–37
    core plays involved, 132
    graphic organizer, 133
    individual chart completed over course of unit, 136
    inductive thinking, 133
    learning objectives, 132
    procedure, 133–34
    quick guided reading of text, 136–37
    recognize patterns, 135
    rotation of partners or small groups, 136
    sample, 135
    on whiteboards, 136
expert performance
    in English, 14
    playbook demystifies, 47
    psychology of, 21–31
explicit modeling instruction, 56

F

Faulkner, William, 222
feedback, 22, 52–53
    dynamic aspects of, 53
    ideal, 52
    in musical chairs, 118
    in quotation game, 255
    single sentence, working on, 202
    teacher, 143, 202
    timeliness of, 52–53, 202
    in tournament of scholars, 243
    in writing conference memo, 210
feedback memo, 287
Fogarty, Robin J., 23, 29
Frankenstein (Shelley), 151, 222
free play, 9
French Revolution, 158
Frost, Robert, 148

G

gallery walks, 110
game of English, 217–18. *See also* scrimmage
Google Form
    used for class digital evidence chart, 137–38
    used for conference memo, writing, 214
    used in musical chairs activity, 119
    used to complete revision chart, 263
grammar dice, 181-187

grammar plays
    grammar dice, 181
    human sentences, 188
    sentence combination, 175
    sentence imitation, 170–71
graphic organizers, 53–54
Great Expectations (Dickens), 72, 74, 152, 200
The Great Gatsby (Fitzgerald), 121, 131, 172
    selected quotations from, 253–55
    Tom Buchanan (character), 236
    guided discovery, 38–40
    in English classroom, 40–45
    self-thinking players and, 38–39

H
Hardy, Thomas, 159
Hawthorne, Nathaniel, 147
Henry, Patrick, 67
Herberger, Sepp, 7
Hill, Chris, 35, 39, 42
hippocampus, 19, 117
human sentences
    grammar plays, 188
    learning objectives, 188
    physical movement and cognition, 189
    procedure, 188–92

I
Iliad (Homer), 157
imagery, 66
induction, 54
inductive classroom teachers, 54
inductive-predictive instruction, 54, 235
inductive thinking, 133
instruction, 38, 52
    explicit modeling, 56
    inductive-predictive, 54
intellectual challenge, 21, 55

J
juxtaposition, 73–74, 90

K
Kerns, Gene, 23
key words, 103
King Lear (Shakespeare), 159

L
L1 play, 66–67
    Beowulf discussion quiz, 230
    crafting composition, 90–92
    details, 66–67
    diction, 66
    imagery, 66
    modified, 78–86
    nonfiction passage, applying to, 86
    passage from novel, applying to, 77–81
L2-L1-L2 play, 82, 165
    Beowulf discussion quiz, 230
    syntax, 128
L2 play
    Beowulf discussion quiz, 230
    conceptual associations, 67–70
    crafting composition, 90–92
    nonfiction passage, applying to, 88–89
    passage from novel, applying to, 79
    thesis statements with, 93
    thesis statements without, 93
L3 play, 70–76
    Beowulf discussion quiz, 230
    contrast, 72–73
    crafting composition, 90–92
    juxtaposition, 73–74
    nonfiction passage, applying to, 89–90
    passage from novel, applying to, 89–90
    repetition, 71
    shift, 74–76
labeling
    core plays involved, 194
    learning objectives, 194
    procedure, 194
    sample, 196
    writing strategies, 195
large table discussions with student moderators, 110–11
learning. *See also* teaching
    environment, 7
    movement linked with, 16–18
    neurotransmitters, impact of, 59–60
    situations, 55
Lemov, Doug, 23
literary news conference, 233–40
    core plays involved, 233
    directions for all students, 234–35
    follow-up questions in, 236
    holding the conference, 236–37

inductive-predictive instruction, 35
learning objectives, 233
ontological questions in, 239
original questions generated by reporters, 239
performers role-playing characters, directions for, 234
procedure, 233–37
questions about character in, 236
reporters, directions for, 234–35
rubric, 241
sample L1-L2 chart for, 240
sample performer chart with answers to questions, 241
logic glue, 102–5
helpful transitions for students, 227
paragraph chart, 140–43
Lord of the Flies (Golding), 100–1

M
Macbeth (Shakespeare), 159, 222
Marx, Karl, 156
mastery handout, 270, 272
McCarthy, Cormac, 74, 115
memory
circuits, 49, 50
long term, 202
movement and, 18–19
musical chairs activity and, 120
retrieval activities and, 288–89
memory assignment, 200
memory circuits/memory networks, 48
developing, 23, 61
grammatical long-term, 188
long term, 194
paragraph chart, 140
strengthening of, 50, 58, 198
memory work, 197–200
challenging tasks, 198
core plays involved, 197
Great Expectations, 200
learning objectives, 197
movement of handwriting, 198
procedure, 198–99
sample memory assignment, 200
metacognition, 56, 195
metacognitive activities, 39, 56–57
in classroom, 57
explicit modeling instruction and, 56
peer editing, 204

revision chart and, 218, 258
metacognitive skills
explicitly teaching and modeling, 56
neural network in brain and, 140
Miracle-Gro. *See* brain-derived neurotrophic factor
mirror neurons, 20
modified L1 play, 83
motivation, 22
movement, 14, 57–59
brain chemistry and, 19–21
cerebellum and, 57
of handwriting, 48–57, 198
link with learning, 16–18
memory and, 18–19
peer-editing, 205
movement variations applied to classroom
boardwork, 108–9
gallery walks, 110
large table discussions with student moderators, 110–11
rotation (individual, partner, triad, large group), 109
multiple paragraphs, 166, 169
musical chairs, 116–23
myelin, 29, 30, 58

N
negative emotional states, 20
neural networks, 114
grammar dice and, 182
metacognitive skills trigger, 56, 140, 195
resting time, 51
retrieval activities and, 59, 171, 288
strengthening of, 23
neurogenesis, 19
neurons, 13, 28, 33, 48, 59. See also brain
BDNF. *See* brain-derived neurotrophic factor
cerebellar activity and, 219, 223
in cerebellum, 17
during complex and challenging tasks, 55, 198
memory, 18
mirror, 20
neuroplasticity, 133
physical movement and, 19
physical or kinetic action and, 17, 117
scrimmage and, 36–37
neuroplasticity, 48, 133, 182

neuroscience, 48. *See also* brain research
    deductive method, limitations of, 42
    documents, 44
    metacognitive skills, 56
    research, 16, 21, 36
    Revision Chart activity, 218
neurotransmitters, 59–61
    acetylcholine, 60, 235
    brain-derived neurotrophic factor, 19, 60, 189
    dopamine, 19, 20, 57, 60, 235
    endorphins, 20
    learning, impact on, 59–60
    negative emotional states and, 20
    norepinephrine, 20–21, 60, 235
    oxytocin, 20
    serotonin, 20, 60
norepinephrine, 60, 235
    negative emotional states and, 20
    stress-induced discharge, 20–21

O

O'Connor, Flannery, 64, 70
Odyssey, 220, 220, 243
organization, 96–100
    ideas (associations) introduced in topic sentence, 99–100
    paragraph, 102, 104, 105
    by place, 98–99
    by time, 98
organization words, 102, 104, 105
    paragraph chart, 140–43
organizing evidence, get creative with
    The Adventures of Huckleberry Finn, 168–69
    core plays involved, 166
    learning objectives, 166
    procedure, 166–67
    sample, 168–69
oxytocin, 20

P

paragraph chart, 37, 97, 140–43
paragraph organization, 102, 104, 105
    by idea, 169
    paragraph chart, 140–43
    single body, 169
    by time, 169
    by time and idea, 169
pattern recognition, 58–59. *See also* memory

peer-editing
Pete, Brian, 23
physical movement
    brain breaks and, 51
    human sentences and, 189
    in musical chairs, 117
    role of, 13
    triggers brain-derived neurotrophic factor, 19
play, 14
playbook
    bookmarks, 267–69
    core, 64–65
    designing for English student, 47–48
    by English coach, 26–27, 50
    metacognitive skills and, 56
    quiz, 284–86
Positive Coaching (Thompson), 7
practice environment. *See* learning environment
pre-existing knowledge, 22
prefrontal cortex, 20–21
pronouns, 103
psychology of expert performance, 21–31
    deliberate practice, 22–23
    english coach, profile of, 25–31
    secondary english teachers, lessons for, 24–25

Q

questions for discussion, in scrimmage activities, 219–22
quotation game, 250–57

R

Ratey, John, 19
reading plays chart. *See also* core plays
    Level One, 66–67
    Level Three, 70–76
    Level Two, 67–70
reflection activity, 218
The Reivers (Faulkner), 222
relationship arguments, in Aristotle's topics, 154–60
    cause-effect relationship arguments, 156–60
    contrary relationship arguments, 155–56
repetition, 22–23, 58, 71
    deliberate practice and, 30
    English coach uses, 28–30
    neurological development, relationship

with, 29
  sentence imitation and, 171
retrieval activities, 59, 288–89
revision chart (activity), 218, 258–64
rotation (individual, partner, triad, large group), 109

S

SAID. See Specific Adaptation to Imposed Demands
Saint Leo University, 18
The Scarlet Letter (Hawthorne), 187, 220
scoring guide (plays), 270–71
  conclusion, 271
  introduction, 270
  paragraphing, 271
  style, 271
  thesis, 271
  topic sentences, 271
scrimmage, 36–37
  discussion quiz, 223–32
  English, 37–38
  grammar dice, 182
  literary news conference, 233–41
  overview of, 217–18
  peer-editing, 204
  players, 36
  questions for discussion, types of, 219–22
  quotation game, 250–57
  revision chart, 218, 258–64
  students reflecting on performance, 218
  tournament of scholars, 242–49
  training environment, 36
self-thinking players, 38, 42
sentence combination, 175–180
sentence creation, isolating plays in
sentence imitation, 170–74
serotonin, 20, 60
Shakespeare
  King Lear, 159
  Macbeth, 159, 222
  Sonnet 29, 75, 130
Shelley, Mary, 151
shift, 74–76
similarity arguments, in Aristotle's topics, 151–52
  from literary work, 151–52
  not from literary work, 152
Simmons, Craig, 47
skill, 14
Snow, Sam, 38

Sonnet 29 (Shakespeare), 75, 130
Specific Adaptation to Imposed Demands (SAID), 8, 32–35
struggle, 30–31
  intellectual, 30
  as neurological requirement, 31
synapse(s), 17, 19, 59, 117
syntactical patterns, practicing four
  core plays involved, 167
  learning objectives, 162
  literary source, based on, 163
  procedure, 163–64
  sample, 165
"Simon the Cyrenian Speaks," 165

T

A Tale of Two Cities (Dickens), 77–83, 156, 199, 220, 240
teaching. *See also* learning
  Aristotle's topics for invention, 144–61
  enduring method of, 61
  English teacher's playbook, 56
  worksheet method of, 61
Teaching a Stone to Talk (Dillard), 86–92
The Terrain of Comedy (Cowan), 222
thesis statement, 92–93
Things Fall Apart (Achebe), 224
Thompson, Jim, 7
Tolstoy, Leo, 158
topic sentence (TS), 94–95
topic string, 100–2, 104, 105
  breaks, 100–1
  paragraph chart, 140–43
  revision to maintain the topic string, 101
tournament of scholars, 37, 242–49
training
  deliberate practice, 8–10
  environment, 7, 243
  SAID principle, 8
transitional words
  connected to time, place or idea, 96
  traditional, 103
Twelve Angry Men (play), 146, 155

U

Unlocking Student Talent (Fogarty), 29

V

Vygotsky, Lev, 55, 198

W

Wilkins, Steve, 222
Wooden, John, 44
Woolf, Virginia, 71
word glue, 102, 103, 104
    paragraph chart, 140–43
working memory, 21
worksheet method of teaching, 61
writing
    conceptual associations, 68–69
    conference memo, 210–14
    journal, 112–13
writing journal, 112–13
    individual student journal, uses of, 113
    learning objectives, 112

Z

zone of proximal development (ZPD), 55, 198

www.ingramcontent.com/pod-product-compliance
Lightning Source LLC
Chambersburg PA
CBHW081540300426
44116CB00015B/2702